**Active
Science**

Teacher's Guide

**Mike Coles
Richard Gott
Tony Thornley**

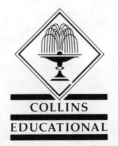

**COLLINS
EDUCATIONAL**

Collins Educational, 8 Grafton Street,
London WIX 3LA

© Coles, Gott, Thornley 1988

First published 1988

ISBN 0 00 327456 X

Designed by Jacky Wedgwood and
David English

Typesetting and artwork by
Burns & Smith, Derby

Printed and bound by Scotprint Ltd,
Musselburgh

The authors and publishers are grateful to
Bob Lock for supplying additional material
for this Guide. The authors are also grateful
to the many colleagues who helped in the
preparation of this course.

CONTENTS

INTRODUCTION

Active Science is a complete science course for lower secondary schools. As well as having a coherent content framework, the course also emphasises skills and processes through a detailed assessment scheme. The course is intended for use with the full ability range.

Aims of the course

Active Science should:

1. Allow pupils to work scientifically in a wide range of contexts often related to everyday experiences and materials.

2. Encourage a knowledge and understanding of scientific fact and process which will support further scientific studies.

3. Enable the learner to gain first-hand experience of thinking and working scientifically.

4. Encourage the pupil to take some responsibility for his or her own learning.

5. Provide opportunities for the learner to develop his or her study skills, especially those of reading and information handling.

6. Provide tasks that challenge pupils of differing interests and aptitudes, but that will enable pupils across the ability range to make positive achievements.

7. Encourage the development of linguistic and mathematical skills.

8. Provide feedback to both teacher and learner through an assessment scheme which is formative and which covers a range of scientific capabilities.

9. Be interesting and motivating by employing a wide range of activities together with clear achievement targets set through the assessment scheme.

The place of *Active Science* in science education

The colourful, attractive appearance of pages from *Active Science* will have a 'primary' feel to many teachers. The scheme uses contexts and materials which are familiar to many pupils who have experienced primary school science. The activities associated with them are, hopefully, sufficiently demanding to stretch these pupils as they move steadily into more abstract and less familiar contexts. The open-ended nature of many of the activities should enable pupils to find their own level; the structure provided at the start of most activities will help those pupils who are less confident at working scientifically.

Where liaison is good with feeder primary schools, it will be possible for teachers to share some of the contexts and activities between the schools. Whilst the scheme has been designed for 11–13 year-olds, primary teachers will have little trouble in adapting ideas and activities for their older classes.

Middle-school teachers will find the range of material and the assessment scheme particularly helpful in planning for a continuous and coherent scientific experience for their pupils. With the added flexibility offered by middle-school curricula, the ideas and resources in *Active Science* can be exploited to the full. Pupils' achievements and profiled records of their progress can become the basis of useful transfer documents. Where the transfer age is 12, careful liaison will be necessary in order that continuity for pupils is preserved. In many ways Book 2 is more demanding than Book 1 and this should be considered when areas of study between a school and its feeder school are being discussed.

Active Science is a practical, process-based course and will support broad and balanced GCSE science courses, whether combined, co-ordinated or integrated. The content and skill areas have been selected to offer pupils following the course the best chances of a continuous and challenging scientific education. The assessment scheme will be a sound preparation for the GCSE courses, particularly those where the onus is on the pupils to understand the assessment scheme and take added responsibilty for their learning.

The third year is a problem area for some schools, particularly if the GCSE courses used are explicitly two-year courses. *Active Science* can be adapted to form the basis for a third-year course. There is sufficient course material, and the assessment scheme has the features needed to assess the higher levels of attainment. The adaptation would need to be done carefully to allow the introduction of GCSE syllabus-specific content where necessary.

How to use *Active Science*

Active Science has been designed as a complete course. The pupils' books and copymasters contain a comprehensive range of materials to support both pupil and teacher. The teaching material has been organised into 12 units which reflect broad content themes. Within each unit an essentially practical approach is taken which covers the main scientific skills of using equipment, communicating and interpreting information, observing, planning investigations, and investigating and making. Opportunities for development of these skills are a central part of the course; they are fully integrated into the content areas covered. The range and nature of the skills are in line with recent government publications on science education. Practical investigations and reading material can be selected and adapted to suit the limitations of time and resources and, of course, the experience of the pupils.

Signals in the Pupil's Book are used to indicate supporting worksheets and opportunities to assess skills. The worksheets are an extra resource which support or extend activities in the Pupil's Book. Many of the worksheets stand alone and form a useful resource in themselves.

Extras

Every topic has an Extras section which aims to broaden the study area, form a basis for homework or extend more-able pupils.

Timing and progression

The course is intended to be a flexible resource from which teachers can select material appropriate to their own pupils. There are few limitations on the order in which the material can be used. In general, Unit 1 should be used as the start of a child's secondary-school science career, but the material within the Unit can be used in any order. The other Units in Book 1 can then follow. Some of the material, because one page builds on a preceding one, should be used sequentially. For example, Unit 5 is best worked through from 5.1 to 5.13, and Unit 6 from 6.1 to 6.12. More details are given in the notes for each Unit.

Book 2 is generally more demanding than Book 1, and is intended for second-year pupils. Units 7 to 11 could be taken in any order, although again some of them need to be used sequentially. Unit 12 differs from the other units: it has no skill assessment and no unifying content framework. It provides the starting point for a number of pupil investigations that could be used to finish the pupils' first or second-year science course.

Readability

The reading age of a range of the material in Book 1 has been assessed. The vast majority of it, including all the activities, comes out at between nine and ten. Some of the comprehension passages and one or two of the test questions are of necessity harder and have a reading age of about eleven. Failure to include such material would deprive many pupils of the chance to develop skills which are important. Yet there is then a danger that pupils with low reading ages will get lost and either give up or become disruptive. It is for each class teacher to judge the suitability of the text or questions for his or her class.

Apparatus requirements

Active Science is a practical course and will require a good stock of basic equipment to sustain it, However, the course does not make use of expensive specialist items which are not likely to be found in scientific departments in secondary schools. A Van de Graaff generator is possibly the most specialist item that features in the course. Consequently, while the course involves much practical work, this is unlikely to lead to increased costs.

An apparatus list for each Unit is provided in this Guide. Equipment is listed for all the experiments described in the Pupil's Book and on the worksheets, but not for the Extras. Any relevant teacher demonstrations have also been included. Pupils often have to design their own experiments in *Active Science*. In these cases, the equipment listed is a suggestion as to what may be needed.

This Guide also contains ideas you might use to amend or extend the investigations in the Pupil's Books. These suggestions are usually simple, but you will need to organise your own equipment for them.

Where 'Pupils' are specified, about 15 sets of apparatus will be needed, depending on the class size. Where 'Teacher' is specified, one of each item should be enough, unless the text specifies more.

Video resources

A list of relevant video material is included at appropriate points in this Guide. Some material is referred to on several occasions, and you will need to judge when a particular video is most appropriate to support your teaching. Some of the material is no longer broadcast, but copies will probably still be available in most schools and local authority teachers' centres.

Sources of the videos are:
- *Seeing and Doing* (Independent Television)
- *Science – Start Here* (Independent Television)
- *Living and Growing* (Independent Television)
- *Scientific Eye* (Independent Television)
- *Exploring Science* (British Broadcasting Corporation)
- *Starting Science* (Independent Television) – no longer broadcast
- *Science Topics* (British Broadcasting Corporation)
- *Environments* (Independent Television)
- *A Place to Live* (Independent Television)

THE ASSESSMENT SCHEME

This is a major resource for teachers. The aims of the assessment scheme are to:

- provide feedback to teachers which can be a formative influence,

- be fully integrated into,and a natural part of, the teaching and learning arising from the scheme,

- be structured and designed to be easily used by teachers,

- involve pupils in recognising attainment targets and subsequently evaluating their performance,

- provide a record of achievement.

There are two main components in the scheme: assessment of knowledge and understanding through the end-of-unit tests, and continuous assessment of skills and processes.

End-of-unit tests

Pupils' knowledge and understanding of each Unit can be assessed using the test material provided in the Copymasters. Any written test of knowledge, understanding, skills or processes has some drawbacks, particularly for the least-able pupils. We suggest that teachers look carefully at the questions before choosing those which are most appropriate for the pupils being assessed. For the least able, it may well be more appropriate to rely on the continuous assessment element, dispensing with the more formal tests.

Continuous assessment

Many forms of continuous assessment, including those outlined in the report of the National Curriculum Science Working Group, *Co-ordinated Science* – the Suffolk Development, and Records of Achievement, rely on the use of criteria. Often, these criteria are expressed, necessarily, in very general terms and this generality can lead to difficulties in interpretation.

To try to solve this problem in *Active Science*, a set of general criteria across five profile elements has been developed, together with specific criteria (marking guidelines) for each of the assessment opportunities flagged in the Pupil's Book. Newly-qualified teachers and those who are not specialist science teachers will find these guidelines particularly supportive.

The five elements are:

1 Basic skills

This element includes such things as the use of apparatus and measuring instruments, and the construction of graphs, charts and tables. The assessment is based on a 'can-do' approach.

2 Communicating and interpreting

The ability to record accurately and to read from and interpret data in the form of prose or numbers is a key part of science. Three criteria levels are used to assess pupil performance, the first and third being described, whilst the second is left to be inferred by the teacher.

3 Observing

The definition of observation used in this book does not include measurement, which is dealt with under the 'Basic skills' heading. Observation here is to do with pupils' ability to use their past experience, at home as well as at school, to pick out the important features of objects or events. Pupils will initially require some help here. They will need to know, for example, that when they are asked for a description of an object they must think about what the *scientifically important* things are.

4 Planning investigations

The marking guidelines for Planning investigations and for Investigating are based on a simple checklist. This checklist can be used in a number of ways. It can be used to check the plan or investigation, and the information used to decide which criteria level the pupil has reached. It can also be used by the teacher as a guide to what the important features of the task are. Or it can be ignored, assessment relying on the criteria levels alone.

5 Investigating and making

Investigations can be checklisted in the same way as Planning investigations. Constructional activities are assessed against criteria only: no checklist is included for these.

Pupil activities in the Pupil's Books are marked by toned boxes to indicate that they may be used to assess particular skills. This does not apply to Unit 12, where no assessment guidelines are provided. All marked assessment oportunities have specific criteria in the *Teachers Guide* to aid the teacher's assessment. Throughout the course, there are many other possible opportunities to assess skills. Once the criteria become familiar, they can be used whenever assessment is needed or is convenient.

The criteria used in the assessment scheme have been described both in general terms (in this Teacher's Guide) and specifically for each activity (see, for example, the teacher's notes for spread 1.2, Testing other candles (Planning investigations)). Two levels of achievement or performance are defined: levels 1 and 3. Teachers (and pupils) can create additional levels to suit their needs: intermediate (level 2,) higher (4) or lower (0). This will become easier with practice.

Profiles and records of achievement

Included in the Copymasters is a pro-forma class record sheet which will allow a record to be kept of individual or group performance across the profile elements.

An averaging procedure at the end of each term or year will result in a ready-made profile of skills which, together with the end-of-unit tests, will give a comprehensive report for pupil, school and parents.

Pupil self-assessment

Giving pupils the opportunity to record their own progress is an important feature of the *Active Science* course. Its educational value does not lie in the objective value of the assessment, but in the fact that pupils have to reflect on the work they have done and pass judgement on themselves. In general they find this useful and motivating. The teacher will find it equally useful in terms of the light it sheds on pupils' self-perception. Pupil self-assessment sheets are given for each Unit, (except Unit 12) in the Copymasters. They can be retained by the pupil to fill in at regular intervals, or stored in a file for occasional or end-of-unit use. One way to encourage pupils to make use of them is to reduce them to exercise-book size, and to stick them in each pupil's book when he or she starts that Unit.

Practical tests and the end-of-course test

Two practical tests are included which could be used towards the beginning of the course. They involve various measuring instruments and scales. The end-of-course test has five components, based on the five profile areas of basic skills, communicating and interpreting, observing, planning investigations and investigating and making. This test could be used to give an end-of-course profile. It may also prove useful in assessment for the National Curriculum. Full apparatus lists and marking guidelines are included in the Teacher's Guide. A pro-forma report to parents suitable for use with this end-of-unit test is included in the Copymasters.

General criteria

Basic skills: practical

LEVEL 1	LEVEL 3
Can make simple measurements using familiar instruments (such as thermometers and rulers) with easy scales involving integers, in familiar situations. Can estimate familiar quantities to a reasonable degree of accuracy, maybe an order of magnitude or better. Can follow simple instructions for practical work. Can use basic laboratory equipment in familiar situations.	Can use familiar instruments in various situations including ones that are novel. Can make measurements with less familiar instruments which may have complex scales in straightforward situations. Can estimate simple quantities with a fair degree of accuracy and less familiar ones within an order of magnitude. Can carry out chemical tests carefully and reliably.

Basic skills: written

LEVEL 1	LEVEL 3
Tables Can read from and complete simple two-column tables involving verbal or numerical data – a table of temperature against time, for instance – including appropriate labels and/or headings.	Can read from and complete tables with two or more columns – a table of melting and boiling points and other properties for metals, say. The tables may contain decimal quantities and multipliers in the column headings; e.g. 'hundreds of degrees centigrade'. Can construct, from scratch, two-column tables from raw data.
Graphs Can read from, and complete, bar charts and line graphs (given marked axes) for straightforward data involving integers.	Can read from, and complete, bar charts and line graphs for straightforward data which may involve decimals. Can interpolate and extrapolate, i.e. read values between labelled lines on the graph or predict values outside the range of the data. Can construct graphs from scratch for data involving simple integer values.
Charts Can read from and complete simple charts – for example a linear flowchart involving few elements.	Can read from, complete and construct simple charts, including flowcharts with branching elements.

Communicating and interpreting

LEVEL I	LEVEL 3
Patterns Can describe and interpret patterns in simple data presented in the form of a table, graph or chart. Can generalise from some, more familiar, data – for instance 'the temperature is falling more at first and then less as it cools'.	Can describe and interpret patterns in more complex data; including simple data presented in multiple-column tables, graphs with decimal quantities or charts with many/branching elements. Can generalise from simple, but not necessarily familiar, data.
Describing and reporting Can describe an experiment they have carried out. The description will include the basic elements. Library/resource research focuses on the most readily accessible and obvious features.	Can describe an experiment they have carried out accurately and sequentially and draw appropriate general conclusions. Library/resource research identifies important features and presents the information in a logical and well structured way. May actively seek further sources of information.
Comprehension Can locate single items of information in a passage, given specific references to aid the search.	Can locate two or more items of information; given specific references or more general guidelines to aid the search. Can collate items of information in response to a more general question and produce a precis/summary of those items or passages from a text. Can integrate other knowledge to support an answer.

Observing

LEVEL I	LEVEL 3
Describing objects and events Selects the most obvious features – shape, colour, size, etc. For instance, a drawing/description of a can collapsed by evacuating it might include terms such as 'squashed, a blue and yellow can; . .'	Uses appropriate theoretical ideas to select what to observe. The description of the can may now only indicate that the force causing the collapse was acting inwards on the can.
Looking for similarities and differences Focuses on obvious features such as shape, colour and size. Differentiation between insects, for instance, may be on size or colour.	Uses appropriate theoretical ideas in deciding which are the key similarities and/or differences. May use correct terminology – head, thorax, abdomen say – in description. May go beyond what can be seen, linking observed features to habitat or feeding habits.
Classifying Again focuses on obvious features – pieces of material may be grouped on the basis of colour, size or shape, for instance.	Uses appropriate theoretical ideas to decide on the groupings – metals or non-metals perhaps – depending on the concepts being studied.

Planning investigations

LEVEL 1	LEVEL 3
Identifies the key variables which define the investigation – what to alter and what to measure (the independent and dependent variables). For instance; in a comparison of the effectiveness of brake blocks, the type of block would be altered and the 'stopping power' measured.	Identifies the key variables and suggests a feasible way of putting them into practice – for instance by using two or more blocks and measuring the stopping distance for the same initial speed. Suggests ways of controlling other relevant factors – the type of bike, the rider (mass) and so on. Suggests a suitable scale for quantities involved by, say, mentioning that the bike should be going at a sensible speed to start with.

Investigating and making

LEVEL 1	LEVEL 3
Investigating	
Identifies the key variables which define the investigation – what to alter and what to measure (the independent and dependent variables), but fails to put them into practice. For instance; an investigation into the rate of growth of seedlings planted in different fertilisers would involve altering the fertiliser type *and* measuring the rate of growth.	Identifies the key variables and develops a suitable method for operationalising them (putting them into practice) – choosing several types and using a fixed quantity of fertiliser and measuring the height of the seedlings before and after a known time period, say. Controls other relevant factors – environment, watering, etc. in this example. Chooses a suitable scale for the quantities involved – quantity of fertiliser, number of seedlings, length of time before re-measuring and so on. Measures to an accuracy appropriate to the investigation – an accuracy of seedling height of 1mm is unnecessary, 10cm inadequate.
Constructing	
The solution to the task will work in principle but not in practice. Alternatively, an adequate design may not be put together well enough to work.	The solution will work in principle and has been put into practice effectively. If appropriate, the apparatus could be calibrated (although it may be impractical to do so) – a wind-speed indicator which worked over a range of marked wind speeds. The solution has evolved through trial and error in a series of practical investigations and shows improvements in elegance and efficiency as a consequence.

Summary of assessment components in *Active Science*

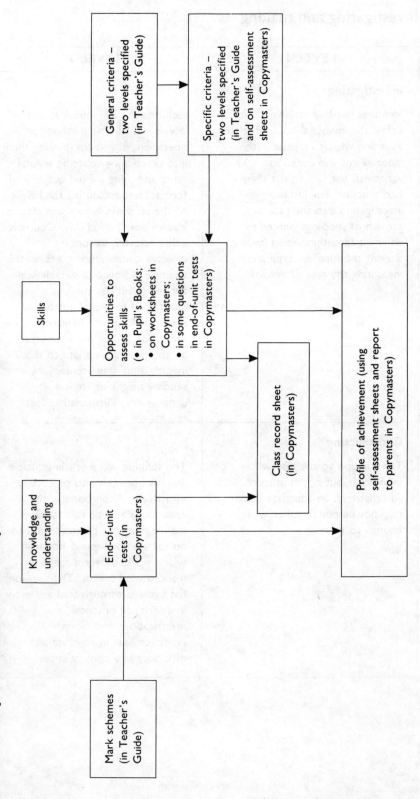

WHAT IS SCIENCE?

Introduction

Unit 1 covers the main aspects of working scientifically. The topics which illustrate this are independent of the Units that follow. The topics can be taken in any order. The aim is for the teacher to capture the pupils' interest and provide an opportunity for the class to get to grips with the skills that are to be assessed during the course. Basic skills are given extra emphasis in this Unit.

The activities have been very carefully chosen to provide good openings for discussion on methods of working, including safety matters.

There is no written test for this Unit. Instead, a practical test has been devised which can be used at some point after the Unit has been completed. A mark scheme and apparatus list are included in this Guide.

Assessment opportunities

Basic skills

1.2 Using a measuring cylinder

1.5 Using a Bunsen burner safely

1.6 Completing a line graph for a pendulum

1.8 Using weighing scales and estimating quantities

1.8 Measuring small quantities

1.10 Using a thermometer

Communicating and interpreting

1.3 Designing a winner

1.9 Buying a bike

Worksheet 1.10B Cooling kettles

Observing

1.4 Mosquitoes, ants and bees

1.5 Sorting the substances

Planning investigations

1.2 Testing other candles

1.9 Take a brake

Investigating and making

1.3 Changing speed

Worksheet 1.10C Lids and cups

1.1 Fires

Apparatus list

Pupils: Wax candle (no bigger than 4cm)
        Petri dish to catch wax drips
        Heatproof mat
Teacher: to demonstrate fire-extinguishing:
        Matches
        Sand tray
        Large cloth or tea towel
        Meths

You might try

Night lights (chubby, squat, wax burners) – these tend to last well and are more stable than most candles.

1.2 Air and fire

Apparatus list

Pupils: Candle (no bigger than 4cm)
        Petri dish
        Heatproof mat
        Plastic measuring cylinders, preferably 250cm^3
        Stopwatch or clock
Teacher: An assortment of other candles
        Range of glass containers (jam jars or beakers), volume 100cm^3–1000cm^3
        Matches

Worksheet 1.2B Volume

Pupils: Centimetre cubes
        Cuboid shapes (e.g. books, boxes, blocks) to measure

Video resources

Scientific Eye, 'Fire and Flames'.

You might try

For the glass containers, try using half-pint, pint and one-litre (roughly 2 pints) beer mugs – they seem to give pupils a more tangible idea of an increase in size. Ask: 'Does doubling the size double the burning time?'

Another option is to test the size of the flame – some types of wax give much higher flames than others.

Assessment criteria

Testing other candles (Planning investigations)

Checklist – the plan included:

Identification of key variables:
   To alter   – the size of candle.
   To measure – the time of burning.

Putting it into practice effectively:
   Altered by   – using at least two sizes.
   Measured by – timing from covering to extinction.
   Controlled   – the beaker used to cover the candle (and hence the volume of air).

Validity of results:
   Scale   – sensible choice of range of sizes.
   Accuracy – use of stopclock/stopwatch

LEVEL I	LEVEL 3
Identified the problem by using at least two different sizes of candle and attempting to judge the time of burning.	Identified the problem correctly. Used two or more sizes of candle and timed burning from covering to extinction sufficiently accurately (stopclock) to distinguish between different candles. Used same, suitably sized, beaker to cover candles.

1.3   Making a model dragster

Apparatus list

Pupils: Empty drink tin with 5mm + hole punched in base
           Card
           Scissors
           Paper clip
           Wooden or metal rod, about 15cm long; < 1cm diameter
           Wooden or metal rod, < 5cm long; < 1cm diameter
           Rubber band about 10cm long unstretched
           Wood or plastic bead with hole through
           Stopwatch or stopclock
           Metre rule
Teacher: Assorted rubber bands

Video resources

Scientific Eye, 'Forces and Friction' and 'Gravity' (although both are better used in Unit 11).

You might try

Washing-up liquid bottles work well; especially with rubber-band 'tyres'. (They also make good 'spinners' if you wish to extend the idea of energy in an elastic band.) Pupils found that 'knicker-type' elastic worked well, especially for slow vehicles.

Assessment criteria

Changing speed (Investigating and making)

Checklist – the investigation included:

Identification of key variables:

To alter — the number of winds of the rubber band or its width or length (for instance).

To measure — the dragster's speed.

Putting it into practice effectively:

Altered by — using at least numbers of winds; or widths; or lengths of the bands.

Measured by — timing a fixed distance (or vice versa).

Controlled — the size of can, the working surface, the number of winds, or widths, or lengths of the bands as appropriate.

Validity of results:

Scale — number of winds (where that is to be altered) significantly different, timed over sensible distance (> 1m)

Accuracy — sufficient to differentiate speeds using stopclock and ruler; repeat measurements if necessary.

LEVEL 1	LEVEL 3
Identified the problem by using at least two different numbers of winds of the band (in this example) and attempting to judge or compare the speeds.	Identified the problem correctly. Used two or more significantly different numbers of winds of the rubber band, and timed the motion over a distance of at least 1m accurately enough (stopclock and ruler) to allow for valid conclusions.

Designing a winner (Communicating and interpreting)

Answers to questions:
3. A number which measures air resistance.
4. About 0.4.

5. Streamlining reduces the air resistance.
6. Weight over rear wheels; soft tyres.
7. So that more weight over front wheels will give better control (of the steering) by reducing lift.
8. Explanation or sketch which shows the centre of gravity being moved backwards, for instance by moving the engine back.

LEVEL 1	LEVEL 3
Located single items of information given specific references – questions 3, 4 and 5 in particular.	Located one or more items of information and collated information into a logical order given more general references – i.e. most of questions answered correctly.

1.4 Sorting animals

Apparatus list

Any available information on insects.

Video resources

There is a very good example of how to use a key in *Scientific Eye*, 'Crimebusters'.

You might try

Any number of variations using information about animals – depending on your preference, the time of year, location and environment.

Assessment criteria

Mosquitoes, ants and bees (Observing)

LEVEL 1	LEVEL 3
Similarities and differences based on features such as colour and size.	Similarities and differences based on features such as number of legs, segmentation of body, etc. reflecting an attempt to create sensible theoretical categorisation.

(Note: these observations are difficult for pupils at this age. They are unlikely, as yet, to have a theoretical framework against which to discriminate between important and trivial details.)

1.5 Heating substances

Apparatus list

Pupils: Eye protection (EACH)
              Bunsen burner; heatproof mat
              Test-tube holder
              Medium Pyrex test tube
              Tongs
              Spatula
Teacher: Sodium chloride
              Marble chips (limestone will do)
              Zinc oxide
              Copper foil (20 2cm × 5cm strips)
              Copper (II) sulphate fine crystals
              Bread (one or two slices)

You might try

Heating other foods also works well. They are best heated gently in water, e.g. dried pea, jelly, Bovril, rice grains, tea, etc.

Assessment criteria

Sorting the substances (Observing)

LEVEL I	LEVEL 3
Categorisation based on obvious features but ones not relevant in the context of the exercise – for instance, their appearance prior to heating.	Categorisation based on idea of permanent change on heating.

1.6 A pendulum clock

Apparatus list

Pupils: String (about 1m)
              Scissors
              Plasticine (about 100g)
              Stopwatch or stopclock
              Graph paper
Teacher: Electric balance

You might try

Ask the Music Department to lend you their metronome. How does altering the position of the weight affect the pointer's movement?

Children often claim that a rigid arm makes a better pendulum timer. Ask: 'Is a metronome an upside-down pendulum?'

1.7 Timers

Apparatus list

Pupils: Stopwatch or stopclock
The rest is a little unpredictable! Try:

        Card
        Sellotape
        Marbles (a few only)
        String
        Old plastic containers (e.g. squeezy bottles)
        Measuring cylinders ($100cm^3$, $250cm^3$)
        Dry sand
        Filter funnels (large plastic)
        Springs (springy ones!)
        Plasticine
        Candle (about 10cm) and Petri dish for drips

Teacher: Hammer
        Nails
        Craft knife

You might try

'Clocks' can be made from burning string or vibrating rulers. Pupils could test how accurate their own estimates of time are (e.g. by counting: 'Mississippi one, Mississippi two . . .' etc.).

A useful way of stretching pupils is to add the extra condition that at certain regular intervals an audible or visual signal must be given.

1.8 How to weigh things

Apparatus list

A set of scales

Pupils: Beam (e.g. wood; 30cm × 2cm × 2cm)
String
100g Plasticine
10g masses (× 10)
100g masses (× 10)
Stand and clamp
Containers (e.g. disposable cups)
Teacher: Electronic balance

A micro-balance

Pupils: Straw (art straws are best)
Needle
Bolt (10–15mm to fit straw tightly)
Aluminium yoke
Wood block, spatula and rubber band to make scale
Sticky ticker-tape
Graph paper (mm squares)
Forceps
Scissors
Teacher: Sugar grains
Salt grains
Rice
Craft knife
Electronic balance (0.01g if possible)

Video resources

Scientific Eye, 'Floating and Sinking' (although this is more appropriate in Unit 2).

You might try

If you can get a plank, children love weighing themselves (and you!).

For the micro-balance, use paper straws for best results. Pupils who work fast could investigate why plastic straws are less satisfactory.

1.9   Choosing a bike

Apparatus list

No specific equipment is needed; but a bike would be useful in the lesson.

Video resources

Scientific Eye, 'Forces and Friction' and 'Getting Things Clean' (although both are more appropriate later).

You might try

In the Extras, washing powders are good for comparison.

A more difficult comparison is to ask pupils to investigate types of flooring. Which would they recommend for schools? Or which would be best in each of the rooms in a house?

Assessment criteria

Buying a bike (Communicating and interpreting)

Answers to questions:
1. Halford's Pathfinder.
2. Peugeot Crystal.
3. Alloy frame, ten or more gears, drop handlebars, alloy rims and hubs, quick-release wheels and toe clips.
4. Sports tourers have more gears and drop handlebars.
5. Alloy frame and rims.
6. Lower drag factor, lower air resistance due to lower profile.
7. Sensible arguments based on gears, riding position, cost etc.

LEVEL I	LEVEL 3
Located single items of information given specific references – questions I and 2 in particular.	Located one or more items of information and collated information into a logical order given more general references – questions 3, 4 and 5. Used other knowledge to support answers – questions 6 and 7.

Take a brake (Planning investigations)

Checklist – the plan included:

Identification of key variables:
   To alter   – the type of brake blocks.
   To measure   – how well it stops the bike (for instance).

Putting it into practice effectively:

Altered by — using three types of block.

Measured by — timing or measuring stopping distance, or the appropriate lab test.

Controlled — the type of bike, the rider, the force applied to brakes, etc.

Validity of results:

Scale — bike moving sufficiently quickly.

Accuracy — use of tape measure and stopclock (or other appropriate instruments).

LEVEL I	LEVEL 3
Identified problem by using at least two types of brake blocks and attempting to judge or compare the stopping distances.	Identified the problem correctly. Used three blocks and timed or measured the stopping distance with appropriate accuracy (stopwatch and/or tape measure) for a bike moving quickly. Controlled other variables, speed, rider, bike, force applied to brake, etc. where appropriate.

1.10 Keeping things warm

Apparatus list

Pupils: Eye protection (EACH)
            Polystyrene cup and lid*
            Plastic cup*
            Thermometer 0–110°C*
            Bunsen burner, heatproof mat, tripod, gauze
            Stopwatch or stopclock
            Stirring rod*
            Pyrex beaker (250 or 400cm^3)*
            Powdered soup

Teacher: Thermos flasks*
            China mugs*
            Matches*

*These items should be washed thoroughly in detergent and then rinsed before use.

Worksheet 1.10C Lids and cups

Pupils: Polystyrene and plastic cups and lids
            Thermometer 0–110°C
            Pyrex beaker (250 or 400cm³)
            Measuring cylinder, plastic 250cm³
            Plastic funnel
            Stopclock or stopwatch
            Graph paper
Teacher: Electric kettle to boil water

Video resources

Starting Science, 'Saving Energy' (although this might be used in Unit 8).

You might try

Include a tin camping mug among the containers – it is good for allowing pupils to feel the heat loss.

Get pupils to find out if the temperature of the *outside* of a container (judged by feeling the outside) has a connection with the rate of heat loss.

Assessment criteria

Worksheet 1.10B Cooling kettles (Communicating and interpreting)

Answers to questions:
1.   72°C.
2.   36°C plus or minus 1°C.
3.   17–18 minutes.
4.   about 15–16°C.
5.   One is a better insulator than the other. Suitable sketch graph.

LEVEL 1	LEVEL 3
Table of data constructed and graph drawn with help in setting up axes. Simple data read from graph.	Table of data constructed and graph drawn. Data read, including that requiring interpolation or extrapolation. Sketch graph drawn appropriately.

Worksheet 1.10C Lids and cups (Investigating and making)

Checklist – the investigation included:

Identification of key variables:

    To alter   – the type of cup: lid or no lid.

    To measure – how good the cup is at keeping things hot.

Putting it into practice effectively:

    Altered by   – using two identical cups, one with lid, one without;
                       using two different types of cup, both with (or without) lid.

    Measured by – time for fixed temperature drop or temperature drop in fixed
                       time.

    Controlled   – the volume of liquid; the initial temperature of the liquid.

Validity of results:

    Scale   – sensible volumes of liquid; initial temperature and time interval.

    Accuracy   – temperature measurements sufficiently accurate to
                       discriminate, say within 1 or 2°C.

LEVEL 1	LEVEL 3
Identified problem by using two cups with and without lids and then two different types of cup. Attempted to judge how well they kept the liquid hot.	Identified problem correctly. Used two identical cups with and without lids, and containing a sensible volume of liquid. The liquid was initially at a high enough temperature to allow for sensible temperature drop over 5 or 10 minutes. Temperature measured sufficiently accurately. Repeated with different types of cup.

YEAR I TESTS
PRACTICAL TEST
READING INSTRUMENT SCALES

Introduction

These two tests are intended to be used at an appropriate stage during the first year of the *Active Science* course. They are suitable at any time after the end of Unit I, when the pupils have had a chance to develop their basic scientific skills.

Apparatus list

Question I Cards with inked lines and labelled A and B. Line A 43mm; line B 87mm. 30 cm ruler.

Question 2 Roll of gummed paper – for instance, the type used for ticker timers. 30cm ruler.

Question 3 $100cm^3$ measuring cylinder, $500cm^3$ beaker of sand, kitchen (or other type) scales which will read about 200g with reasonable accuracy, funnel.

Question 4 Rubber band and suitable forcemeter, i.e. one that reads between; say one-third to two-thirds of full scale with the rubber band. 30cm ruler.

Question 5 $130cm^3$ of coloured water (ink used as dye) in $250cm^3$ beaker, syringe reading to $2cm^3$, spare syringe. (This syringe could be replaced by an easier one to manipulate – 5 or $10cm^3$ with suitable alterations to question.)

Question 6 $100cm^3$ measuring cylinder with $65cm^3$ of water. $25cm^3$ cylinder with $17cm^3$ water.

Question 7 0–110°C thermometer, the question sheet should be somewhere near a sink.

Question 8 Retort stand, boss and clamp, Im length of string, suitable object to act as a pendulum bob (Plasticine, large nut), stopclock or stopwatch, piece of Plasticine and needle or similar to act as fiducial point. 30cm ruler.

Question 9 Electronic clock and clockwork stopclock set to 38 seconds and I minute 39 seconds respectively.

Question 10 Match, Bunsen burner (not connected to supply and without rubber tube), test tube in rack. The question sheet should be positioned near to a sink.

Question II Bunsen burner, mat, matches, test tube, test-tube rack, supply of water (tap or beaker), test-tube holder or clip, goggles.

Question 12 2 boiling tubes, 2 test tubes, four delivery tubes (see diagram), retort stands, bosses and clamps.

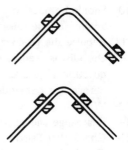

Question 13   Kitchen roll, tray large enough to soak single piece from the roll, 500 and 1000cm^3 beakers, supply of water, kitchen scales, 25 and 100cm^3 measuring cylinders, plastic funnel.

Question 14   Pile of A4 writing paper, either 130 (say) sheets, or a pile of exactly 100 sheets with label to that effect, 15 or 30cm ruler.

Question 15   Ball of Plasticine, about 50cm^3, ruler.

Question 16   Expendable steel spring, set of 6 × 100g slotted masses and hanger (with most springs this should not exceed the elastic limit), metre rule, retort stand, 2 bosses and clamps. Retort stand set up, spring and ruler on bench.

Administration

The questions represent no more than examples which may be used, modified or augmented as required. Some questions will take considerably longer than others. This problem can be overcome to some extent by putting two or more questions together at one station. An alternative is to add a number of written questions – drawing a line graph from a set of data for instance – which pupils can carry on with if they have time to spare at any question.

   With circuses of this type it is often possible to utilise the services of the lab technician for the general tidying up and maintenance of the questions; both during the question and, more particularly, at the changeover from one to another.

   If this is not possible, the apparatus can in some cases be duplicated so that the pressure of servicing the apparatus at changeover can be removed or reduced.

Notes on particular questions

Question 5   Asks pupils to use a syringe. The volume of water in both the beaker and the syringe must be checked at the changeover point (an extra syringe can be supplied which can then be checked at any time during the next question time).

Question 7   Close to a sink.

Question 8   Check that the apparatus has been dismantled ready for use by the
              next pupil.
Question 10   Should be near to a sink (pupils are required to estimate the
              volume of the sink).
Questions 11 Require the teacher to observe the pupils work. At question 11 a
and 12   checklist is used to monitor their safe working with the Bunsen; at
              question 12 the apparatus must be checked against the diagram
              before it is dismantled.
Question 13   Will require a general tidying up.
Question 14   Rearrange pile of paper.
Question 15   Check that Plasticine is in a ball.
Question 16   Check that masses have been removed.

Practical test

Mark scheme

The answers given here are typical values only. The ranges for accuracy suggested
here can be changed to suit the ability, age and experience of the group – the
ones included here are examples only.

1. 43mm
    9cm

2. 12.6cm ± 2mm

3. 110 ± 5g (accuracy depends on the scale in use).

4. 7 ± 1N (say).

5. in beaker 130 ± 10cm^3
    in syringe 1.8 ± 0.1cm^3

6. a. 65 ± 1cm^3
6. b. 17 ± 0.5cm^3

7. a. 19°C ⎫
    b. 30°C ⎬ (approximate values only)
    c. 12°C ⎭

8. Time for ten swings = 10 seconds
    Time for one swing = $\dfrac{10 \text{ swings}}{10 \text{ seconds}}$ = 1 swing (every second).

9. 38 seconds
    1 minute 39 seconds (accuracy depends on choice of instrument).

10. Typical values are given for each question. Pupils tend to be poor at
    estimating – error limits of 10%, 50% or even more may be appropriate.
    a. 4.5cm
    b. 8m
    c. 200g
    d. 120mm^2

e. 3kg

f. 15–20cm^3

g. 20 litres

11. Checklist:
- Bunsen lit from 'underneath'
- with air hole closed
- adjusted to give small blue flame
- test tube held in clip
- angled away from danger
- tube moved in flame to 'spread' heat.

12. Checklist:
- tube 1 correctly selected.
- correct delivery tube selected.
- tube 2 correctly selected.
- fixed together correctly and without undue force.

Positioning, or tubes in relation to each other, adequate.

13. A towel will soak up 10–30cm^3 of water (typically).

Methods: weighed towel before and after soaking, OR squeezed water out and measured volume, OR measured volume of water before and after.

14. Thickness of 100 sheets = 9mm

Thickness of one sheet = 9/100 = 0.09mm

15. 50cm^3 ± 10 (say).

16. Apparatus used appropriately.

Extension measured (not length).

Appropriate accuracy ± 5mm, say.

Table headed appropriately with mass or weight; extension.

Five or six measurements taken.

Typical values:

Mass (g)	Extension (cm)
100	4.5
200	8.5
300	12.0
400	16.5
500	20.0
600	23.5

Reading instrument scales

Mark scheme

1. What is the reading on this balance? a. 770g
   b. 364g

2. What is the length of the pencil? 17cm

3. How long have these stopclocks been running for?
   a. 3 minutes 16 seconds
   b. 11 minutes 7 seconds

4. What is the reading on the forcemeter? 26N

5. How much water is there in this measuring cylinder?
   $47cm^3$
   ($46-48cm^3$ should be accepted)

6. How much water is there in this beaker? $70cm^3$ (65–75)

7. How much water is there in this jug? $330cm^3$ (320–340)

8. How much water is there in this syringe? $1.4cm^3$

9. What is the temperature reading on these thermometers?
   a. 19°C
   b. 57°C

10. What is the reading on this thermometer?
    19.5°C

Mark allocation

Either one mark for each answer within, say, one (or two) scale divisions (where appropriate) of the instrument, or:
3 marks for each answer within 1 scale division
2 marks for each answer within 2 scale divisions
1 mark for each answer within 5 scale divisions

UNIT 2 WATER

Introduction

The main concepts of this Unit are:
- water as a finite resource
- water as a habitat
- purification of water
- dissolving
- evaporation
- states of matter
- displacement and density
- dehydration

These concepts are developed, and scientific skills practised, in the context of the everyday experiences of pupils. Spread 2.12 offers water in food as a context for broader investigations. Most of the Units in the *Active Science* course have a final double-page spread of this type.

The main themes in this Unit can be taught in any order, although the sequence used in the book helps with continuity.

Assessment opportunities

Basic skills

2.1   Using a microscope

2.3   Drawing a bar chart of rainfall figures

2.3   Following instructions for setting up glassware

2.4   Using a top-pan balance

2.9   Following instructions and drawing a line graph for boiling water and melting ice.

Communicating and interpreting

2.5   Clean water and disease – comprehension

2.6   Using water to dissolve things – report on experiment

2.12 Dried food – interpreting data

Observing

2.4   Living things in water

End-of-Unit-test, Question 3, Water animals.

Planning investigations

2.8   What is the best way to dry a cloth?

2.12 How much water is there in fresh food?

Investigating and making

2.2   Making a roof

2.5   Can I drink it?

Worksheet 2.6   How well does sugar dissolve?

2.1 Water from different places

Apparatus list

Pupils: Glass or TPX plastic measuring cylinder, 100cm³
            Microscope and slide
            Teat pipette
            Watch glass
            Pyrex beaker 250cm³

Teacher: Plasticine
            Matches
            Samples of water from different places – but beware of local pollution of ponds, streams etc.

You might try

A more accurate test of water clarity is to read typed script through the tube of water until this becomes too difficult. Pupils could also investigate if all types of water magnify the same when a drop is put over print.

2.2 Too much water

Apparatus list

Pupils: Atlas map of the UK for p.28 (there is also a weather map for 31 January 1953 on worksheet 3.2)
            Balsa wood strip: about 50cm × 5mm × 5mm (wood spills are a possible substitute)
            Balsa or PVA adhesive
            Medium-gauge polythene bag of reasonable thickness
            Card
            Scissors
            Modelling knife
            Cutting board (heatproof mat will do)
            Drawing pins
            Paper towel
            Beaker

You might try

Making a roof

Pupils could try different tile patterns.

If you can get some straw, the properties of a thatched roof are worth investigating.

As a further investigation, test the pitch (angle of slope) of a roof.

Assessment criteria

Making a roof (Investigating and making)

LEVEL I	LEVEL 3
The idea behind the structure was appropriate but it didn't give an adequate dry area due to poor design and/or poor workmanship.	The idea was sound and the design incorporated ideas contained in the text – overlapping slates for instance. Modifications were incorporated in the light of experience. The final structure was stable and a satisfactory method of measuring dryness was developed.

2.3   Too little water

Apparatus list

Pupils: Eye protection (EACH)
           Conical flask, 150–250cm^3
           Bung and delivery tube to fit
           Stand and clamp
           Bunsen burner, heatproof mat, tripod, gauze
           Test tube
Teacher: Matches
           Sea water (or 1molar sodium chloride solution)

You might try

Set pupils this extension investigation task: You live in a very hot, dry country and you fetch all your water in a bucket. You also have to store your water in a bucket. Investigate ways of keeping the water at its best.

2.4   Water and life

Apparatus list

Finding out how much water is in a plant

Pupils: Fresh plant leaves
Teacher: Electric balance
           Oven pre-warmed at about 60°C

Living things in water

Pupils: Hand lens
            Microscope and slide
            Worksheet 2.4 (Key to small water organisms)

Teacher: Sample of pond water

Video resources

Seeing and Doing, 'Pond Life'.
A Place to Live, 'Wings over the Pond', 'Tiger in the Pond'.
Science – Start Here, 'Rainy Days'.

You might try

'Living things in water' could be extended to include a comparison between life in fresh water and sea water.

Assessment criteria

Living things in water (Observing)

LEVEL 1	LEVEL 3
The drawing showed obvious features – size, colour and overall shape, for instance.	The drawing emphasised features such as segments of body and/or linked features to motion/habitat of animal (even if incorrectly from an 'expert' point of view).

2.5 Drinking water

Apparatus list

Pupils: A little unpredictable, but try:
            Glass or TPX plastic measuring cylinder, $100cm^3$
            Microscope and slide
            Teat pipette
            Watch glass
            Pyrex beaker $250cm^3$
            Thermometer $0-110°C$
            Bunsen burner, heatproof mat, tripod, gauze
            Test tube

Teacher: Matches
            Samples of water from different places (but beware of local pollution).

You might try

An interesting problem-solving exercise for pupils is to ask them to find a good way of purifying water – without giving them extra help. Pupils have even been known to try putting charcoal in water, a method of purification mentioned in the Bible!

Assessment criteria

Can I drink it? (Investigating and making)

Checklist – the investigation included:

Identification of key variables:

To alter   – the source of the water.

To measure – the 'cleanliness' of water.

Putting it into practice effectively:

Altered by   – using at least two sources of water.

Measured by – a variety of tests involving evaporating, observing with a microscope, etc.

Controlled   – the volume used each time

the procedures, e.g. clean glassware.

Validity of results:

Scale   – sensible volume of water used.

LEVEL 1	LEVEL 3
Identified the problem correctly by attempting to test at least two different samples.	Identified the problem correctly. Used two or more samples of water and a number of different tests of cleanliness. Used a sensible volume of water as appropriate to each test. Controlled the volume of the different samples where necessary and observed procedures such as using clean glassware.

Clean water and disease (Communicating and interpreting)

Answers to questions:

4. 2200 houses.
5. Wells and rainwater.
6. 60 000 people.
7. Sketch of water wheel showing blades dipping into river and driving water up some sort of channel. Some source of power attached to wheel.
8. Suitable redefinition: poor quality, dirty etc.
9. Not enough water, provide new waterworks (to process more water from the river).

LEVEL 1	LEVEL 3
Located single items of information – questions 4, 5 and 6 in particular.	Collated items of information and present a precis of that information. Can integrate other knowledge to support an answer – questions 7, 8 and 9.

2.6 Dissolving

Apparatus list

Pupils: 6 test tubes
Test-tube rack
Filter funnel
Filter paper
Spatula
Worksheet 2.6 (How well does sugar dissolve?)

Teacher: Sugar
Salt
Liquid detergent
Custard powder
Tea
Iron filings
Vinegar
Coffee
Soap
Powder paint
Washing soda (sodium carbonate)
Flour
Copper (II) sulphate fine crystals (POISON!)
Chalk powder (calcium carbonate)
Rice
Cooking oil
Baking powder

(The solids are best kept permanently in labelled Petri dishes.)

You might try

Pupils could identify the colours in stalagmites and stalactites and find out what caused these colours. One colour is caused by iron compounds, but iron filings do not dissolve. Pupils could find out how the iron colour got there.

Wookey Hole caves have one chamber where all the stalactites were shot down by a man using them for target practice in fun. Why is this a great shame from the scientific point of view?

Assessment criteria

Using water to dissolve things (Communicating and interpreting)

LEVEL 1	LEVEL 3
The description included the basic elements of the work they had carried out. The results were recorded and a conclusion drawn which was not in conflict with the evidence but which was specific rather than general.	The description was accurate and presented the details in a logical and sequential fashion (even if the experiment itself was not particularly well executed). Data was collated into some form of ordered prose or table and subsequently used to form the basis of categorisation. Conclusions were drawn on the basis of accumulated evidence and were at an appropriate level of generality.

Worksheet 2.6   How well does sugar dissolve? (Investigating and making)

Checklist – the investigation included:

Identification of key variables:
  To alter   – stirring, or water temperature, or volume of water.
  To measure – rate of dissolving.

Putting it into practice effectively:
  Altered by   – one stirred regularly, or continuously, the other not stirred; hot and cold water; large and small volumes.
  Measured by – timing from putting powder into water until all dissolved.
  Controlled   – time for stirring; or volume of water; or water temperature, as appropriate.

Validity of results:
  Scale   – sensible volume of water and chemical, amount of stirring, etc.
  Accuracy   – suitable accuracy of measurements of water volume and amount of chemical (measuring cylinder and 'teaspoon'), care over 'end point' of dissolving, use of stopclock, repeat measurements.

LEVEL I	LEVEL 3
Identified the problem by using at least two temperatures (for example) and attempting to judge how long it took to dissolve.	Identified the problem correctly. Used two or more temperatures (for instance) and held other factors (stirring, or water volume) constant. Used a stopwatch or clock to time from putting powder into water to when all dissolved. Used sensible, measured and equal volumes of water and powder.

2.7 Water and washing

Apparatus list

Pupils: 'Dirty' cloth, about 30cm × 5cm to cut up into eight pieces ('dirt' could be made by pre-soaking an old cloth in diluted permanent ink, and then drying the cloth)
Scissors
Soap powder
Detergent
Stirring rod
Washing-up bowl
Stopwatch or stopclock
Access to hot water

Video resources

Scientific Eye, 'Getting Things Clean'.

You might try

Pupils could make their own laboratory 'washing machine' using a large plastic sweet jar, shaken by hand. Remind them to work out ways of keeping tests fair.

Pupils could investigate how different abrasives might work in washing. Does each one have its own job?

2.8 Drying

Apparatus list

Pupils: Cloth, about 30cm × 5cm, to cut up
Scissors
String (for washing line)
Teacher: Electronic balance
If available, hot-air blowers/fans

Video resources

Scientific Eye, 'Drying Out'.

You might try

Pupils could make their own 'tumble-drier' as a problem-solving task. One idea is a plastic sweet jar with holes in it. Ask: 'How could you make it more like a tumble-drier?'

Assessment criteria

What is the best way to dry a cloth? (Planning investigations)

Checklist – the plan included:

Identification of key variables:
   To alter   – cloth flat or crumpled, temperature, draught.
   To measure – the rate of drying.

Putting it into practice effectively:
   Altered by   – using flat and crumpled cloth for instance, with other variables under test held constant.
   Measured by – mass of cloth before and after the drying process (for instance).
   Controlled   – the area by measuring cloths or overlapping them and trimming to size;
                    initial wetness;
                    time for drying.

Validity of results:
   Scale   – Sensible size for cloths, reasonable time allowed to elapse before weighing.

LEVEL I	LEVEL 3
Identified the problem by using flat and crumpled cloths, or cloths at two different temperatures, etc. and 'seeing how long they took to dry'.	Identified the problem correctly. Changed one variable at a time, e.g. using flat and crumpled cloths at the same temperature. Used sensibly sized pieces of cloth and allowed sufficient time for drying. Weighed cloth before and after same drying time. Controlled other variables (e.g. initial wetness) as appropriate.

2.9   Ice, water and steam

Apparatus list

Pupils: Eye protection (EACH)
Pyrex beaker 250cm^3
Stirring rod
Thermometer 0–110°C
Crushed ice, about 100cm^3
Bunsen burner, heatproof mat, tripod, gauze
Worksheet 2.9 (Sketch graphs)
Teacher: Matches
Graph paper

Video resources

Science – Start Here, 'Cold Weather'.

You might try

Pupils could investigate the principle behind gritting roads. What is used? Why?
   The history of steam engines (as opposed to steam locomotives) is interesting applied science.

2.10   Floating and sinking

Apparatus list

Pupils: Access to sink or washing-up bowl
50g+ of Plasticine
Teacher: Electronic balance
Variety of objects: some that float, some that sink (e.g. cork, rubber, plastic, wax, wood, paper, metal, etc.)
Aluminium blocks of different sizes
Wood blocks of different sizes

Video resources

Scientific Eye, 'Floating and Sinking'.
Science – Start Here, 'Shipshape'.

You might try

Ask pupils to make a simple hydrometer from a match and Plasticine. They should use it to compare the support given by different types of water. It can also be used to compare sugar solutions.

2.11 Water at work

Apparatus list

No specific equipment is needed for this topic.

You might try

Making a simple gravity-turned water-wheel shows how water can be put to work at very little cost.

There is a very large water-driven wheel at the Welsh National Slate Museum in Llanberis which drives all the machinery in the foundry, e.g. the lathes and drills.

2.12 Investigating water in food

Apparatus list

Rehydrating spaghetti

Pupils: about 25g spaghetti
Pyrex beaker, 400cm³, clean
Bunsen burner, heatproof mat, tripod, gauze
Teacher: Electronic balance
Colander or large food strainer
Rice

How much water is there in fresh food? (if done as an investigation)

Pupils: Samples of food (e.g. bread, crisps, cheese)
Pyrex beaker, 250cm³
Teacher: Oven pre-warmed to 60°C
Electronic balance

You might try

Fresh foods which are good to test for water content include oranges, apples, tomatoes, potatoes, bananas, a melon, cucumber, strawberries, and cabbage or lettuce (to link back to 2.4).

Assessment criteria

Dried food (Communicating and interpreting)

Answers to questions:
1. 50p.
2. Milk.
3. Fresh apple; dehydrated potato, apple, peas, meat and milk.
4. Dried food, any sensible reason.
5. Dried food, processing costs (for instance).
6. Correct list for several foods.

LEVEL 1	LEVEL 3
Located single items of information correctly, questions 1 and 2.	Located items correctly, questions 1, 2, and 3. Interpreted the table in response to more general questions, 4 and 5, and used the table as a basis for collecting further information, question 6.

How much water is there in fresh food? (Planning investigations)

Checklist – the plan included:

Identification of key variables:

To alter	– the type of food.
To measure	– the amount of water.

Putting it into practice effectively:

Altered by	– using different foods.
Measured by	– initial and final mass of food (when mass no longer decreasing).
Controlled	– initial weight of samples, temperature for drying.

Validity of results:

Scale	– suitable mass of food, temperature and drying time.
Accuracy	– appropriate scales or balance.

LEVEL 1	LEVEL 3
Identified the problem by using two different foods and attempting to judge their loss in mass.	Identified the problem correctly. Used the same initial mass of two or more different foods, dried them at the same (appropriate) temperature until their masses were no longer decreasing and measured their masses with appropriate accuracy.

Unit 2 Test

Mark scheme

1. a. 18p.
    b. Sewage.
    c. 2p.

2. a. For example:

Material	Shrink test	Fade test	Crease test
A	No	No	Quite
B	No	No	A bit
C	No	A bit	Quite
D	A lot	No	Very

   b. Choice backed up by sensible reasons.

3. a. Description including major reasons – 'walks' on water, four long legs, two shorter ones, antennae, etc. (pupils are likely to use everyday words; the marking is based on their appreciation of the important features rather than accurate vocabulary).
    b. Such things as: one lives on the water, one underneath; shape of body, 'hairs', segmentation, etc.

LEVEL 1	LEVEL 3
The description focused on obvious features such as colour, shape and number of legs. The differences noted were similarly 'everyday'.	The description was based on an attempt to identify the important features of the animal; for instance, the size of the body in relation to legs and its possible link with its ability to 'float'. Differences similarly based on sensible structure–function arguments, even if technically 'wrong'.

(This question can be used to assess Observing.)

4. Selection of tests drawn from work in the Unit. For instance, filtering, evaporating, etc.

5. Could you follow the guide? Does it contain all the major points referred to in the diagram in the text? (e.g. overlapping tiles, etc.).

6. a. Stirring, increasing the volume or temperature of the water, grinding the sweet.
   b. Does the plan:

      - identify the variable to alter, e.g. stirring, temperature?
      - suggest how this is to be put into practice?
      - identify the dependent variable, rate of dissolving?
      - decide how this can be measured, e.g. time for a fixed mass to dissolve completely?
      - mention some things to control, the mass of the sweet, volume and temperature of water, etc?

7. a. 100 children.
   b. 112–113 children.
   c. Oldtown.
   d. Yes. *Overall*, there were more children with many bad teeth in Oldtown even though there were fewer with no bad teeth.

8. a. Dirty, greasy, dirty, greasy.
   b. Temperature of water, volume of water, volume of soap powder, time of washing, stirred or not stirred, equal amount of dirt, equal amounts of grease, equal-sized pieces of cloth.

9. a. Paper, rags, sticks and coarse grit.
   b. Filter.
   c. Grit and sand.
   d. Stay 'floating' in the water.

10. a. Table 1.
    b. Welsh.
    c. Table 3.
    d. – Suitable choice of scale.
       – Axes labelled 'average household bills' and 'Year'.
       – Equal interval scale for 'average household bills'.
       – Bars labelled with year and equal width and separation.
       – Bars correctly plotted.
       – Title.

AIR

Introduction

Starting with the effects of moving air as evidence for the presence of air, the Unit moves on to discuss air pressure. Striking practical activities are used to introduce this concept. Further activities on the uses of air may or may not be interpreted in terms of air pressure: the pupils are encouraged to make their own decisions about some of the phenomena described.

A final set of laboratory activities precedes an optional description of gas structure and the kinetic theory. The composition of air leads into a longer study of oxygen and its role in burning and respiration. The mechanics of breathing are included, as well as ventilation and the heating of buildings. Flight is the theme of the longer investigation on the final spread.

It is advisable to use the progression in the Unit as a teaching sequence.

Assessment opportunities

Basic skills

3.1 Using a top-pan balance

3.7 Testing for carbon dioxide

3.9 Drawing a bar chart about breathing

3.11 Drawing a line graph about how long air lasts

Communicating and interpreting

3.3 Airy questions

3.10 How do fire-fighters ventilate a fire?

Unit test, Question 3, Comprehension on discovery of oxygen

Observing

3.2 Taking air away

3.5 Finding out about air

3.7 Observing burning

Planning investigations

3.4 Testing the propeller

Unit test, Question 2, Bounce of a football

Investigating and making

3.1 Measuring the speed of air

3.9 Extras 2: Breathing rates

3.12 Flying machines

3.1   Is air real?

Apparatus list

Air experiments

Pupils: Medium-gauge A4 size polythene bag
$10cm^3$ + plastic syringe
Jam jar or milk bottle or Pyrex beaker
Washing-up bowl or access to sink with plug

Weighing air

Pupils: Balloon
Washing-up liquid squeezy bottle (large)
Bung to fit squeezy bottle

Teacher: Electric balance
Vacuum pump
Glass lemonade bottle with bung, pressure tubing and tubing clip
connected
Safety screen

Measuring the speed of air

Pupils: A little unpredictable but try:
Any scrap card or plastic boxes and cups
Egg boxes
Assorted rubber bands
Sellotape and glue (PVA)
String
Drawing pins
Assorted pieces of wood ($5-30cm \times 2cm \times 4cm$ is useful)
Stand and clamp

Teacher: Fan or air blower if available

You might try

When pupils are blowing air into a plastic bag, they could also test to see how much weight it can support. (This links to spread 3.2.)

When making a wind-speed measuring device, most children opt for one that spins. Encourage some to try a flap-style device, since it is easy to relate wind speed to how many degrees the flap moves up.

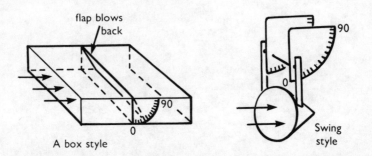

flap blows
back

A box style

90

90

0

0

Swing
style

Assessment criteria

Measuring the speed of air (Investigating and making)

LEVEL 1	LEVEL 3
The idea behind the indicator was sound but its construction was inadequate due to poor choice of materials or workmanship (too much friction in a bearing for instance).	The idea was sound in principle and worked in practice. The design utilised ideas presented in the text and an attempt was made to check that the design would work for various wind speeds (i.e. that it could, in principle, be calibrated).

3.2 Living under the atmosphere

Apparatus list

Testing air pressure

Teacher: Vacuum pump
Safety screen
Gallon or 5-litre oil can fitted with bung and tubing to connect to pump

Using air pressure

Teacher: Wooden board about 30cm × 30cm × 2cm
Medium or heavy-gauge polythene bag, about A4 size
Tubing
Antiseptic solution
Wire to fix bag to tube

Measuring air pressure

Pupils: Party blower
Balloon
Art straws
Sellotape
Transparent PVC tubing (about 50cm)
Teacher: Aneroid barometer if available

You might try

In the experiment 'Using air pressure', a camping air-bed works well.

If pupils have not tested the supportive strength of air in 3.1, they will find it interesting to see whether six inflated balloons can support the lightest or the heaviest child – or even the teacher!

Assessment criteria

Taking air away (Observing)

LEVEL 1	LEVEL 3
The sketch/description showed a crushed can.	The sketch/description indicated that the pupil had 'observed' that the can was pushed in from all sides – i.e. that the air pressure acts in all directions.

3.3 Air at work

Apparatus list

Pupils: Materials to make a poster, e.g.:
          Coloured sugar paper
          Pritt Stick
          Felt marker pens
          Scissors

Video resources

Starting Science, 'Sources of Energy', 'Helicopters'.
Scientific Eye, 'Keeping Cool'

You might try

Pupils are likely to enjoy designing and making their own kites, then testing them, modifying the design, testing again, and so on.

Assessment criteria

Airy questions (Communicating and interpreting)

LEVEL 1	LEVEL 3
The poster included photographs or diagrams and copies of explanatory text.	The poster included relevant photographs and diagrams which were used as part of a logical and coherent description of the operation of the animals/apparatus.

3.4 Using air to move

Apparatus list

Pupils: Scrap plastic containers (to cut up)
            Scissors to cut plastic
            Cork to mount plastic in
            Craft knife and cutting board
            Large steel needle to make an axle
            Small blocks of wood (about 10cm × 4cm × 2cm)
            Drawing pins
            Poster materials (see 3.3)

You might try

Pupils could make a model submarine from a plastic lemonade bottle. They could raise it by blowing in air through slits in the side. Pupils could also add a propeller and test their design in the shallow end of a swimming pool.

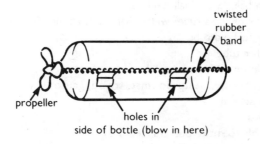

twisted
rubber
band

propeller

holes in
side of bottle (blow in here)

Pupils could also try this problem-solving task. There is a weight at the bottom of a tank, and they have to find a way of raising it to the surface without human effort. (Suggest they use air bags if nobody has any ideas.)

Pupils could also make a rocket from a washing-up liquid bottle and test it outside.

Assessment criteria

Testing the propeller (Planning investigations)

LEVEL 1	LEVEL 3
Identified the variable – how 'good' the propeller is – by trying to measure force or wind speed, but suggested method would not work due to inappropriate choice of instrument or method of putting it into practice.	Identified the variable correctly. Suggested sensible apparatus for measuring force or wind speed. Suggestions showed recognition of likely order of magnitude of quantities to be measured.

3.5 What is air?

Apparatus list

Teacher: This is a 'circus' of experiments:
  Eye protection (some experiments)
  Air freshener
  Medium-gauge A4 polythene bag with closure
  Access to freezer compartment
  2 candles on Petri dish bases
  Matches
  Aluminium foil pieces, about 3cm x 1cm
  Empty large plastic drink bottle with top
  2 plastic syringes, 10cm^3 + connected by tubing
  500cm^3 round bottom flask with glass tube through bung
  Pyrex beaker
  3 boiling tubes in test-tube rack
  Labelled bottles of boiled (distilled) water and pond water
  Bunsen burner, heatproof mat, test-tube holder
  Squash ball, 'Supa' ball, golf ball
  Perspex or glass tube, wider than balls, about 50cm long
  Clamp to hold tube
  Bung for tube
  Treacle tin with push-on lid
  Bunsen burner, heatproof mat, tripod, gauze
  Safety screen
  Matches
  Materials to make posters (see 3.3)

You might try

The following two demonstrations are very enjoyable for pupils:

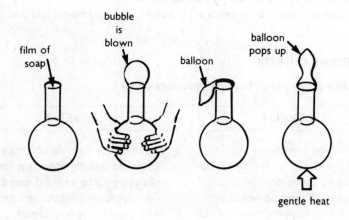

They also link to spread 4.2.

Assessment criteria

Finding out about air (Observing)

LEVEL 1	LEVEL 3
Reports on the obvious features of the experiments – for instance smell, movement of tin foil, etc.	Attempts to select observations on the basis of some theory of what air is – even if that theory is incomplete.

3.6 The ingredients of air

Apparatus list

Pupils: Small candle on cork base (as a float)
           Gas jar or cylinder that the base will fit inside
           Washing-up bowl
           Chinagraph marker pencil
           Measuring cylinder (100 or 250cm^3)
Teacher: Matches

3.7 Oxygen

Apparatus list

Burning in oxygen

Pupils: Eye protection (EACH)
           Combustion spoon
           Bunsen burner, heatproof mat
           Test-tube rack
           5 test tubes of oxygen (with bungs!)
Teacher: Matches
           Equipment to fill test-tubes with oxygen
           Lime water
           Copper foil pieces (about 4cm × 1cm)
           Steel wool
           Sulphur (small pieces)
           Wood spills
           Magnesium ribbon

Observing burning

Pupils: Eye protection (EACH)
           Bunsen burner, heatproof mat, tripod
           Tongs
           Sand tray
           Worksheet 3.7A (Observing burning)

Teacher: Cooking oil
           Scrap paper
           Small iron nails
           Coal (very small pieces)
           Polythene bag cut into small pieces
           Packet of crisps
           Flakes of paint
           Wood shavings
           Marble chips
           Matches
           Aluminium foil
           Grass
           Wool (small pieces of material are best)

(These are best kept permanently in labelled Petri dishes.)

Worksheet 3.7B   Find the kidnappers

Pupils: Bunsen burner, heatproof mat, tripod
           Sand tray
           Tongs

Teacher: Pieces of as many different types of paper as possible, preferably all
           the same colour
           Matches

Video resources

Scientific Eye, 'Fire and Flames'. (This may have been used in Unit 1.)

Assessment criteria

Observing burning (Observing)

LEVEL 1	LEVEL 3
Reports on obvious features; colour and extent of flame, smoke, etc.	Includes other observations linked to an attempt to classify the materials by their structure or type.

3.8 Breathing I

Apparatus list

Pupils: Boiling tubes or conical flasks fitted as shown:

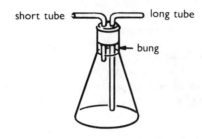

short tube   long tube

bung

Candle in Petri dish

Teacher: Limewater
            Ice
            Antiseptic

Video resources

Good Health, 'Love your Lungs'.

You might try

Extras 2 could be used to pursue the question of *why* we breathe faster during and directly after exercise.

3.9 Breathing 2

Apparatus list

Pupils: Stopwatch or stopclock
            Large (A3) medium-gauge polythene bag
            Washing-up bowl
            Rubber tubing
            Large plastic beaker

You might try

A bell jar with a rubber diaphragm is a useful working model of what happens during breathing.

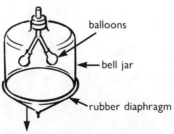

balloons

bell jar

rubber diaphragm

Assessment criteria

Extras 2 (Investigating and making)

The written account indicated that the investigation had included:

Identification of key variables:
To alter	– the age of those being tested.
To measure	– the rate of respiration.

Putting it into practice effectively:
Altered by	– testing at least two people.
Measured by	– number of breaths per minute (or equivalent).
Controlled	– state of activity, sex, etc.

Validity of results:
Scale	– sensible length of time used to count breaths; significant difference in age between those tested.
Accuracy	– use of stopclock or equivalent; repeated measurements.

LEVEL I	LEVEL 3
Identified the problem by testing at least two people of different age. Judged respiration rate in some way, even if qualitative.	Identified the problem by testing more than two people of significantly different ages. Measured respiration rate by counting breaths over at least one minute when people at rest (or same level of activity).

3.10 Ventilation

Apparatus list

Pupils:	Heatproof mat
	Candle (< 4cm high) on Petri dish
	Card to make into chimney
	Scissors
	Cardboard box (a shoe box with lid is ideal)
	Polythene (to make a 'window')
	Tissue paper
Teacher:	Sellotape/glue
	Matches

You might try

In the experiment on testing chimneys, if you have a piece of apparatus to show convection currents, it is easy for children to build chimneys and then test how well they work.

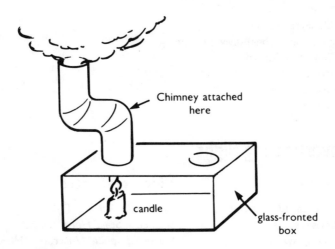

Chimney attached here

candle

glass-fronted box

Assessment criteria

How do fire-fighters ventilate a fire? (Communicating and interpreting)

Answers to questions:
1. Because air is needed for burning, apparently making matters worse.
2. Clears hot air and smoke, improves vision for fire-fighters.
3. Burns faster (spread to nearby buildings).
4. Sensible list drawn from text, e.g. is there anybody trapped?; then find out about building, location of stairs, skylights, etc. and adjacent properties; ventilate building, top then bottom; tackle seat of blaze while hosing outside.
5. Already plenty of air.
6. Blast of smoke, etc. on opening at top if other way.
7. Slows down spread of fire.

LEVEL 1	LEVEL 3
Located single items of information given specific references – questions 1 and 2 in particular.	Located and collated information to produce list of jobs (questions 1–4). Could bring other knowledge to bear, e.g. question 5. Could make sensible inferences from presented information, e.g. questions 6 and 7.

3.11 Living without air

Apparatus list

Pupils: Washing-up bowl
$400cm^3$ + Pyrex beaker or gas jar
Measuring cylinder
Chinagraph pencil
PVC (or rubber) delivery tube
Candle in Petri dish
Stopwatch or clock

Teacher: Graph paper
Antiseptic

3.12 Investigating flight

Apparatus list

Pupils: Thin card (A4 piece)
Scissors
Art straw
White paper (A4 piece)
Glue (Pritt and PVA)
Stand and clamp
Thread

Video resources

Animals in Action, 'Flying'.
Science – Start Here, 'Flight'.
Starting Science, 'Aircraft', 'Helicopters'.
Scientific Eye, 'Lighter Than Air'.

You might try

If you can get any examples of birds' wings through the Royal Society for the Protection of Birds, pupils could compare these with the shape of their aerofoil.

Ask: 'Is a helicopter blade the same shape as an aerofoil?'

Assessment criteria

Flying machines (Investigating and making)

Checklist – the investigation included:

Identification of key variables:

To alter   – the length of wings, or shape of aerofoil, or length or shape of tail, etc.

To measure   – how far it flies.

Putting it into practice effectively:

Altered by   – systematic change to one of variables.

Measured by – distance of flight.

Controlled   – other factors, how launched, etc.

Validity of results:

Scale   – changes to shape, etc. big enough to produce measurable effect.

Accuracy   – several repeats for each change.

LEVEL I	LEVEL 3
Identified the problem by changing the length of wings, for example, and 'seeing how far the plane went'.	Identified the problem by changing one factor at a time and measuring how far the plane flew, averaged over several flights with other conditions controlled. Changes to structure not so small as to be unlikely to produce measurable effects.

Unit 3 test

Mark scheme

1. a. About 20 to 30km.
   b. Stratus, cumulus, altocumulus and cirrus.
   c. 50km.
   d. 100mb.
   e. The plane would 'explode' – the air would rush out from the pressurised cabin to the atmosphere where the pressure is lower.

2. The plan included:

Identification of key variables:
   To alter   – how much the ball is blown up.
   To measure   – the bounciness.

Putting it into practice effectively:
   Altered by   – counting number of pumps or measuring pressure using one of the gauges.
   Measured by – rebound height for fixed height of release.
   Controlled   – surface used, method of release of ball.

LEVEL I	LEVEL 3
Identified the problem by changing pressure of ball and attempting to measure or judge the bounciness.	Identified the problem by systematically changing the pressure in the ball by counting the number of pumps or measuring the pressure. Dropped the ball from the same height onto the same surface and measured the rebound height (or similar).

(This question can be used to assess Planning investigations.)

3. a. Hydrogen.
   b. Sun's rays focused on powder.
   c. Candle burning and active mouse.
   d. Priestley, because he had made (separated) the gas.

LEVEL 1	LEVEL 3
Located single items of information given specific references as in parts a and b.	Located one or more items of information – part c – and collated evidence in support of an argument – part d.

(This question can be used to assess Communicating and interpreting.)

4. a. Algiers
   b. Luxembourg.
   c. 6.
   d. The further north, the cooler it is.
   e. Luxembourg, lower temperature because of fog.

5. a. Class B.
   b. Fire blanket, carbon dioxide, foam or powder.
   c. Water.

6. a. West.
   b. Edinburgh windiest, London least windy.
   c. Isobars.
   d. The atmospheric pressure along each line is the same.

7. a. 1.6g
   b. 0.8g
   c. Bottle not completely empty, inaccurate scales.

8. a. Arrows showing force directed inwards on can.
   b. Sketches showing the same number of particles, rather fewer and almost none inside the can.
   c. As air is taken out, more particles are hitting the outside of the can than the inside, so net force inwards causing can to collapse.

9. Graph A is cloud cover because the rainfall can be zero when it is cloudy but there cannot be rain if there is no cloud cover.

10. a. 'Blow forrard tanks' makes front of boat 'lighter' than back, causing the boat to rise at the front. 'Blow aft tanks, flood forrard' reverses the effect, making the front go down.
    b. Blow BOTH front and aft tanks.

UNIT 4 MATERIALS

Introduction

A general introduction of the three states of matter precedes separate studies of solids, liquids and gases. Subsequent spreads lead into:
– rocks and concrete as building materials
– structure as a way of increasing strength
– strength, stability, cost and aesthetics in design
– plastics
– fibres and fabrics, their structure and heat insulating properties.
The final investigation is built around the very light materials that are needed to construct a model hot-air balloon.

The topics in this Unit can easily be re-ordered to suit the teacher's preference.

Assessment opportunities

Basic skills

4.5 Drawing a bar chart for concrete

4.7 Using a newton meter

4.10 Using a thermometer

Communicating and interpreting

4.3 Liquids

4.8 What plastics are

Unit test, Question 9, Cups and lids

Observing

4.1 Using materials

4.2 Gases expand when they are warm

Unit test, Question 4, Describing a bridge

Planning investigations

4.11 Extras 5: Comparing the balloons

Unit test, Question 7, Comparing sleeping bags

Investigating and making

4.6 A model bridge

4.7 Costing it out

4.9 Is yarn stronger than its fibres?

4.1 Using materials

Apparatus list

Observing materials

Pupils: A4 piece of plain paper
Sugar paper
Felt pens
Pritt
Scissors
Worksheet 4.1 (Talking about materials)

A materials machine

Pupils: Balloon
50g sand
30 pins
30 art straws (30cm maximum)
1m of string
Aluminium foil (10cm × 2cm)
PVA glue
$100cm^3$ plastic beaker
2 yoghurt pots
Elastic band (about 10cm)

You might try

Extras 1: Why not extend the supermarket problem to include unsuitable packaging? For example – why aren't cereals sold in bottles? How can wine be sold in boxes? And so on.

Assessment criteria

Using materials (Observing)

LEVEL 1	LEVEL 3
Groups based on everyday features of objects – shape, size, colour, etc.	Groups based on ideas of solids, liquids and gases, or other appropriate 'scientific' basis for categorisation.

4.2 What a gas!

Apparatus list

Pupils: $500cm^3$ round-bottomed flask
Bung with glass tube to fit flask
Beaker

Video resources

Scientific Eye, 'Lighter Than Air'.

You might try

A fun experiment is to test how long lemonade stays fizzy. This is done by placing a crown-type bottle top in lemonade in a Pyrex evaporating dish or tall wine glass. When you put the bottle top in with the corrugated edge pointing down, it will somersault. Pupils can time how long it keeps somersaulting. When it stops, it has failed the 'fizzical'!

Assessment criteria

Gases expand when they are warm (Observing)

LEVEL I	LEVEL 3
The record showed a variety of observations – including those not relevant in the context of the activity, such as condensation.	The record concentrated on those observations (bubbles and sucking back) linked to expansion and contraction of the air.

4.3 Drip ... Drip ... Drip ...

Apparatus list

Liquids

Pupils: Piece of A4 plain paper
           Paints or crayons if available

When is a liquid not a liquid?

Pupils: Eye protection (EACH)
           Piece of wood with a varnished or plastic surface, about 30cm × 5cm
           Bunsen burner, heatproof mat, gauze, tripod
           Beaker
           Glass rod
Teacher: Cornflour (300g +)
           Matches
           Electronic balance

You might try

Extras: Pupils could find out whether all motor oil has the same thickness at different temperatures. They can make their own 'runniness' meter as follows:

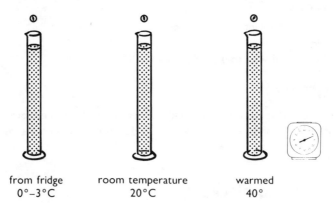

from fridge   room temperature   warmed
0°–3°C   20°C   40°

They can then see if the marbles fall at the same speed.

Ask: 'If you took your car from Iceland to the Sahara Desert, should you change the oil? Why?'

Assessment criteria

Liquids (Communicating and interpreting)

LEVEL 1	LEVEL 3
The report presented information taken from the lesson and from pupils' general knowledge.	The report was an imaginative collection of ideas from a variety of sources and included various ways of presenting information – diagrams, stories, adverts, etc. as well as straightforward information. It had a coherent theme.

4.4 Solids

Apparatus list

Looking at solids

Teacher: A wide-range of materials (solids, liquids, gases). Should include things like powders, crystals, Blu-tack, rubber, Sellotape, polythene, gelatine or jelly, ice as well as metal, rock, wood.

Worksheet 4.4   Solids, liquids and gases

Pupils: Eye protection (EACH)
          Bunsen burner, heatproof mat, gauze, tripod
          Sand tray
          Tongs
Teacher: Matches
          Solder (cut into 5cm pieces)
          Ice
          Pieces of wax (old candles are fine)

You might try

An investigation of materials which links rubber gloves to brake blocks is to test the best rubber for shoe soles. Pupils should devise their own tests, as far as practicable. (This links to 11.6.)

4.5   Rocks and blocks

Apparatus list

Using stone

Pupils: Hand lens
          Nail
          Teat pipette
Teacher: Electronic balance
          Samples of limestone, slate, sandstone and granite for pupils to test

Concrete: making

Pupils: Paper to protect benches
          Plastic teaspoons
          Spatula
          Old plastic or card cups for mixing concrete in
          Wooden mould (best made from loose pieces of 10cm × 1cm × 1cm
          wood on a base). Each group needs 3 moulds.
          Teat pipette
          Worksheet 4.5 (Making a concrete mixture)
Teacher: Cement
          Sand
          Fine gravel
          Bucket for waste concrete

Concrete: testing

Pupils: Eye protection (EACH)
          String
          100g and 1kg masses

Video resources

Scientific Eye, 'River of Rock', 'Earth Ltd'.

You might try

Perhaps a better way of testing concrete which avoids sudden collapsing and falling weights is to let pupils make a 'bashometer':

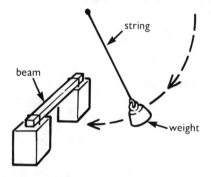

Pupils must wear eye protection for this.

4.6 Making things stronger

Apparatus list

Compression and tension

Pupils: Thin twigs

A model bridge

Pupils: Art straws
            Thread
            PVA glue
            Thin card
            String
            10g masses
            Scissors

Shaping a stronger bridge

Pupils: 3 or 4 A4 sheets of thin card
            Scissors
            10g and 100g masses
            String

A bridge competition

Pupils: A4 sheet of thin card
            Scissors
Teacher: 10g and 100g masses
            Sellotape
            String

Worksheet 4.6 Strong straw structures

Pupils: Art straws
             Scissors
             PVA glue
             Pipe cleaners cut into 5cm pieces if available
             Newspaper
Teacher: Brick (several if possible)

Video resources

Scientific Eye, 'Shape and Strength'.

You might try

Pupils could test the best *shape* for support, as well as the beam itself, especially to show compression.

   When they are testing beams, children could test the difference that an arch makes to the amount of weight that the beam will take.

Assessment criteria

A model bridge (Investigating and making)

Checklist – the investigation included:

Identification of key variables:
   To alter   – the load on the bridge.
   To measure – the sag.

Putting it into practice effectively:
   Altered by   – adding masses to centre of bridge, for instance.
   Measured by – the distance the centre moves down from no load condition.
   Controlled   – the method of adding weights.

Validity of results:
   Scale   – sensible choice of masses to give reasonable deflection in a number of steps, at least three different loads.
   Accuracy   – sufficient to discriminate between readings.

LEVEL I	LEVEL 3
Used at least two masses and attempted to judge the sag of the bridge.	Used three or more masses in the same position on the bridge and measured the sag from the rest position with appropriate accuracy. Masses chosen to give several readings before collapse.

4.7   Design a stool

Apparatus list

Pupils: Plasticine
            Newton meter (0–IN and 0–10N)
            Straws
            Scissors
            Blu-tack
            A4 piece of thin card
            Thread
            10g masses

You might try

Ask: 'Why did old-fashioned milking stools have only three legs?'
   Extras: Ask: 'Why can racing cars go round corners at far greater speeds than, say, London-type taxis? Is it just because they have bigger engines?'

Assessment criteria

Costing it out (Investigating and making)

LEVEL 1	LEVEL 3
Stool met requirements of area and thickness but the design or construction was such that stability and/or strength was inadequate.	Stool met all requirements and was designed and/or developed using ideas from the Unit with an eye to simplicity and efficiency.

4.8   Plastics everywhere

Apparatus list

Pupils: Eye protection (EACH)
            Bunsen burner, heatproof mat
            Worksheet 4.8 (Key for identifying plastics)
Teacher: Matches
            Samples of plastics to include:
            Squeezy bottles
            Old cassette tape
            Nylon curtain fittings
            Polythene bag
            Plastic cup
            Yoghurt pot
            Polystyrene packing
            Artificial-fibre cloth

Video resources

Scientific Eye, 'Earth Ltd'.

You might try

You could take 'Testing plastics' further and ask pupils whether all plastics that look alike are of the same strength. Pupils could test a variety of plastic carrier bags.

Assessment criteria

What plastics are (Communicating and interpreting)

LEVEL 1	LEVEL 3
Description contained main features drawn directly from the material in the text and followed that sequence and structure.	Description contained all features in text and linked them together into a well-ordered and logical sequence. Other information relevant to the task was introduced as appropriate to make a coherent account.

4.9   Fibres and fabrics

Apparatus list

Pupils: Thin (0.5cm) strips of paper or plastic
　　　　　Scissors
　　　　　Masses 10g, 100g, 1kg
　　　　　Wool if available
　　　　　Knitted material
　　　　　Woven material
Teacher: Sellotape
　　　　　Hole punch
　　　　　Cotton
　　　　　Hand lenses

You might try

Extra: Let pupils test a variety of materials to see which type is best for making young children's pyjamas. Take great care over flammability tests. Many synthetics also produce toxic fumes when they burn.

Assessment criteria

Is yarn stronger than its fibres? (Investigating and making)

Checklist – the investigation included:

Identification of key variables:
    To alter   – 'spun' or not 'spun'.
    To measure – the strength of the yarn.

Putting it into practice effectively:
    Altered by   – using separate 'fibres' and spun ones.
    Measured by – e.g. load required to break 'yarn'.
    Controlled   – length, technique of loading, total number of fibres.

Validity of results:
    Scale   – sensible widths and lengths of 'fibres' and choice of masses.
    Accuracy   – load increased in sufficiently small increments to give reasonable measurement of breaking force.

LEVEL I	LEVEL 3
Used separate 'fibres' and spun 'fibre' and attempted to judge which broke first.	Used separate and multiple 'fibres' of same length and width. Measured breaking strain sufficiently accurately by choice of load increments.

4.10   Keeping warm

Apparatus list

Pupils: Potato (medium-sized) heated to 70°C. A few spare potatoes of different sizes could be useful.
              Thermometer (0–110°C)
              Rubber bands
Teacher: Variety of insulating material, (e.g. fabrics, plastic bubbles, loft insulation, feathers, fur (!)).

Video resources

Scientific Eye, 'Keeping Warm' (this has the full story of Scott and Amundsen), 'Keeping Cool'.
Starting Science, 'Keeping Warm and Safe' (first part), 'Saving Energy'.
Science – Start Here, 'Cold Weather'.

You might try

Set pupils this task: 'Without spending any money, can you build a shelter in the school grounds that would keep you warm?'
    Pupils could find out how well different sweaters keep them warm.

4.11 Investigating hot-air balloons

Apparatus list

Pupils: Tissue paper or thin polythene bags
           Scissors
           Sellotape
           General-purpose glue
           Paper clips
Teacher: Hot-air blower or hair drier

Video resources

Starting Science, 'Helicopters'.
Scientific Eye, 'Lighter Than Air'.

You might try

Thin tissue paper works fairly well in this investigation.

If the weather is cool and there is no wind, heating the balloons inside the school and taking them outside seems to give them better lift. Ask: 'Why?'

Assessment criteria

Extras 5 (Planning investigations)

Checklist – the plan included:

Identification of key variables:
   To alter   – the size of the balloon.
   To measure   – the amount of lift.

Putting it into practice effectively:
   Altered by   – using two or more balloons of different diameters (volumes).
   Measured by – forcemeter, or load to just stop it lifting, or equivalent.
   Controlled   – temperature of air (or source of heat).

Validity of results:
   Scale   – some suggestion that balloons would need to be quite different in size.

LEVEL 1	LEVEL 3
Identified the problem by using two or more balloons and looking to see 'how good they were'.	Identified the problem by using two significantly differently sized balloons with air at the same temperature. Lift measured by some suitable quantitative method.

Unit 4 test

Mark scheme

1.

Solids	Liquids	Gases
wood	water	air
billiard ball	vinegar	exhaust fumes
salt	treacle	breath
glass	fog	(fog and smoke
smoke		may also be
jelly		classified as
ice cream		gases)

2. Polystyrene.

3. a. Hydrogen.
   b. Natural gas.
   c. Oxygen.
   d. Carbon dioxide.

4.

LEVEL 1	LEVEL 3
Description of bridge based on overall shape, colour and size, for instance.	Selection of features described based on an understanding of key structural parts – the keystones of the arch bridge, or the pivot of the cantilever, for example.

(This question can be used to assess Observing.)

5. a. Material or plastic which is flexible but waterproof.
   b. Rubber which is spongy and grips well.
   c. Steel for strength.
   d. Steel for its springiness.

6. a. Wool, silk.
   b. Nylon, polyester, acrylic, viscose.
   c. Group 4.

7. Checklist – the plan included:

Identification of key variables:
   To alter   – the type of sleeping bag.
   To measure – how well it keeps in the heat (thermal conductivity).

Putting it into practice effectively:

Altered by   – using both types.

Measured by – putting a source of heat (e.g. large tin can of hot water) inside the bags and measuring its fall in temperature for a fixed time.

Controlled   – the initial temperature of the water, the size of the can and the volume of the water.

LEVEL 1	LEVEL 3
Identified the problem by attempting to measure how 'good' the two sleeping bags are at keeping the heat in.	Identified the problem by wrapping the sleeping bags around identical sources of heat and measuring the rate of fall of temperature of the sources.

(This question can be used to assess Planning investigations.)

8. a. Cotton (or wool) because of their high absorbency, cotton rather cheaper.
    b. Silk (or wool) for appearance.
    c. Wool because it is warm and hard wearing (or other sensible arguments).

9. a. The polystyrene cup with lid.
    b. The plastic cup without a lid.
    c. The lid makes most difference (8° difference compared to 4° for the type of material).

LEVEL 1	LEVEL 3
Could describe and interpret simple patterns in data – parts a and b.	Could interpret data from multiple column or complex data and form a generalisation – part c.

(This question can be used to assess Communicating and interpreting.)

10. a. Balloon rises, stays up longer.
    b. The gas becomes hotter, therefore lighter, giving extra lift.
    c. Burn the gas and then throw out the canister.

LIFE

Introduction

The unit begins with a study of the features of living things. A large amount of factual material is needed to support this, and it is arranged in alphabetical order at the back of the Pupil's Book in a Reference Section. As a result, most of the Unit is made up of single pages which include references to the factual section.

Sorting and classification are features of this Unit, which starts with cells, their function and reproduction. Reproduction in plants is followed by reproduction in animals. This section is dominated by human reproduction, which is firmly set within the context of family life. There is a short description of methods of contraception. A consideration of death, generations and a study of populations conclude this Unit.

The nature of the Unit will mean that most teachers will want to follow the teaching sequence in the text. A careful study of the school policy on sex education will determine the need to stress certain aspects and, perhaps, ignore others.

Many video resources are available to support this topic. The ITV video series *Living and Growing* is relevant from spread 5.7 on. It contains some sensitive material and is perhaps more appropriate for slightly older pupils. However, the programmes are well made, and it is worth considering their use. The *Exploring Science* videos 'Life Goes On – Fertilisation' and 'Life Goes On – Reproduction and Survival' could be used at any point between 5.7 and 5.11 inclusive.

Assessment opportunities

Basic skills

5.3 Looking at cells under a microscope

5.10 Drawing a line graph of the growth of an embryo

Worksheet 5.3A Using a microscope to look at cells

Communicating and interpreting

5.7 New animals

5.13 Extras: evolution chart

Unit test, Question 6, Average height of children

Observing

5.2 Sorting organisms into groups

Unit test, Question 3, Describing an elephant

Planning investigations

5.5 Extras 2: growing mushrooms

5.6 Growing seeds

Investigating and making

5.4 What does yeast need to reproduce?

Worksheet 5.5 Growing cuttings

5.1 Dead or alive?

Apparatus list

Teacher: Any reference material on the origin of the Earth.

Video resources

Scientific Eye, 'What is Life?'.

5.2 Sorting out living things

Apparatus list

Pupils: Poster material (paper, Pritt Stick, sugar paper, scissors)
Teacher: Any books illustrating living organisms.

Video resources

Scientific Eye, 'Crimebusters'. This is very good for showing how a key is used.

Assessment criteria

Sorting organisms into groups (Observing)

LEVEL I	LEVEL 3
Groups based on everyday classification scheme – e.g. animals are furry and have four legs – or obvious features of colour or size.	Groups based on a more scientific classification scheme (even if that scheme is not strictly correct). For instance, plants, animals with backbones, animals without, etc.

5.3 Cells

Apparatus list

Pupils: Microscope and slide
            Cover slip
            Mounted needle
            Worksheet 5.3A (How to use a microscope to look at cells)
            Worksheet 5.3B (How to make a plant cell slide)
Teacher: Scalpel
            Onion, tomato and pond slime (beware of pollution) if possible
            Prepared slides of cells

Video resources

Exploring Science, 'Life Goes On – Cells'.

You might try

The 'My Body' project has a very good idea for making a model of a cell.

5.4 New cells from old

Apparatus list

Pupils: 3–4 conical flasks or boiling tubes
            Bungs and delivery tubes to fit flasks/tubes
Teacher: Yeast (preferably fresh)
            Sugar
            Electronic balance
            Lime water

Assessment criteria

What does yeast need to reproduce? (Investigating and making)

Checklist – the investigation included:

Identification of key variables:
   To alter   – sugar, water and temperature.
   To measure   – yeast growth.

Putting it into practice effectively:
   Altered by   – varying the sugar concentration, or the amount of water or
                    the temperature using appropriate apparatus.
   Measured by – counting the bubbles per minute or equivalent.
   Controlled   – the sugar, water or temperature as appropriate, the amount of
                    yeast.

Validity of results:
   Scale   – sensible volumes of water, sugar and yeast, sensible range of
                    temperatures (up to about 40°C), counts at least 20 bubbles
                    (say).
   Accuracy   – quantities measured out with suitable accuracy.

LEVEL I	LEVEL 3
Identified the problem by attempting to judge, for example, the rate of gas production for different temperatures.	Identified the problem by counting the number of bubbles produced per minute (or a time sufficient to give, say 20 bubbles) for at least two significantly different temperatures measured by thermometer. The same quantities of yeast, water and sugar measured out with sufficient accuracy to give reliable results.

5.5 New plants

Apparatus list

Taking cuttings

Teacher: Seed trays
Rooting compost
Hormone rooting powder
Assortment of plants to test
Scalpels
Worksheet 5.5 (Growing cuttings)

Making seeds

Pupils: Flower with clearly visible anthers
Scalpel
Cutting board
Hand lens/microscope and slide

What is inside a seed?

Pupils: Broad been seed
Scalpel
Cutting board
Hand lens

Video resources

Exploring Science, 'Life Goes On – Fertilisation', 'Life Goes On – Cells'.
Seeing and Doing, 'Flowers'.
Scientific Eye, 'Plants for Food'.

You might try

Geraniums are excellent for taking cuttings.
Marrow plants are good if you want to collect pollen and cross-fertilise by brushing it on to the female part of the flower.
Pupils could be asked to find out why the growing of cucumbers is so different from growing marrows.

Assessment criteria

Extras 2: growing mushrooms (Planning investigations)

Checklist – the plan included:

Identification of key variables:
To alter – the material the mushrooms are grown in.
To measure – the rate of growth.

Putting it into practice effectively:
Altered by – using at least two materials (animal or plant matter).
Measured by – height or mass of mushrooms after fixed time.
Controlled – the number of spores, environment.

Validity of results:

Scale — sensible number of mushrooms used to allow for variation; sensible time before measurement.

LEVEL I	LEVEL 3
Identified the problem by planting the mushrooms on two types of material and looking to see how well they grew.	Identified the problem by planting the same number or weight of spores on the two types of material and weighing them after the same growing time. Grown in the same environment.

Worksheet 5.5: Growing cuttings (Investigating and making)

Checklist – the investigation included:

Identification of key variables:

To alter — the type of cutting.
To measure — the success rate of cutting.

Putting it into practice effectively:

Altered by — using at least two types of cuttings.
Measured by — whether the cuttings take or not.
Controlled — environmental conditions, amount of watering.

Validity of results:

Scale — used several cuttings (to allow for variation), waited sensible time before judging effectiveness.

LEVEL I	LEVEL 3
Identified the problem and attempted to follow the instructions for producing at least two cuttings. Looked to see if the cuttings had taken.	Identified the problem by using several samples of each of the cuttings. Kept conditions of temperature, moisture and light constant for the different types. Looked to see if they had germinated after an appropriate time.

5.6 Sowing seeds

Apparatus list

How do seeds spread?

Pupils: Dried pea
Piece of A4 paper
Teacher: Sellotape

Growing seeds

Teacher: Old Petri dishes (or seed trays)
           Seeds to grow (assorted fast growing)
           Seed compost or soil

Video resources

Scientific Eye, 'Plants for Food'.
Starting Science, 'Metamorphosis' (just the part on seed growth).

You might try

Most schools grow cress and broad beans. Why not try runner beans? They grow
quickly, which appeals to children, and they are easy to measure. Children are
even more impressed if you grow beans on either side of the classroom and allow
the beans to climb up string to form an arch across the ceiling.

Assessment criteria

Growing seeds (Planning investigations)

Checklist – the plan included:

Identification of key variables:
   To alter   – the temperature, amount of light or water or the type of soil.
   To measure – percentage germination.

Putting it into practice effectively:
   Altered by   – using at least two temperatures, or light levels, etc.
   Measured by – the number of germinated seeds after a fixed time from fixed
                 initial number.
   Controlled   – the temperature, water, light or soil, depending on the test,
                 the batch of seeds, environment.

Validity of results:
   Scale   – significant difference between temperatures, or light and dark,
                   wet or dry; sandy or clay soils. Sensible number of seeds used
                   (or results collected across class), waited sensible length of time.

LEVEL I	LEVEL 3
Identified the problem by using at least two seeds in different conditions and looking for signs of germination.	Identified the problem by, for instance, using many seeds planted in the same soil, at the same temperature and watered equally (using a measured quantity of water per day) but one set in the dark and one in the light. Noted the number germinating after a suitable time.

5.7 New animals

Apparatus list

No specific apparatus is needed.

Video resources

Animals in Action, 'Parenthood'.
Scientific Eye, 'What is Life?'

Assessment criteria

New animals (Communicating and interpreting)

LEVEL 1	LEVEL 3
Reproduced the main element of each description – one reproducing by cell division, the other by unfertilised eggs.	Gave a summary of the features of the reproduction of the two organisms, including their characteristics and rate of reproduction.

5.8 New humans 1 – a love story

Apparatus list

No specific apparatus is needed.

5.9 New humans 2 – eggs and sperms

Apparatus list

Pupils: Worksheet 5.9 (The menstrual cycle)

5.10 New humans 3 – 'I'm pregnant!'

Apparatus list

Pupils: Graph paper

Video resources

Good Health, 'One of the Family', 'Still One of the Family'.

5.11 New humans 4 – 'Girl or boy?'

Apparatus list

Pupils: Worksheet 5.11 (Growing taller)

You might try

At this stage, children often ask how or what decides whether an embryo becomes a boy or a girl. They also ask about multiple births, and identical and ordinary twins.

5.12 Families

Apparatus list

No special apparatus is needed.

Video resources

Animals in Action, 'Parenthood'.
Science – Start Here, 'I'm Special'.
Exploring Science, 'Life Goes On'.

You might try

For this request, you will need to bear in mind children's family circumstances. Ask children to bring in photographs of their grandparents (especially if any photos show the grandparents aged 12 or 13). Children are often amazed at how many similarities others can see between them and their grandparents.

5.13 Populations

Apparatus list

No special apparatus is needed.

Video resources

Good Health, 'One of the Family', 'Still One of the Family'.

You might try

Some countries have been trying to encourage people not to have children. Ask: 'Can you name one such country? Why do you think that country is trying to reduce its population growth?'

   At least one country is now urging its people to have lots more children. Ask pupils what might have happened there.

Assessment criteria

Extras: evolution chart (Communicating and interpreting)

Answers to questions:
1. a. Flowering plants.
   b. Protofish, trilobites.
   c. 200 approx.
2. Fish; sensible reason for decline of species (e.g. changes in living conditions, increase of predators).

LEVEL I	LEVEL 3
Located single items of information from tree – questions 1(a)–(c).	Located single items correctly. Interpreted table in light of knowledge of 'large animals' – question 2. Used library or other resources to find out about the decline in the species and presented the information appropriately.

Unit 5 test

Mark scheme

1. a. A hard outer case in which an insect changes from a larva to an adult.
   b. Tiny insects that live in plant sap. Female aphids can reproduce without having their eggs fertilised.
   c. A cell that a new plant can develop from. It does not have a food store like a seed.

2. a. How many germinate or how well they grow after a certain time.
   b. Variation between seeds.
   c. To act as a control to check that the fertilisers are better than water.

3.

LEVEL I	LEVEL 3
Description centred on general features of shape, size and colour.	Description attempted to link structure to function. For instance the trunk used for grasping objects, skin for protection, ears for cooling.

(This question can be used to assess Observing.)

4. a. They have backbones, soft skin, adults breathe air and have five fingers and toes.
   b. Chordates (or chordates, animals and organisms).
   c. Bryophyta.
   d. Arachnids, insects, millipedes, centipedes and crustaceans.
   e. Mammals.

5. Choice of group based on sensible biological classification. For instance non-living plant, animal (or sub-groups of animals).

6. a. 56.5 inches.
   b. 61.5 inches.
   c. 5 to 6 inches.
   d. Life span gradually increasing over the century for both boys and girls. Difference in height slightly reduced.
   e. Medical advances and improvements in agriculture, for instance.

LEVEL 1	LEVEL 3
Single items of information taken from chart correctly – parts (a) and (b) in particular.	Information taken from chart correctly. Pattern in data noted and described. Used previous knowledge to explain pattern sensibly – most answers correct.

(This question can be used to assess Communicating and interpreting.)

7.

Part A	Part B
Cytoplasm	is where a cell makes and stores chemicals.
The nucleus	controls what the cell does.
A cell wall or membrane	holds the cell together.
A chromosome	contains information to allow cells to divide.
Tissue	is a lot of cells joined together.

8. a. Suitable bar chart drawn, horizontal axis labelled 'country', vertical axis 'life span' (or equivalent), bars correctly plotted and drawn.
   b. Western nations higher than Third-World countries, due to better medicine and relative abundance of food.

9. a. Pollen reaches ovule which develops into a seed.
    b. Cuttings produce plant identical to parent. Seeds can produce quite different plants.
    c. Advantages – survival rate higher, numbers easier to control and predict, etc.
       Disadvantages – no variation in plants, so no improvement, easier to store many seeds, can be kept a long time.

10. The plan included:

    – changing the treatment of the conker (age, pickling, roasting);
    – devising a test for strength that would work;
    – keeping other factors constant, such as size, age, etc. (depending on what is being tested).

ELECTRICITY

Introduction

The approach and illustrations in this Unit are based on 'batteries, bulbs and wires' and are independent of any manufactured systems. This is a deliberate policy, as the authors feel that children understand simple wires and bulbs better than spring or plastic connectors. However, it should not be too difficult for teachers to interpret the diagrams and equipment for use with circuit boards if they so wish.

The following areas are covered in this Unit:
- electric circuits
- magnetic effect
- heating effect (including fuses)
- batteries, and the introduction of volts
- distribution of domestic electricity
- earthing and safety in general
- static electricity
- signals that use electricity
- the nervous system as an electrical system.

The final investigation focuses on home-made batteries.

The Unit is developmental and, unless the class already understands electric circuits, teachers are advised to follow the suggested sequence.

The only relevant video material we have found to support this Unit is *Science – Start Here*, 'Full Circuit', and this could be used with spread 6.2 or 6.3.

Assessment opportunities

Basic skills

6.2 Drawing circuit diagrams

6.7 Safety first – wiring a plug

Worksheet 6.2 Electrician's diagrams

Worksheet 6.7A Wiring a plug

Worksheet 6.7B Wiring a table lamp – following instructions

Communicating and interpreting

6.8 Making electricity – lightning

6.9 Where there's smoke there's fire

Unit test, Question 7, Using electrical appliances

Observing

6.1 Extras 2: looking inside a torch

6.4 Making a buzzer

Planning investigations

6.6 Are volts valuable?

Unit test, Question 5, Light bulbs

Investigating and making

6.4 Testing magnets

6.11 Making a model signal

6.12 Investigating home-made batteries

6.1   Switch on!

Apparatus list

Switches and bulbs

Pupils: 1.5V battery in holder
            Connecting wire (several pieces)
            2 × 1.25V bulbs in holders
            Wire cutters/strippers
            Screwdriver
            Soft wood about 5cm × 2cm × 1cm
            Paper clip
            Drawing pins
Teacher: Assortment of switches
            Assortment of bulbs

Worksheet 6.1   Steady as you go

Pupils: A4 card
            1.5V battery in holder
            Connecting wire (several pieces)
            1.25V bulb in holder
            Wire cutters/strippers
            Screwdriver
            Aluminium foil
            Pritt Stick

You might try

If children have mastered the ideas behind bulbs and switches, set them the task of sending a message to a partner along a length of corridor, using one bulb and a switch. This poses two problems: (a) how to make a code, (b) how to magnify the bulb's brightness using a reflector (cooking foil is good for this).

Assessment criteria

Extras 2: looking inside a torch (Observing)

LEVEL 1	LEVEL 3
Drawing showed an incomplete understanding of the nature of an electric circuit – a broken or shorted circuit for example.	Drawing showed the key features of the torch in a complete circuit. The circuit included the switch, battery and bulb.

6.2 Circuits

Apparatus list

Pupils: 1.5V battery in holder
          Connecting wire (several pieces)
          3 × 1.25V bulbs in holders
          Wire cutters/strippers
          Screwdriver
          Worksheet 6.2 (Electrician's diagrams)
Teacher: Assorted conductors and insulators (e.g. metals, plastic, wood, magnet, old integrated circuits, etc.)

6.3 Electricity at home I

Apparatus list

Pupils: 1.5V battery in holder
          Connecting wire (five pieces)
          1.25V bulb in holder
          Wire cutters/strippers
          Screwdriver
          2 × soft wood about 5cm × 2cm × 1cm
          Paper clips
          Drawing pins
          Worksheet 6.3 (Keeping track of electricity)

You might try

The idea of wiring a model is always popular with pupils. Dolls' houses become far more realistic with working lights. Other popular models include lighthouses, airfield runways and even a speedway track with lights.

6.4 Magnets

Apparatus list

Testing magnets

Pupils: 1.5V battery in holder
          Connecting wire (a long piece)
          Wire cutters/strippers
          Screwdriver
          15cm nail
          Compass
          Pins
Teacher: Soft iron cores if available
          Assorted nails

Electric buzzers

Pupils: Power pack (4V d.c.)
Hacksaw blade
Stand and clamp
5cm+ nail
2 crocodile clips
Screwdriver
3 pieces of connecting wire
1 long piece of thin insulated wire
Wire cutters/strippers
Emery paper
Soft iron C-core
Worksheet 6.4 (How an electric bell works)
Teacher: Electric bell if available

Permanent magnets

Pupils: Strong permanent magnet
Pins
Petri dish
Washing-up bowl
Teacher: Assorted materials to test if they are magnetic

You might try

Pupils can make a model railway signal arm as a good application of this topic.

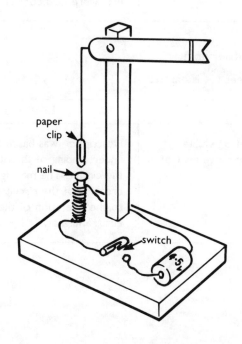

Assessment criteria

Testing magnets (Investigating and making)

Checklist – the investigation included:

Identification of key variables:
    To alter   – the material of the core, the characteristics of the coil.
    To measure – the strength of the magnet.

Putting it into practice effectively:
    Altered by   – varying the number of coils, for instance.
    Measured by – number of pins held or equivalent.
    Controlled   – the length and diameter of the coil, the core material, the
                    voltage (number of batteries).

Validity of results:
    Scale   – significant change in number of turns on coil.

LEVEL 1	LEVEL 3
Identified the problem by changing the number of coils, in this example, and attempting to judge the strength of the magnet.	Identified the problem by using at least two, significantly different, numbers of turns for the coil with the same material as the core, and measuring the strength by counting the number of pins held. Other factors, such as voltage, coil shape etc. were held constant.

Making a buzzer (Observing)

To be used if worksheet 6.4 is omitted.

LEVEL 1	LEVEL 3
Description focused on visible features such as the movement of the hacksaw blade.	Description was based on an understanding of the operation of the circuit. The making and breaking of the circuit was linked to the operation of the electromagnet.

6.5 Getting hot

Apparatus list

Heat from a car headlamp

Pupils: Power pack 12V d.c.
              Headlamp bulb in holder
              Connecting wire
              Beaker 250cm^3
              Thermometer 0–110°C
              Stopclock or stopwatch
Teacher: Other assorted 12V bulbs in holders

Hot wires

Pupils: 1.5V battery in holder
              Connecting wire
              Paper clip mounted as switch
Teacher: Steel wool
              Other thin (30swg+) wire
              Fuse wire if available

6.6 Batteries

Apparatus list

Is big better?

Pupils: 1.25V bulb in holder
              Connecting wire
Teacher: Assortment (at least 15) of 1.5V batteries of different sizes

Are volts valuable?

Pupils: 1.5V battery in holder
              1.25V bulb in holder
              Connecting wire
              9V or 12V battery (a car battery is possible)
              Bulb in holder, rating to match battery
Teacher: Rechargeable battery if possible
              Watch battery
              Demonstration voltmeter (0–12V)

What are volts?

Pupils: 3×1.5V batteries in holders
              Connecting wire
              1.25V bulb in holder

Are volts valuable? (Planning investigations)

Checklist – the plan included:

Identification of key variables:
　　To alter　　– type of battery.
　　To measure – how 'good' the batteries are.

Putting it into practice effectively:
　　Altered by　　– using the two types of battery.
　　Measured by – measuring how long the batteries will operate some electrical device.
　　Controlled　 – the device used in test, new batteries.

Validity of results:
　　Scale　　　 – selected a device which uses enough current to flatten the batteries in a reasonable time.

LEVEL 1	LEVEL 3
Identified the problem by using two batteries and seeing how long they lasted.	Identified the problem by using the two types of new battery in identical circuits with a device which needs a high current (e.g. a cassette player) and measuring the time before failure.

6.7 Electricity at home 2

Apparatus list

Pupils:　　Mains plug to wire
　　　　　3-core cable
　　　　　Wirecutters/strippers
　　　　　Screwdriver
　　　　　Worksheet 6.7A (Wiring a plug)
　　　　　Worksheet 6.7B (Wiring a table lamp)

6.8 Big voltages

Apparatus list

Making electricity
Teacher:　Van de Graaff generator and accessories

Worksheet 6.8 Building up electricity
Pupils:　　Electrostatic strips and dusters
Teacher:　Range of materials to test, e.g. metal, wood, plastic, rubber (balloon), cloth, etc.

You might try

There is still a great deal of fun to be found in the usual static electricity experiments. Children never cease to be amazed by the bending of water.

Ask children to find out about lightning conductors. Why are they made narrow and pointed when they are designed to 'collect' lightning? Why not make them as big and flat as possible?

Teaching note on electrostatics

Experiments on electrostatics can leave some pupils with the idea that the positive and negative electricity which gives sparks can be used to explain current electricity. Two sorts of electricity leave the positive and negative ends of the battery and 'fight' in the bulb, making a 'spark' – the light. You can avoid this confusion by stressing that sparks are a visible flow of electricity, not a 'fight'.

Assessment criteria

Making electricity – lightning (Communicating and interpreting)

LEVEL I	LEVEL 3
Basic information copied from a single source.	Information collected from one or more sources and presented as a clear argument in suitable language.

6.9 Electrical signals I

Apparatus list

A burglar alarm

Pupils: 1.5V battery in holder
           Connecting wire
           Aluminium foil
           1.25V bulb in holder

Teacher: Bell or buzzer and power pack
           Mercury switch if available
           Microelectronics kit to make simple alarm if available

A fire alarm

Many possibilities exist here. The pupils may use electrical circuits with a bimetallic strip switch, or an electronic device if they are given guidance. What is needed will depend on the teacher and resources available.

You might try

Extend the burglar alarm idea to include a pressure switch under the mat. Add a buzzer instead of a light.

Pupils can make a simple 'latched' control box with a toggle switch (carefully positioned).

Assessment criteria

Where there's smoke there's fire (Communicating and interpreting)

Answers to questions:

3 Any detector can set the alarm off.
4 Detector for white smoke would not work for black – as it uses the idea of reflected light. Similar argument in reverse for black smoke.
5 Either type acceptable with adequate supporting reason.
6 Parallel, so that any detector will complete the circuit, setting the alarm off. Correct diagram selected and adequately reproduced.

LEVEL I	LEVEL 3
Located single items of information – question 3.	Located single items correctly. Interpreted diagrams correctly to explain need for two types of sensor, question 4, and used previous knowledge to support answer, questions 5 and 6.

6.10 Electricity in living things

Apparatus list

Testing your nerves

Pupils: Paper clip or 5cm of thin wire (about 26swg)

Reaction speed

Pupils: Metre rule marked in centimetres
Teacher: Calculator

You might try

Extend the reaction time experiment to include adults – perhaps for homework. Pupils could find out if reaction times slow down with age.

Pupils could also find out whether sportsmen and sportswomen have quicker reactions, whether certain jobs help, and whether it is possible to improve reaction time with practice.

6.11   Electrical signals 2

Apparatus list

Pupils: $4 \times 1.25V$ bulbs in holders
1.5V battery in holder
Connecting wires
$8 \times 5cm$ pieces of thick copper wire $< 16swg$

Assessment criteria

Making a model signal (Investigating and making)

LEVEL 1	LEVEL 3
Rails set up adequately. Simple circuits connected to light bulbs but not in correct sequence.	Rails set up correctly with most of appropriate circuits (possibly after some help from other groups or teacher).

6.12   Investigating home-made batteries

Apparatus list

Testing fruit

Pupils: Voltmeter 0–5V
$5 \times 1cm$ strips of metals: copper, zinc, magnesium, lead, iron nail etc.
Emery paper
Connecting wire and crocodile clips
LED

Teacher: Variety of fruits, potato, tomato etc.

Testing a rechargeable battery

Pupils: Eye protection (EACH)
Power pack (6V d.c.)
Connecting wires and crocodile clips
Lead plates about $3cm \times 6cm$
$250cm^3$ beaker
6V 0.06A bulb in holder

Teacher: 2molar sulphuric acid (1 litre)

You might try

If possible, pupils could try a Florida grapefruit (the pink kind), which seems to work well.

At home they can try using a 2p piece and a milk-bottle top as the electrodes.

Assessment criteria

Making batteries (Investigating and making)

Checklist – the investigation included:

Identification of key variables:
  To alter   – the type of fruit, for instance.
  To measure – the voltage generated.

Putting it into practice effectively:
  Altered by   – using at least two types of fruit.
  Measured by – using a voltmeter across the electrodes.
  Controlled   – the separation and size of the electrodes.

Validity of results:
  Accuracy   – separation of electrodes measured with sufficient accuracy.

LEVEL I	LEVEL 3
Identified the problem by using at least two fruits and noting the voltmeter readings.	Identified the problem by using at least two types of fruit and measuring the voltage for identical, or the same, electrodes placed at the same, measured, distance from each other.

Unit 6 Test

Mark scheme

1 a. A, C, D and F
   b. Correct explanation based on open or short circuit.
   c. Correctly amended.

2   A Series.
     B Parallel.
     C Parallel.
     D Series.
     E Mixture.

3 a.

Part	Material
A	wood or plastic
B	steel or brass
C	steel or brass
D	wood or plastic

   b. Suitable explanation based on conduction and insulation. Some may indicate that springiness of part C is important.

4

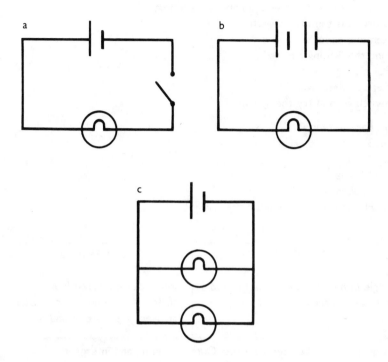

5 a. They don't say what they mean by 'best'.
   b. Checklist – the plan included:

Identification of key variables:
   To alter   – the type of bulb.
   To measure – how long it lasts.

Putting it into practice effectively:
   Altered by   – using both bulbs.
   Measured by – timing from switching on to failure.

LEVEL 1	LEVEL 3
Identified problem by using both bulbs and looking to see which one lasted longest.	Identified problem correctly. Used several bulbs (to allow for variation) and timed how long they lasted.

(This question can be used to assess Planning investigations.)

6 Decide whether you are going to try yourself or whether you are going to ring an electrician.
   Find the mains fuses with a torch if necessary.
   Switch off the main switch.
   Remove cover.
   Find the lighting circuit fuse.
   Put a new fuse in.
   Replace the cover.
   Switch on and try the lights.

7 a. Parallel twin PVC
   b. 3 amp.
   c. 3 amp.
      13 amp.
   d. Rubber/textile braided.
      Flexible but tough and heat-resistant.

LEVEL 1	LEVEL 3
Single items of information located in tables – part a.	Information located from two tables. Knowledge used to support answers – parts b, c and d.

(This question can be used to assess Communicating and interpreting.)

8 a. Suitable graph plotted with sensibly chosen scales, axes labelled, points correctly plotted and smooth line drawn.
   b. Slightly more than 4 minutes.
   c. About 2 minutes.

9 a. 3cm (to be sure).
   b. More sensitive across the arm than along it.
   c. Position of nerves running along the arm. Sensitivity across will be governed by nerve spacing.

10 a. Sensible choice backed up by good reason.
    b. Pressure (for instance), detects weight on seat.
    c. Flashing light.

HEALTH

Introduction

The first section of the Unit deals with eating and food. This covers:
- nutrition and food constituents
- healthy eating habits
- food additives
- preserving food
- digestion
- teeth.

The next content area is fitness. The emphasis here is on the benefits of keeping fit and the scientific reasoning behind the value of exercise. This leads into sports science and the need for specialised skills and training.

The Unit is completed with a series of activities concerned with the prevention of ill health. These activities are supported by a range of up-to-date information on illness, accidents and first aid. This section covers aspects of:
- safety in the home
- disease (causes and prevention)
- smoking
- heart disease
- cancer
- first-aid techniques.

The three content areas (food, fitness and illness) could be taught in any order, but the sequence *within* them is important and is worth following.

Assessment opportunities

Basic skills

7.1 Testing for protein, glucose, starch and fat

7.2 Drawing a bar chart on energy use

7.3 Testing milk for sourness with Resazurin

7.8 Drawing graphs about illnesses

Communicating and interpreting

7.4 Where the food goes

7.8 Sickness and health

Observing

7.3 Extras 1: Ways of preserving food

7.5 Teeth

Planning investigations

7.1 Water in living things

7.5 Extras 1: Comparing toothbrushes

Investigating and making

7.2 Extras 1: Food preferences of birds

7.4 Saliva at work

7.7 Testing the model leg

7.1 Why eat?

Apparatus list

Water in living things

Pupils: Fresh plant material
           Fresh meat
           2 watch-glasses
Teacher: Electronic balance
           Oven at 60°C

Testing food

Pupils: Eye protection (EACH)
           Test tubes and test-tube rack
           Bunsen burner, heatproof mat
           Test-tube holder
           Reagent: biuret reagent (or alternative)
                      Benedict's solution
                      iodine solution
           Brown paper or greaseproof paper
           Worksheet 7.1 (Energy in food)
Teacher: Range of foods to test

Video resources

Scientific Eye, 'Plants for Food', 'Microbeasts and Disease'.
Good Health, 'Healthy Eating', 'Dr Sweettooth'.
Science – Start Here, 'Food'.
Your Living Body, 'Feeding'.

You might try

Water in plants and water in meat are a good link back to 2.12 in Book 1.
Spread 2.12 might help pupils decide which plant is best.

The class could do a survey of what children eat at lunchtime when they have a choice. Ask pupils how they would alter the school menu to make sure everyone was getting enough protein, carbohydrate, minerals, vitamins and roughage. (Cost need not be an important element at this stage.)

Pupils could relate food science to history by finding out what diseases sailors caught through lack of vitamins. Why couldn't they take fruit to last their whole voyage? Pupils could find out how Captain Cook got over the problem with his sailors (he took sauerkraut and forced the men to eat it!).

Children are always surprised if you calculate the quantities of sugar or oil in food (e.g. sugar in a Mars bar or oil in peanuts) and then actually measure out these amounts.

Assessment criteria

Water in living things (Planning investigations)

Checklist – the plan included:

Identification of key variables:
   To alter   – the type of food
   To measure – the amount of water

Putting it into practice effectively:
   Altered by   – using the same amount of different foods.
   Measured by – weighing before and after drying, for instance.
   Controlled   – drying time and temperature, freshness of food.

Validity of results:
   Scale   – sensible amount of food, drying time and temperature.

LEVEL I	LEVEL 3
Identified the problem by using two types of food and suggesting some way of finding the water content, even if the method was inappropriate.	Identified the problem by using equal amounts of the two, fresh, foods. Weighed them before and after drying for a sufficient length of time at a high enough temperature (or until no loss in weight).

7.2 Healthy eating

Apparatus list

Pupils: Worksheet 7.2A (Energy cost of activities)
            Worksheet 7.2B (Square meals)

Video resources

Good Health, 'Healthy Eating', 'Dr Sweettooth', 'Exercise and Rest'.
Your Living Body, 'Feeding'.

You might try

It may be interesting to have a class discussion on why fast-food places (burger bars, pizza bars, fried-chicken takeaway shops) are so popular. Are 'square meals' unfashionable now, whereas fast foods are trendy?

   Many advertisements for chocolate bars claim that these give you energy. Pupils can collect chocolate-bar wrappers and study the lists of ingredients to check if these claims are true. They could design a wrapper and invent a name for a new chocolate bar that makes the buyer think the product is full of energy.

Assessment criteria

Extras I: Food preferences of birds (Investigating and making)

Checklist – the investigation included:

Identification of key variables:
   To alter   – type of food.
   To measure – which type birds prefer.

Putting it into practice effectively:
   Altered by   – using equal amounts of different foods.
   Measured by – counting the number of birds (of a particular type) at each
                 food, or how much food goes, or similar.
   Controlled – how the food is presented, the time each is available.

Validity of results:
   Scale   – sensible amount of food used and left for reasonable length of
                 time. Data taken for sensible number of birds.

LEVEL I	LEVEL 3
Identified problem by using at least two types of food and looking to see which birds preferred.	Identified the problem by using two or more types of food in equal and sensible quantities, presented in such a way as to give each food an 'equal chance'. Measured the mass of food eaten or similar.

7.3 Additives and treatments

Apparatus list

Pupils: Eye protection (EACH)
         Bunsen burner, heatproof mat
         Test tube
         Test-tube holder
         Test-tube rack
Teacher: Range of food labels with food content on 2 pints of untreated (green-top) milk, or pasteurised milk that has been left out for 24 hours
         Cotton wool
         Campden tablets (used in wine-making)
         0.1molar ethanoic acid (or vinegar)
         Resazurin dye (for testing milk)
         $2cm^3$ syringe
         Sticky labels

Video resources

Good Health, 'Healthy Eating', 'Germs, Germs, Germs'.
Scientific Eye, 'Microbeasts and Disease'.

You might try

Tell pupils that they have been asked to make 'instant Irish stew', or 'instant turkey curry', or 'instant chicken chow mein' to be sold in airtight packets. What groups of E-number additives might pupils include in their list of ingredients and why?

Assessment criteria

Extras 1: Ways of preserving food (Observing)

LEVEL 1	LEVEL 3
List excludes fresh foods but does not indicate how the food has been preserved.	List based on various stated ways of preserving food.

7.4 Food processing

Apparatus list

Pupils: Eye protection (EACH)
3 boiling tubes
3 test tubes
Test-tube holder
Test-tube rack
Stirring rod
Benedict's reagent
Bunsen burner and heatproof mat
Stopwatch or stopclock
Worksheet 7.4 (The digestive system)

Teacher: Model of digestive system if available
Bread
Made-up saliva solution (alpha-amylase) (Stress that pupils must follow hygiene rules when using fluids of biological origin – wash out and disinfect test tubes after use, etc.)

Video resources

Good Health, 'Healthy Eating'.
Science – Start Here, 'Food'.
Your Living Body, 'Feeding'.

Assessment criteria

Where the food goes (Communicating and interpreting)

LEVEL 1	LEVEL 3
Chart shows major steps in chain correctly labelled and ordered.	Chart shows all stages. Labelling indicates what happens to food at each stage and how long each stage takes.

Saliva at work (Investigating and making)

Checklist – the investigation included:

Identification of key variables:
To alter   – the temperature of the saliva, or chewing, or type of food.
To measure – how well it works.

Putting it into practice effectively:
Altered by   – using equal amounts of saliva at two or more temperatures, for instance.
Measured by – glucose test.
Controlled   – 'chewing' or not, the type of food.

Validity of results:
Scale   – sensible amounts of food, saliva and time for reaction to occur; sufficiently wide range of temperatures.

LEVEL 1	LEVEL 3
Identified the problem by using saliva at two different temperatures and looking to see which 'worked best'.	Identified the problem by using equal amounts of food and saliva at two or more significantly different temperatures. Food left for sufficient length of time before using glucose test.

7.5 Teeth

Apparatus list

Pupils: Assorted animal teeth and jaws
          Dental mirror if available (plus antiseptic)
          Worksheet 7.5 (A tooth chart)

Video resources

Good Health, 'Dr Sweettooth', 'White Ivory'.

You might try

Although enamel is hard, pupils are still amazed at what happens to a tooth suspended in Coke for a few nights.

Pupils could design the 'toothbrush of the future' and explain their ideas. They should think about: bristles (shape, material, length), handle length, shape of toothbrush. Could the handle contain an automatic toothpaste dispenser? What would be the differences between toothbrushes for very young children and for adults?

Assessment criteria

Teeth (Observing)

LEVEL 1	LEVEL 3
Answer suggests various uses of teeth but fails to link their shape to their function.	Answer links shape of teeth to their function – cutting short grass, grinding, etc.

Extras 1: Comparing toothbrushes (Planning investigations)

Checklist – the plan included:

Identification of key variables:
  To alter – the type of toothbrush.
  To measure – how well they clean teeth.

Putting it into practice effectively:
  Altered by – using both brushes.
  Measured by – using disclosing tablets, for instance, or how well they clean some model teeth.
  Controlled – time of brushing, type and amount of toothpaste, initial 'dirtiness' of teeth.

Validity of results:
  Scale – sensible length of time of brushing.

LEVEL 1	LEVEL 3
Identified problem by using both brushes and attempting to judge how well they cleaned teeth.	Identified problem by using both brushes for same length of time with same amount and type of toothpaste (or none) on different days. Suggested suitable method of measuring how clean teeth were.

7.6 Go for it!

Apparatus list

Pupils: Worksheet 7.6 (Height and weight)
Teacher: This is a circus of activities. At least one of each:
           Several stopwatches or stopclocks
           Large (5-litre capacity) medium-gauge polythene bag
           Washing up-bowl
           1 litre beaker
           Blackboard chalk
           Box (rigidly fixed) for sit-and-reach test (see text)
           Box or bench for step-ups (40cm high)
           Bathroom scales (kg)
           Metre rules

Video resources

Good Health, 'Love Your Lungs', 'Exercise and Rest'.
Scientific Eye, 'Fitness and Sport'.
Your Living Body, 'Bones and Muscle', 'Breathing', 'The Heart and Bloodstream'.

You might try

Younger children are fascinated by listening to the heart with a stethoscope and counting the beats, rather than just taking a pulse rate. A simple stethoscope can be made using tubing and a funnel.

7.7 Exercise

Apparatus list

Pupils: A4 card to make model leg
           Scissors
           Brass paper fasteners
           Assorted elastic bands
           Plasticine
           Stand and clamp
Teacher: Table-tennis ball
           Squash ball

Video resources

Scientific Eye, 'Fitness and Sport'.
Good Health, 'Exercise and Rest'.

You might try

Ask pupils whether all members of a sports team need the same skills and level of fitness. For example, in American football, a quarterback throws the ball, a running back sprints and catches, and a line backer is a 'crusher'. If the needs are different, ask pupils what these differences could be.

Assessment criteria

Testing the model leg (Investigating and making)

LEVEL 1	LEVEL 3
The idea for the leg was adequate but it didn't work well.	The idea for the leg was adequate. It was well constructed and the position of the muscle tested and adjusted to produce the best result. The redesigned leg (to kick a ball) was well thought out and incorporated sensible modifications.

7.8 Sickness and health

Apparatus list

This part of the Unit is mostly reference material. Additional material to support the text on these topics will be helpful:
- accidents
- illness
- medicine
- smoking (some teachers may like to demonstrate a 'smoking machine' at this point)
- heart disease
- cancer
- first aid

Pupils: Worksheet 7.8 (What would you do?)

Video resources

Good Health, 'Look After Yourself', 'Germs, Germs, Germs', 'Keeping Safe'. *Scientific Eye*, 'Fitness and Sport', 'Microbeasts and Disease'.

You might try

Pupils could find out how, in history, smoking began. Ask whether they think there will be a time when no one smokes any more (this topic could be discussed in groups and pupils could list reasons for their group's view).

Assessment criteria

Sickness and health (Communicating and interpreting)

The large number of activities here prevents the use of marking guidelines for each example. The general criteria at the front of the Teacher's Guide can be used to generate such guidelines.

Unit 7 Test

Mark scheme

1 a. 1895 (about).
   b. 1939.
   c. Trials reduced the death rate, then mass immunisation reduced it even more quickly to a very low level.

2 a. 4%.
   b. 51%

3 a. 850.
   b. 394.
   c. Quite a number of accidents for those less than four years old, then less, then a big increase with age.
      The pattern: babies and old people are most likely to suffer falls.

4. Fred and Winston, because it included vegetable, filler, main food and a drink.

5 a. Country Store.
   b. Niacin, riboflavin and thiamin.
   c.

Cereal	Energy in kJ
Weetabix	1400
Frosties	1515
Rice Krispies	1500
Ricicles	1510
Crunchy Nut Cornflakes	1605
Country Store	1470

6 a.

Boys	Distance	Girls	Distance
John	6 m	Maria	5 m
Alexander	8	Nargis	4.5
Nico	4	Sarah	4
Ali	6.5	Diana	3
Edward	6	Debbie	3.5
Carl	6	Fatima	3
Jim	7		

   b. Different pupils have different-strength arms, but, on average, boys are stronger than girls.

7.   2½–6 months   diphtheria
                     tetanus
                     whooping cough
                     polio

      4–8 months   diphtheria
                     tetanus
                     whooping cough
                     polio

      10–14 months   diphtheria
                     tetanus
                     whooping cough
                     polio

      1–2 years   measles

      5 years   diphtheria
                     tetanus
                     polio

      10–13 years   tuberculosis
                     German measles (rubella)

8.   Does the plan:
      – identify the variable to be changed: the weight of the stick?
      – suggest how this is to be put into practice?
      – identify the independent variable: how well it hits the ball?
      – say how this can be measured?
      – mention some things to control: the speed of the hockey stick, for
        instance?

9 a. A virus infection of the stomach.
      Eating too much.
      Drinking too much.
   b. Less than 24 hours.
   c. Eat nothing, drink small quantities of water every two hours, then go on
      to semi-solid food (dry biscuits, etc.) before returning to normal diet.
   d. Continuous pain, lasts more than 24 hours, temperature more than 38°C,
      undue anxiety.

10 a. Mexico.
   b. Bite from infected mosquito. Take anti-malarial tablets and avoid
      mosquitoes! Use insect repellent, cover arms or use screens.

UNIT 8 ENERGY

Introduction

The approach adopted in the Unit is first to explore pupils' understanding of energy, before creating opportunities for pupils to extend this understanding through a range of activities. The topics covered include:
- energy consumption and fuels
- fossil fuels
- fuels and choice of fuel
- generating electricity
- conservation of energy
- solar energy
- photosynthesis
- energy chains
- paying for energy
- nuclear energy
- alternative energy sources.

The investigation at the end of the Unit is set in the context of a café. The suggested activities are based on an energy audit and energy conservation.

There are many possible teaching sequences for this Unit.

Assessment opportunities

Basic skills

8.5   Drawing a pie chart of energy usage

8.6   Testing leaves for starch

Communicating and interpreting

8.4   Making fuels into electricity

8.8   Is cost everything?

8.11 Five-minute special

Observing

Worksheet 8.7   Key to soil and leaf litter animals

8.9   Saving money at home

Planning investigations

8.6   Extras 1: Geranium plants and starch

8.8   Which is cheapest?

Investigating and making

8.2   Comparing fuels

8.7   Making a good compost heap

8.10 A solar heater

8.1 What is energy?

Apparatus list

Pupils: Materials to make a poster display
             Newspaper and magazine material to search for energy items

Video resources

Scientific Eye, 'Earth Ltd'.
Good Health, 'Exercise and Rest'.
Starting Science, 'Making Things Move'.

You might try

This spread could be linked to the dragster that pupils made in 1.3. They could investigate how the energy stored in the elastic band depends on the number of twists.

8.2 Fuel

Apparatus list

Pupils: Eye protection (EACH)
             Heatproof mat
             5cm string
             Ignition tube
             Test tube
             Test-tube holder
             Thermometer 0–110°C
             Small crucible
Teacher: Diesel fuel (paraffin is an alternative)
             Meta fuel tablets

Video resources

Scientific Eye, 'Fire and Flames' (this may have been used in Unit 1).

You might try

Extend Extra 1 to let pupils find out the advantages and disadvantages of diesel fuel as compared with petrol.

Assessment criteria

Comparing fuels (Investigating and making)

Checklist – the investigation included:

Identification of key variables:
   To alter   – the type of fuel.
   To measure   – the amount of heat given out.

Putting it into practice effectively:
   Altered by   – using both types of fuel.
   Measured by – rise in temperature of fixed volume of water, for example.
   Controlled   – the volume fuel, time of heating, method of heating.

Validity of results:
   Scale   – sensible amounts of water and fuel; sensible time for heating.

LEVEL I	LEVEL 3
Identified the problem by using both types of fuel and attempting to measure or judge the heat output of the fuels.	Identified the problem by using known volumes of each fuel to heat a sensible, known volume of water. Measurements made of temperature before and after heating for a sensible time.

8.3 Where do fuels come from?

Apparatus list

Coal, oil and gas

This is information about the three fuels. Supporting material would be helpful, if available.

Making fuels easier to use

All these experiments need care: eye protection, bench protection, etc. Appropriate safety precautions are essential.

Oil: If doing the investigation see Worksheet 8.3A (Making oil into useful fuels) below.

Coal: It is best to have a set of tubes set aside for this (messy!). See diagram in Pupil's Book for details of equipment. Crushed good-quality coal is also needed.

Wood: See diagram on Worksheet 8.3B (Improving wood as a fuel) for details of equipment. Small wood chips (not shavings or sawdust) are needed.

Worksheet 8.3A Making oil into useful fuels

Pupils: Eye protection (EACH)
              Bunsen burner, heatproof mat
              Test tube with delivery tube
              Bung fitted with a thermometer and stirrer
              Four test tubes, labelled A, B, C, D
              Test-tube stand
              Ceramic wood soaked with crude oil
              Stand and clamps

Worksheet 8.3B Improving wood as a fuel

Pupils: Eye protection (EACH)
              Test tubes fitted with bungs and delivery tubes
              Bunsen burner, heatproof mat
              Beaker of cold water
              Small wood chips (not sawdust)

8.4 Which fuel should I use?

Apparatus list

Pupils: Eye protection (EACH)
              Bunsen burner, heatproof mat, tripod
              Sand tray to burn fuels in
              Tongs
Teacher: All the fuels should be in lumps less than $1\,cm^3$ (but not powdered)

Wood	Coke
Coal	Coalite
Peat	Paper
Charcoal	

You might try

Pupils could extend their investigations by finding out if the *size* of the piece of fuel matters – for example, they could compare logs with wood pieces with wood shavings.

Assessment criteria

Making fuels into electricity (Communicating and interpreting)

LEVEL 1	LEVEL 3
The 'page' included basic information drawn from easily obtainable sources.	The 'page' contained information from a number of sources and was presented in a variety of forms appropriate to the nature of the information. The structure showed an attempt to produce a logical sequence.

8.5 Running out of energy

Apparatus list

The spread covers the finite lifetime of fuels, and efficiency in using fuels. Any supporting material on these themes would help, but no specific apparatus is needed.

Video resources

Scientific Eye, 'Earth Ltd', 'Fire and Flames' (these may have been used earlier).

You might try

In the United Kingdom alone we print about 24 million copies of newspapers daily. One tree makes about 400 newspapers. Ask pupils to work out how many trees are needed for just one day's papers. (This would link to spread 12.10.)

Tell pupils they have been shipwrecked on a desert island. They have saved the following things from the ship: tools, wood, nails and lots of clear plastic sheeting. How could they get energy using just these things? Would they need as much energy on their island as they do at home now? Pupils could list the things that use up energy at home but that wouldn't be on the island, e.g. television sets.

8.6 Energy from the sun

Apparatus list

Food from the sun

Pupils: Eye protection (EACH)
Hot water from a kettle (or bunsen burner, heatproof mat, tripod, gauze)
Test tube
Beaker 250cm^3
Iodine solution and teat pipette
White tile

Teacher: Geranium plant (leaves)
Meths
Large cork-borer (to get suitable bits of leaf)
Paper towels
Starch solution (to demonstrate iodine colour)
Kettles

Where does starch come from?

This is not done as an investigation in the text, but the teacher may wish to demonstrate it. If so:

Teacher: Fresh pondweed, washed in distilled water
3 clean boiling tubes in rack with bungs
Bicarbonate indicator (just blue)
Aluminium foil

Video resources

Science Workshop, 'Leaves'.
Scientific Eye, 'Plants for Food'.
Science – Start Here, 'Food', 'Plant Life', 'Under the Sun'.

You might try

Some plants prefer growing in the shade. Pupils could plan an investigation to test if these plants make as much starch as others.

There are often plants growing in deep underground caves that are open to the public, e.g. Gough's and Cox's Caves in Cheddar. Can pupils explain how these plants got there?

Assessment criteria

Extras I: Geranium plants and starch (Planning investigations)

Checklist – the plan included:

Identification of key variables:
 To alter   – the colour of light.
 To measure   – the amount of starch in the plant.

Putting it into practice effectively:
 Altered by   – using coloured filters, say.
 Measured by – starch test.
 Controlled   – the brightness of the light, size of leaf (or plant), the time before testing.

Validity of results:
 Scale   – sensible length of time allowed.

LEVEL I	LEVEL 3
Identified the problem by using at least two different colours of light and testing for starch.	Identified the problem by using at least two colours of light of the same intensity and checking similar leaves (plants) for starch after a sensible length of time.

8.7 Energy chains

Apparatus list

Making a good compost heap

This needs a safe place to make compost.

Pupils: Suitable vegetable matter
            Compost accelerator
            Soil
            Worksheet 8.7 (Key to soil and leaf litter animals)

You might try

Are we all secondary consumers? Children find it interesting and surprising if they are asked to build up an energy chain for themselves. Some of these chains have more 'links' than others. What does a vegetarian's energy chain look like?

Assessment criteria

Making a good compost heap (Investigating and making)

Checklist – the investigation included:

Identification of key variables:
    To alter   – whether compost accelerator is used or not.
    To measure   – how 'good' the compost is.

Putting it into practice effectively:
    Altered by   – using the accelerator on one heap only.
    Measured by – for instance, the number of animals, or the state of the vegetation.
    Controlled   – the size of the heap, the material on the heap, the time left before inspection.

Validity of results:
    Scale   – sensibly-sized heaps and amount of accelerator used.

LEVEL I	LEVEL 3
Identified the problem by making two heaps, putting accelerator on one and looking to see which heap was best.	Identified the problem by making two identical and sensibly sized heaps. One heap dosed with accelerator as per the instructions. The quality of heaps 'measured' appropriately.

Worksheet 8.7   Identifying small animals (Observing)

LEVEL I	LEVEL 3
Identified some common animals. Allocated most of them to the correct sub-group on the key.	Used the sub-groups on the key to identify types of animals. Used fine details for further discrimination.

8.8   Using energy

Apparatus list

Which is cheapest?

Teacher: If available, camping stoves of various types to demonstrate (see text). But stress that stoves intended for outdoor use should never be used indoors.

How hot?

Pupils: Eye protection (EACH)
            Bunsen burner, heatproof mat
            Tongs
            Candle
            Spill
            Stopwatch or stopclock
            Tongs

How easy is it to light?

If done, this investigation requires:
Pupils: Eye protection (EACH)
            Spills
            Tongs
            Crucible
            Heatproof mat
Teacher: A range of fuels to test (e.g. petrol, paraffin, meths, diesel fuel, paper, meta blocks)

You might try

Many people enjoy having barbecues. Can pupils suggest why? (Are they cheap? Quick? Easy? Do they keep the house cleaner?)

   Pupils could be asked to design a barbecue that works on a fuel other than charcoal, wood or briquettes.

Assessment criteria

Which is cheapest? (Planning investigations)

Checklist – the plan included:

Identification of key variables:

To alter – the type of stove and amount of fuel.

To measure – which is cheapest for boiling water.

Putting it into practice effectively:

Altered by – using a known amount of fuel in each stove.

Measured by – change in temperature of a known amount of water, for instance.

Controlled – the amount and initial temperature of water, the container, the setting on the stove (if appropriate).

Validity of results:

Scale – sensible amounts of water.

LEVEL I	LEVEL 3
Identified the problem by using each stove and seeing how fast it heated water.	Identified the problem by using measured quantities of fuel in each of the stoves to heat the same, sensible, volume of water in identical containers, until fuel exhausted. Used information to estimate comparative cost.

Is cost everything? (Communicating and interpreting)

LEVEL I	LEVEL 3
Choice made but with little or no supporting evidence.	Choice made with sensible supporting evidence drawn from the information given and from considering the needs of each situation.

8.9 Saving energy

Apparatus list

This spread is about insulation. There are no specific equipment requirements, but samples of insulation materials (e.g. pipe lagging, loft insulation) would be useful.

Video resources

Scientific Eye, 'Keeping Warm' (this may have been used in Unit 4).

You might try

You could tell pupils that they each have a small wooden hut deep in a forest. What could they do to insulate the hut and heat it in the most economical way?

Assessment criteria

Saving money at home (Observing)

LEVEL 1	LEVEL 3
List of some of the more obvious energy saving devices produced.	Comprehensive list of energy saving devices produced. The list draws on an understanding of the causes of heat loss in deciding which are important factors.

8.10 Energy for ever?

Apparatus list

Renewable energy sources

Any information on energy sources (especially video, slides, photos).
Pupils: Worksheet 8.10 (Energy sources)

A solar heater

Pupils: High density A4 polythene bags
            Scissors
            Black and white paper/card
            Sellotape
            Boiling tube
            Plastic tubing (say 50cm) and connector
            Thermometer (0–110°C)
Teacher: A sunny day
            Solar cell and solar water heater to demonstrate if available

Video resources

Environments, 'Rivers and Water', 'Lakes – Reservoirs'.
Scientific Eye, 'River of Rock', 'Earth Ltd'.

Assessment criteria

A solar heater (Investigating and making)

LEVEL 1	LEVEL 3
The device was sound in principle but failed in practice due to inadequate design or workmanship.	The device was sound in principle and worked well in practice. It was well constructed and drew on the ideas presented in the accompanying text. A way of measuring its effectiveness was devised.

8.11 Nuclear energy

Apparatus list

Pupils: Cassette recorder, microphone, tape, if available
Teacher: Any information (especially video/slides) on nuclear energy

You might try

Set up a discussion or a debate where children act out roles in a local community where a nuclear power station is to be built. A vote could be taken at the end.

Assessment criteria

Five-minute special (Communicating and interpreting)

LEVEL 1	LEVEL 3
The programme presented readily available factual material from both sides of the argument.	The programme presented evidence on both sides of the argument. It drew on various sources of factual material and presented them in an interesting and logical way.

8.12 Investigating Joe's Café

Apparatus list

Pupils: Electric kettle
Tea bags
Milk
Sugar
Measuring cylinder, plastic (10 or 25cm³)
Cup or mug
Stopwatch or stopclock

Video resources

Science Workshop, 'Water'.
Scientific Eye, 'Evaporation and Condensation'.

You might try

Extra 1: Many people living alone, especially the elderly, have found jug kettles a great advantage. Pupils could investigate how and why.

Unit 8 test

Mark scheme

1. Suitable axes (more than half the paper used, say), labels on both axes, bars plotted correctly and labelled, titled.

2. a. Cooking.
   b. Transport.
   c. 40% (approx.).

3. Good and bad points mentioned, e.g. such things as cost, cleanliness, ease of use, etc.

4. a. 6900 (approx.).
   b. 9300.
   c. Energy needs increase as you grow, level off as growth stops, boys go on longer because growth continues for longer and is higher because boys, on average, are bigger.

5. a. Large piece of coal.
   b. 22°C.
   c. Small pieces of coal heated water most, smokeless least. But small pieces last for shortest length of time (or similar).

6. Does the plan:
   – identify the variable to change: the number of turns of the key?
   – suggest how this is to be put into practice: counting several different numbers of turns?
   – identify the dependent variable: the distance travelled?
   – decide how this can be measured: ruler, string, tape measure?
   – mention any controls: type of surface, for instance?

7. a. Position at which water enters wheel, overshot uses buckets rather than paddles.
   b. Gives out most energy (power, force) for the same amount of water.
   c. Uses weight of water as well as its speed.

8. a. Heat, light, sound and radiation.
   b. Radioactive dust carried into atmosphere and deposited via rain, eaten by animals, then by us.
   c. X-rays in hospitals and cancer treatment.

9. a. Petrol has: higher top speed
                  greater acceleration
                  uses more fuel
                  car (engine) is lighter in weight
   b. Taxi mainly concerned with running costs, therefore choose diesel.

10. a.

Room	Fall in temperature °C
Entrance hall	21
Living room	15
Small bedroom, double glazing	6
Small bedroom, no double glazing.	9

   b. Small bedroom with double glazing.
      Entrance hall.
   c. Comments on size of rooms, size of windows and whether double glazed or not, draughts in hall, or other sensible suggestions.
   d. Temperature falls rapidly at first because the hall temperature is high compared with the outside, and the hall loses heat fast. As the temperature falls, this difference becomes smaller and the rate of heat loss slows down.
   e. Less than 3, probably about freezing.

SENSES

Introduction

The Unit starts with a study of light and sight, then moves on to cover sound and hearing, taste, smell and touch. At the end of the Unit there is a range of activities about communication, the brain and learning. The specific content areas are:
- the way light travels
- cameras
- reflection and refraction of light
- structure and function of the eye
- sight defects
- the way sound travels
- musical sounds
- noise
- the tongue and taste
- the skin and touch
- structure of the brain
- learning and remembering
- interpreting images

The themes in this Unit could be taught in any sequence.

Assessment opportunities

Basic skills

Worksheet 9.2A   Making a pinhole camera

9.3   Using lenses: microscopes

Communicating and interpreting

9.2   A shadow theatre

9.10   Images – designing a logo

Observing

9.2   Extras 1: coloured objects in street lights

9.3   Extras 3: looking at things in water

Planning investigations

9.4   Extras 1a: can adults see further than children?

9.5   A sound detector

9.7   Tasting tea

Investigating and making

9.4   Far vision

9.6   Musical instruments

9.8   Imitating touch

9.1 Using your senses

Apparatus list

Making sense

Teacher: A circus of 'sensing' activities is appropriate here: 2–3 blocks, same size, different substance (e.g. glass, metal, wood).
Pieces of paper, same size, different colour and thickness.
Test tubes with different colour/temperature liquids in.
Different flavours of crisp. (Care: hygiene problem!)
Identical sealed boxes or tins, different contents (e.g. coins and Plasticine).

Things you cannot sense

Pupils: Magnets
1.5V battery
Teacher: Radio or TV set
Radioactive ore (and GM tube and counter)

You might try

Ask pupils if we can all use every one of our senses. Discusss blindness, deafness and how other senses make up for the lost ones. (This links to 9.4, 9.5 and worksheet 9.10A.)

Children could investigate what happens to our sense of taste when we have a cold. They could try the crisp test with a peg on the nose. Can they still definitely distinguish between the flavours? (This links to 9.7.)

9.2 Looking at light

Apparatus list

A shadow theatre

Pupils: Cardboard box (shoe box is ideal)
Scissors
Greaseproof (or thin white) paper
Bright light source (e.g. 12V bulb and power pack)
White card
Spills
Sellotape

Cheap photos

Pupils: Pinhole camera kit of black card or blackened tin
           Greaseproof paper
           Sellotape
           Worksheet 9.2A (Making a pinhole camera)
           Worksheet 9.2B (Taking and developing photographs)
           Worksheet 9.2C (A modern camera)
Teacher: Access to darkroom with safe-light
           Photographic paper (ready cut to fit cameras)
           Developer
           Fixer
           Opaque sticky tape
           SLR camera if available

Video resources

Scientific Eye, 'Seeing and Believing'.
Your Living Body, 'Seeing and Hearing'.
Science – Start Here, 'Colour'.

You might try

Pupils could look at coloured objects in the classroom through different-coloured filters.

Pupils could also try to write a message, part of which disappears under a filter of a given colour.

Assessment criteria

A shadow theatre (Communicating and interpreting)

LEVEL 1	LEVEL 3
Report included the most significant elements of at least one experiment together with relevant data.	Report included a description of the experiments, together with a well-ordered presentation of the data in tables or other form. Appropriate conclusions were drawn and summarised.

Extras 1: Coloured objects in street lights (Observing)

LEVEL 1	LEVEL 3
Changes in colours noted.	Changes in colours noted in different-coloured light. Link made (or attempted) between colour of light and colour of object in white light.

9.3 Bending and reflecting light

Apparatus list

Bending light

Pupils: 2x1.5V batteries, connecting wire, 2.5V bulb in holder
          Card
          Scissors
Teacher: Assortment of:
          Mirrors and lenses (plane, convex, concave)
          Polythene sheet
          Perspex and glass blocks
          Prisms
          Test tubes with bungs
          Milk bottle

Investigating lenses and mirrors, Using lenses

Pupils: Concave and convex lenses, low and high power
          2x1.5V batteries, connecting wire, 2.5V bulb in holder
          Card
          Scissors
Teacher: Microscope, binoculars, telescope (as available)

Video resources

Scientific Eye, 'Seeing and Believing'.

You might try

Ask: 'If light travels in straight lines, how can you see anything in the shade?'

For making periscopes, you can now buy a mirrored sheet which can be cut up with scissors. This is cheap enough for children to take their finished periscopes home.

Making a kaleidoscope is also a good exercise. Pupils can use some cut-up mirrors and small pieces of coloured gel.

Assessment criteria

Extras 3 (Observing)

LEVEL 1	LEVEL 3
Writing and sketch showed objects as they are, rather than as they appear, or description failed to indicate significant features.	Writing and sketch indicated an awareness that appearance is linked to bending of light at surface of water.

9.4 Seeing things

Apparatus list

How good are your eyes?

Pupils: Metre rules
         Graph paper
         Worksheet 9.4 (Dissecting an animal eye), if done, with dissecting
         instruments.
Teacher: Model of eye if available

Video resources

Your Living Body, 'Seeing'.
Scientific Eye, 'Seeing and Believing'.

You might try

Ask pupils to collect pictures of animals and find out whether all 'hunters', like the lion, have their eyes at the front. Why?

Ask pupils if we can always trust our sight. Then show them some pictures of optical illusions (straight lines that look bent, or lines of equal length that seem different, candlestick/two profiles, etc.).

Assessment criteria

Far vision (Investigating and making)

Checklist – the investigation included:

Identification of key variables
    To alter   – distance of the book, size of print, person reading.
    To measure – ability to read text.

Putting it into practice effectively
    Altered by   – moving book measured distances from eye, changing size of
                 print, etc.
    Measured by – reading of text.
    Controlled   – lighting conditions (observer, size of text as appropriate).

Validity of results
    Scale   – sensible range and number of print sizes; sensible number of
                 readers.
    Accuracy   – distance measured using rule sufficiently accurately.

LEVEL 1	LEVEL 3
Identified problem by trying to read different print sizes at different distances.	Identified problem by measuring distance (accurately enough) when print becomes illegible. Used different readers (and significantly different sizes) in similar lighting conditions.

Extras 1a: Can adults see further than children? (Planning investigations)

Checklist – the plan included:

Identification of key variables:
To alter   – age of person.
To measure – how far they can see.

Putting it into practice effectively:
Altered by   – using people of different age.
Measured by – distance they can distinguish text or diagram.
Controlled   – lighting conditions, size of text.

Validity of results:
Scale   – used more than one person at each age.

LEVEL 1	LEVEL 3
Identified problem by asking people of different age to read some text.	Identified problem by asking people of significantly different ages to read the same text (or equivalent) in the same lighting conditions. Suggestion that several people would be needed at each age to allow for variation.

9.5 Hearing things

Apparatus list

How does sound travel?

Pupils: Balloon
Teacher: Signal generator and speaker
          Model ear if available
          If demonstrating speed of sound (not in text): starting pistol and several stopwatches

A sound detector/Earthquakes

Pupils: Microphone and oscilloscope (or demonstration)
            Large screwdriver

Video resources

Your Living Body, 'Hearing'.
Scientific Eye, 'Hearing and Sound'.
Science Workshop, 'Hearing'.

You might try

As an interesting problem-solving exercise, ask pupils to make something to help them hear better. This work could lead into an investigation of stethoscopes.

When looking at the speed of sound, you could discuss the use of starting guns in races. Sprinters now have a loudspeaker in the lane behind their starting blocks – why? Might this have helped sprinters to break more records? Also, why do sportsmen and women often perform better in front of a home crowd rather than away?

Assessment criteria

A sound detector (Planning investigations)

Checklist – the plan included:

Identification of key variables:
   To alter   – the material.
   To measure   – how well sound passes.

Putting it into practice effectively:
   Altered by   – using different materials.
   Measured by   – height of oscilloscope trace.
   Controlled   – size and shape of materials, volume of test sound, position of
                   materials, e.g. all suspended.

LEVEL 1	LEVEL 3
Identified problem by trying different materials to 'see how well they passed the sound'.	Identified problem by passing known sound through similar-sized pieces of the materials and measuring the size of the trace.

9.6 Making sounds

Apparatus list

Pupils: Equipment to make sounds, e.g.:
            Assorted rubber bands and string
            Hammer/nails/wood to mount bands or string with
            Set of milk bottles or test tubes (CLEAN ones)
            Straws (not plastic)
            Pieces of iron/steel of different lengths (xylophone)
Teacher: If available, a tape of assorted noise nuisance and a cassette player

Video resources

Your Living Body, 'Hearing'.
Scientific Eye, 'Hearing and Sound'.
Animals in Action, 'Signals, Methods of Communication'.

You might try

This topic could be extended to include animals making sounds. Why and how do they make sounds? Are these different from the sounds that humans make? This could include mating calls, warning signals, etc. Pupils could find out whether dolphins or whales 'talk', and how bats 'see' to fly.

Assessment criteria

Musical instruments (Investigating and making)

LEVEL 1	LEVEL 3
Basic instrument was adequate in theory but failed to work satisfactorily in practice.	The instrument was based on ideas presented in the Unit and was successfully developed, by trial and error, from those ideas. It gave a suitable range of notes and the frequency could be adjusted. There was some form of sounding board to amplify the sounds.

9.7 Taste and smell

Apparatus list

Tasting

Teacher: Sodium chloride solution, about 0.1 molar
          Sugar solution, about 0.01 molar
          Lemon juice solution
          Tonic water
(NB These solutions are for tasting so must be made hygienically)
          Assorted crisps of different flavours
          Set of clean teat pipettes (for tasting from)

Smelling

Pupils: Set of test tubes
          Measuring cylinder, 10 or 25cm^3
Teacher: Ammonia solution 1 molar
          Solutions as for taste investigations (above)

You might try

Warning: When pupils are doing taste tests with crisps, the order of the tasting is important. Some flavours linger, even if children wash out their mouths after each test. You might suggest that they leave cheese and onion until last!

A good lesson on taste is to use the Home Economics area and flavour small 'potato burgers'. These can be made with mashed potato and then different flavours added to the mini-burgers. Try:
– the 'El Paso Burger' (red chilli powder)
– the 'Calcutta Burger' (curry powder or its constituent spices)
– the 'Peking Burger' (Chinese-style sauce)
– 'Burger Milano' (basil and tomato purée)
Children are sure to enjoy experimenting with other food flavours and eating the burgers themselves.

Assessment criteria

Tasting tea (Planning investigations)

Checklist – the plan included:

Identification of key variables:
    To alter   – milk before or after tea.
    To measure – the taste.

Putting it into practice effectively:
    Altered by   – putting the same quantity of milk in the same quantity of tea
                       but before or after it.
    Measured by – the taste as reported by several people.
    Controlled   – the strength of the tea.

LEVEL 1	LEVEL 3
Identified problem by asking somebody to see if they could decide whether the milk went in first or not.	Identified the problem by asking several people to decide if there was a difference in taste when the same quantities of milk and tea (of the same strength) were used.

9.8 Touch

Apparatus list

Testing the sensors

Pupils: Plain A4 paper
Assorted small objects with different masses
$100cm^3$ beakers
Thermometer
Teacher: Electronic balance

Imitating touch

Pupils: A4 card
Brass fasteners
Scissors
Sellotape
String
Teacher: Table-tennis balls
Egg if available

Video resources

Your Living Body, 'The Skin', 'The Nervous System'.

You might try

Put some objects in a 'feely bag' and ask pupils to describe them, using only their sense of touch for observing. Encourage good use of descriptive language.

Assessment criteria

Imitating touch (Investigating and making)

LEVEL 1	LEVEL 3
The device was OK in theory but was either too insensitive (broken egg) or did not grip sufficiently (broken egg on floor)!	The device utilised ideas presented in the text and was designed in such a way that its sensitivity could be adjusted to perform the task.

9.9 Using your brain

Apparatus list

Pupils: Plane mirror
            Worksheet 9.9A (Learning)
            Worksheet 9.9B (Reading and remembering)

Teacher: Information about the brain, if available (on video or slides)

Video resources

Your Living Body, 'Brain and Nervous System'.
Animals in Action, 'Signals, Methods of Communication.'

You might try

There is room for discussion on learning in animals. How are dogs trained? How
are circus animals (elephants, sea lions, horses) taught their tricks? How do
parrots learn to talk?

Many animals, once they are retired from a circus, still remember their tricks.
(Bristol Zoo had a polar bear which danced backwards and forwards for much of
the day because that was part of its old circus act.) Why do you think animals
don't forget such tricks?

9.10 Communicating

Apparatus list

Pupils: 2x1.5V batteries in holders
            2.5V bulb in holder
            Short pieces of connecting wire
            2 long pieces (2–5m) of connecting wire
            Paper-clip switch, or equipment to make one

Video resources

Your Living Body, 'Brain and Nervous System'.
Animals in Action, 'Signals, Methods of Communication'.

You might try

Ask pupils to observe people's body language. Discuss their observations of
gestures, postures etc.

Pupils could try sending a fairly long message to each other using just body
movement. (This leads on to dramatic presentation and mime.)

Discuss our ways of greeting people and saying goodbye. Why do we shake
hands? Why do we kiss, or bow? Pupils could find out how people in different
societies greet each other.

Discuss with pupils what messages we interpret from objects or sounds, e.g. flashing blue light, siren, flags on a bathing beach, buoys, ice-cream vans' music and so on. Can pupils think of any others?

The task on logos could be linked to heraldry using coats of arms. Pupils could use reference books showing coats of arms to guess what the original owner did or was interested in. They could then design their own coat of arms.

Assignment criteria

Images (Communicating and interpreting)

LEVEL I	LEVEL 3
The logo contained obvious features such as the initials of the organisation but did not convey any other image.	The logo succeeded in conveying an appropriate image to other groups.

9.11 Overcoming handicaps

Apparatus list

Pupils: Blindfold
            Egg (solid if possible)
            Egg cup
            Egg box
            A4 card
            Scissors
            Sellotape

Video resources

Science Workshop, 'Hearing'.
Scientific Eye, 'Hearing and Sound', 'Seeing and Believing'.

Unit 9 Test

Mark scheme

1. a. Strip and filament.
   b. 50 times per second.
   c. Stop movement.
   d. Dangerous – you could sew your finger if you don't realise the needle is moving.

2. a. Twice its real size, 10cm.
   b. Shadow gets bigger.
   c. Shadow gets thinner, but not shorter, until it is a line, then gets bigger again until back to original.

3. a. Right way up and smaller.
   b. Convex.
   c. Convex mirror, things always same way up and smaller, giving wider angle of view.

4. a. So that he couldn't identify the foods by sight.
   b. So that he couldn't memorise the order.
   c. Some foods could be identified with or without anyone being able to smell them; others couldn't be identified at all; others could only be identified if they could be smelled as well as tasted.

5. a. Suitable drawings, light rays drawn as straight lines.
   b. Black will give a better defined beam, silver will be brighter; either answer OK if sensible reasons offered.
   c. Suitable sketch.

6. Design includes egg box type material for walls, sealed door, some method of ventilation, double glazed window, microphone or equivalent. Use of background sound – music or running taps.

7. a. Does the plan:
      – identify the variable to alter: the terrain?
      – suggest how this is to be put into practice?
      – identify the dependent variable: how well the sound carries?
      – decide how this can be measured by, for example, how far away a sound can be heard?
      – mention some things to control: the volume of the sound for instance?
   b. Hills reflect sound upwards, or similar.

8. a. C.
   b. F.
   c. Comments on price increase with magnification, type of lenses and special features such as rubber protection.

9. Simon.

10. a. 25°.
    b. 40°.
    c. Graph uses sensible axes (at least half of the graph paper), correctly labelled, points plotted correctly, smooth line, correct reading-off of angle.

SUBSTANCES

Introduction

This Unit is mainly about chemistry. Chemical change is the first main topic, and this sets the scene for many of the later themes. The properties of acids are explored, and this group of substances is used to introduce indicators. The issues raised by acid rain are also considered. Alkalis and neutralisation then lead into a study of limestone.

The second half of the Unit looks at some important chemicals, starting with iron and steel. This covers the history of iron extraction and how iron is converted into steels. The different types of steel are studied, and so is rust. Copper is used as an example of a metal which can be extracted from its ore in different ways. This is followed by a study of a non-metallic element, sulphur. The importance of common salt is then stressed: its extraction, history and role in corrosion. The electrolysis of salt serves as an introduction to chlorine. The final spread has water, the chemical, as the focus of several investigations.

The first half of the Unit should be taught in the order given in the Pupil's Book, but the second half can be taught in various sequences.

Assessment opportunities

Basic skills

10.3 Measuring acidity

10.4 Adding acid to alkali – measuring pH

10.10 Identifying gases

10.11 Hard and soft water – following instructions

Communicating and interpreting

10.4 Extras 1: Designing a poster on alkalis

10.6 Rust

Observing

10.1 Finding out about substances

10.6 Burning iron

10.7 Heating copper

Planning investigations

10.2 Acid fizz

10.11 Chemicals in water

Investigating and making

10.4 Which powder is best?

10.8 Keeping food fresh

10.9 Corrosion

10.1 Making new substances

Apparatus list

Pupils: Eye protection (EACH)
           Test tubes and rack
           Spatula

Teacher: Solutions of: ethanoic acid (0.5molar) or vinegar, bleach, copper (II) sulphate 0.5molar, lime water, ammonia (0.5molar)

           Solids in labelled dishes: magnesium ribbon pieces, copper wire pieces, small iron nails, sulphur lumps, sodium hydrogen carbonate, sodium chloride, limestone powder (calcium carbonate), sodium carbonate, iron filings

           Positive guidance on safety should be given to pupils. They should not smell fumes from test tubes too closely, but should first breathe in to fill lungs with air, then point the test tube away and waft a small amount of the vapour towards them and sniff gently.

You might try

This would be a good opportunity to remind pupils of the different hazard warnings and labels.

It may also be a good opportunity to discuss the dangers associated with chemicals at home (especially if these are misused), for example bleach, toilet cleaners, ammonia.

Assessment criteria

Finding out about substances (Observing)

LEVEL 1	LEVEL 3
The classification and subsequent observation were based on everyday features such as colour, shape and smell.	The classification was based on the chemical properties of the materials. The ideas used to generate the classification were modified as more results were obtained.

10.2 Acids

Apparatus list

Pupils: Eye protection (EACH)
            Test tubes and rack
            Spatula
            Teat pipette
            Petri dish (old)

Teacher: Sodium bicarbonate powder   Beer (why not?)
            Calcium carbonate powder   Wine
            Beetroot or blackberry juice   Milk
            Magnesium ribbon
            Emery paper
            Vinegar (or ethanoic acid 0.5molar)
            Coca Cola and any other fizzy drinks
            Orange juice and lemon juice
            Pickled-onion juice

Video resources

Scientific Eye, 'Acids' (also relevant for 10.3–10.5).

You might try

These kitchen substances could also be tested for acidity and alkalinity: sherbet, soap, liver salts, potato, washing-up liquid, sink cleaner, oven cleaner, shampoo. Pupils have even had success testing such things as mustard, eggs, turmeric. Some home-made wines are also excellent for testing.

Assessment criteria

Acid fizz (Planning investigations)

Checklist – the plan included:

Identification of key variables:
    To alter   – type of drink.
    To measure   – acidity.

Putting it into practice effectively:
    Altered by   – using two or more types of drink.
    Measured by   – pH paper or similar.

LEVEL 1	LEVEL 3
Identified problem by using at least two types of drink and 'measuring' acidity.	Identified problem by using several types of drink of different sorts. Measured acidity correctly using suitable indicator.

10.3 Acids: friend or foe?

Apparatus list

Pupils: Eye protection (EACH)
Test tubes and rack
Spatula
Universal indicator or full range indicator paper
Relevant colour chart

Teacher: Dropper bottles of indicator (as above)
Samples of water from different sources (but beware of pollution)

You might try

Making indicators is an enjoyable and worthwhile practical task. Pupils can try red cabbage, fresh beetroot, blackberries or blackcurrants. The petals of blue flowers (particularly blue lupins) make an excellent indicator.

10.4 Alkalis

Apparatus list

Detecting alkalis/Adding acid to alkali

Pupils: Eye protection (EACH)
Test tubes and rack
Spatula
Universal Indicator or full-range indicator paper
Relevant colour chart
Worksheet 10.4A Gardening
Worksheet 10.4B Neutralising

Teacher: Assorted alkalis, e.g. sodium carbonate, sodium hydrogen carbonate, soap solution, oven cleaner, Rennies (or similar), toothpaste, household ammonia (or 0.5molar ammonia), detergent, garden lime (calcium oxide), beetroot or blackberry juice, clean magnesium ribbon, 0.1molar ethanoic or hydrochloric acid, Universal Indicator or full-range indicator solution

Worksheet 10.4B Neutralising

Pupils: Eye protection (EACH)
Test tubes and rack
Spatula
Universal Indicator of full-range indicator solution
Relevant colour chart

Teacher: Samples of soil of differing acidity
Centrifuge
Vinegar
Sodium hydrogen carbonate powder
Some toothpastes

Which powder is best?

Pupils: Eye protection (EACH)
            Test tubes and rack
            Spatula
            Universal Indicator or full-range indicator solution
            Relevant colour chart
Teacher: Assorted stomach powders (e.g. Milk of Magnesia, Bisodol)
            Solution of weak acid (e.g. 0.1 molar ethanoic acid)

Assessment criteria

Which powder is best? (Investigating and making)

Checklist – the investigation included:

Identification of key variables:
    To alter   – type of stomach powder.
    To measure   – how well it neutralises.

Putting it into practice effectively:
    Altered by   – using two or more different types.
    Measured by – quantity needed to neutralise fixed amount of acid.
    Controlled   – strength of acid, indicator.

Validity of results:
    Scale   – sensible quantity of acid.
    Accuracy   – repeats if necessary and appropriate.

LEVEL I	LEVEL 3
Identified problem by using at least two types of stomach powder with some acid and 'looking to see what happened',	Identified problem by using at least two types of stomach powder as per the instructions on the label. Chose a sensible amount of acid, at an appropriate strength, and monitored pH using indicator until neutrality. Measured quantity of stomach powder needed.

Extras I: Designing a poster on alkalis (Communicating and interpreting)

LEVEL I	LEVEL 3
Poster used readily available information to illustrate dangers.	Poster included information from lessons and from other sources to illustrate a variety of dangers to people and objects/ecology, etc.

10.5 Limestone

Apparatus list

Pupils: Eye protection (EACH)
            Bunsen burner and heatproof mat
            Stand and clamp
            10cm of nichrome wire, approx. 22swg
            Teat pipette
            Universal Indicator paper
Teacher: Limestone chips
            Ammonia solution 0.5molar
            Calcium oxide
            Sodium carbonate
            Sodium chloride
            Universal Indicator solution

You might try

Pupils could try this detective game: 'Murder at the chalkface'.

The office manager of a quarry has been killed. The quarry produces lime. A villain called Garrotting Gordon is suspected and, when the police arrest him, he has white powder on his trousers. He says he works in a sugar factory and got the white powder from there. Can the pupils prove whether he is telling the truth or not?

10.6 Iron and steel

Apparatus list

Pupil: Eye protection (EACH)
            Strip of iron (say 2cm x 5cm)
            Strip of steel (say 2cm x 5cm)
            Bunsen burner, heatproof mat
            Spatula
            Tongs
Teacher: Iron filings
            Iron powder
            Steel wool
            Small iron nails

Video resources

Scientific Eye, 'Earth Ltd'.

You might try

The CDT Department could help with comparing the properties of cast iron, wrought iron and steel.

Good rust-proofing is now possible. It is said that we could produce car bodies that never rust. Ask pupils why they think we still have cars that rust.

Assessment criteria

Burning iron (Observing)

LEVEL 1	LEVEL 3
Description of obvious features – sparks, colour of material, appearance after heating, for instance.	Observations chosen in an attempt to describe the link between the behaviour of the material and its size (particles to strip). Description includes sensible attempt at explanation linked to surface area, volume etc.

Rust (Communicating and interpreting)

Answers to questions:
1. 6%.
2. Front wings.
3. Doors, door sills, front and rear wings.
4. Bar chart of correct set of figures, axes labelled and sensibly chosen to fit graph paper, correctly spaced scale, accurately plotted and drawn.
5. Jacking point might collapse.
6. Keep paintwork clean, underseal (or similar), clean salt from underneath in winter, polish (to prevent water 'wetting' the surface).

LEVEL 1	LEVEL 3
Located single items of information, questions 1, 2 and 3. Could complete the bar chart having been given the axes.	Located single items of data. Drew the key features of the bar chart correctly, question 4. Could predict from the data and apply ideas from elsewhere in the Unit and from everyday experience, questions 5 and 6.

10.7 Copper

Apparatus list

Making copper

Pupils: Eye protection (EACH)
           Test tube and rack
           Power pack (4V) or battery and connecting wire
           2 carbon rods
           Crocodile clips
           Beaker 100cm^3
           Crucible
           Pipe-clay triangle
           Worksheet 10.7 (Using acid to make copper)
Teacher: Magnesium ribbon
           Copper (II) sulphate solution 0.5molar
           Iron filings
           Sand tray
           Copper (II) oxide

Heating copper

Pupils: Eye protection (EACH)
           4 pieces of copper, 2cm x 5cm
           Emery paper
           Bunsen burner, heatproof mat
           Tongs
Teacher: Nail varnish
           Pliers

Video resources

Scientific Eye, 'Earth Ltd' (good example of how copper is mined and transformed into rivets).
Search, 'Search Goes Full Circle'.

You might try

The uses of copper as a conductor of electricity and heat could be shown and discussed, including copper saucepans or kettles as examples.

Ask pupils to list all the times they use iron, steel or copper (and its alloys) in a day.

Alloys could be introduced here – what they are and why we have them.

This is also an opportunity to look at the recycling of metals.

Assessment opportunities

Heating copper (Observing)

LEVEL I	LEVEL 3
Description centred on colour of material.	Description relates colour of material to presence of air (and so to chemical reaction).

10.8 Sulphur

Apparatus list

Iron and sulphur, Copper and sulphur

NB Heating iron and sulphur together must be done in a fume cupboard.

Teacher: Eye protection
Iron filings
Sulphur powder
Sulphur lumps
Small iron nails
Magnet
Test tubes
Hammer
Copper wire about 16swg

Sulphur dioxide

Pupils: Eye protection (EACH)
Test tubes in rack
Universal Indicator solution
Bunsen burner, heatproof mat, tripod, gauze
Beaker, 250cm^3
Stopclock or stopwatch
Knife and teat pipette
Apple

Teacher: 1000cm^3 sulphur dioxide solution or Campden tablets
Assorted coloured cloths
Lemon juice
Vinegar
Salt
Sugar

Assessment criteria

Keeping food fresh (Investigating and making)

Checklist – the investigation included:

Identification of key variables:
To alter   – amount of sulphur dioxide solution.
To measure   – how brown the apple becomes.

Putting it into practice effectively:
Altered by   – using different, measured, quantities of sulphur dioxide solution.
Measured by – looking for signs of browning.
Controlled   – initial state and size of the piece of apple.

Validity of results:
Scale   – sensibly-sized piece of apple, suitable length of time before checking for appearance of browning.

LEVEL 1	LEVEL 3
Identified the problem by using different amounts of solution and looking to see what happens to the apple.	Identified the problem by using measured quantities of sulphur dioxide solution on equal, sensibly-sized pieces of apple. Waited for an appropriate time before checking for browning.

10.9 Salt

Apparatus list

Purifying rock salt

Pupils: Eye protection (EACH)
           Bunsen burner, heatproof mat, tripod, gauze
           Beaker, 250cm^3
           Stirring rod
           Conical flask, 150–250cm^3
           Filter funnel and paper
           Pestle and mortar
           Evaporating basin
Teacher: Rock salt (or sodium chloride mixed with small amounts of sand and mud)

Corrosion

Pupils: Eye protection (EACH)
           Bunsen burner, heatproof mat, tripod, gauze
           Beaker, 250cm^3
           Boiling tubes, bungs, rack

Teacher: Rock salt
           Sodium chloride
           Distilled water
           Magnesium sulphate

You might try

Tell pupils that they live by the sea (they may do, anyway!). They have to write a letter, explaining to a friend how and why sea spray affects the family car and their bicycle.

The class could look at salt and sea water, and why it is easier to float in salty water. (This links back to 2.10 and the hydrometer exercise in 2.1).

Assessment criteria

Corrosion (Investigating and making)

There are several possible investigations here. The checklist below is for one of them – rock salt versus pure salt.

Checklist – the investigation included:

Identification of key variables:
    To alter   – the type of salt.
    To measure   – level of corrosion.

Putting it into practice effectively:
    Altered by   – using equal quantities of each type of salt.
    Measured by – area or thickness of corrosion.
    Controlled   – amount of water, access to air, size of test piece of metal,
                     time before measurement.

Validity of results:
    Scale   – sensibly-sized piece of metal and amount of salt and water.

LEVEL I	LEVEL 3
Identified problem by using different types of salt on pieces of metal and looking to see which rusted most.	Identified problem by using the same amount of the two types of salt on the same size pieces of metal with the same volume of water present and the same access to air. Devised some means of measuring the extent of corrosion. Waited suitable time before making measurement.

10.10   Chlorine

Apparatus list

Pupils: Beaker 250cm^3
            Battery or power pack (4V) and connecting wires
            2 crocodile clips
            2 carbon rods
            2 ignition tubes
            Spill
Teacher: Distilled water
            Sodium chloride
            Universal Indicator paper
            Bunsen burner and heatproof mat
            Assorted coloured cloths

10.11   Chemicals in water

Apparatus list

Pure water

Pupils: Eye protection (EACH)
            Beaker 250cm^3
            Battery or power pack (4V) and connecting wires
            2 crocodile clips
            2 carbon rods
            2 ignition tubes
            Spill
Teacher: Distilled water
            Universal Indicator paper
            Bunsen burner and heatproof mat
            Sulphuric acid, 2molar

Chemicals in water, Hard and soft water

Pupils: Eye protection (EACH)
            Bunsen burner, heatproof mat, tripod, gauze
            Beaker, 250cm^3
            Evaporating basin
            4 test tubes in rack
            Worksheet 10.11 (What causes hardness in water?)
Teacher: Samples of water: distilled, hard (add calcium carbonate if necessary),
            sea water, mineral water
            Hydrochloric acid, 1molar in dropper bottles
            Dilute soap solution or soap flakes
            Sodium carbonate
            Commercial water softener
            Electronic balance

Video resources

Search, 'Search in Water'.
Scientific Eye, 'Evaporation and condensation'.
Science Workshop, 'Water'.
Environments, 'Rivers and Water', 'Lakes and Reservoirs'.

Assessment criteria

Chemicals in water (Planning investigations)

Checklist – the plan included:

Identification of key variables:
To alter   – source of water.
To measure   – the amount of dissolved substance.

Putting it into practice effectively:
Altered by   – using the same quantities of at least two sorts of water.
Measured by – weighing (or other) the amount of solid left after evaporation.

Validity of results:
Scale   – sensible amount of water to give weighable quantity of solid.
Accuracy   – instrument chosen to give suitable accuracy of measurement.

LEVEL 1	LEVEL 3
Identified the problem by using at least two types of water and attempting to find out what was dissolved in them.	Identified the problem by evaporating equal and suitable quantities of the different sorts of water and measuring the residue with appropriate accuracy.

Unit 10 Test

Mark scheme

1.

Use	Percentage
Other	30
Fertilisers	30
Detergents	14
Paints	11
Fibres	8
Plastics	5
Cleaning	2

2. a. Sandy soil.
    b. Clay.
    c. Medium loam.
    d. White subsoil, pasty when wet, low in organic matter, alkaline dogwood, viburnam and clematis grow well.

3. a. Blood water.
    b. 11.
    c. Lemon juice, vinegar, lemonade, coffee.
    d. Household cleaner, stomach medicine, toothpaste.

4. a. Norway.
    b. Bulgaria.
    c. Worst polluted are mainly in the north of Europe. The worst polluters are mainly in the south.
       The prevailing winds go from south to north.

5. For instance:
    Keep the pieces of metal damp, (and salty perhaps), but otherwise in the same conditions, leave for several weeks and inspect for extent of corrosion.

6. a. 7.
    b. A, because it needed fewest drops.

7. a. Petrol and lead pipes.
    b. Brain damage.
    c. Petrol burned in engine, lead comes out in exhaust fumes, is breathed in.
    d. Lead-free petrol, replace lead pipes with copper or plastic.

8. A is iron.
    B is steel.
    C is brass.
    D is copper.
    E is aluminium.

9. Suitable choices with reasons.

10. a. 3.
    b. 2.
    c. Iron.
    d. Gold has lowest production figures, will last the shortest length of time and is the rarest in the earth's crust. It is much used in jewellery because it doesn't 'rust' and, because it is so scarce, it is very expensive.

FORCES

Introduction

The first spread in the Unit gathers pupils' perceptions about forces through a study of some common actions. The rest of the Unit then introduces more complex ideas on forces. The main topics are:
- springs
- Isaac Newton, force and weight
- levers
- mechanisms in the human body
- friction
- speed and acceleration
- momentum
- investigating 'bounciness'
- machines.

The final spread is based on an investigation of forces and friction in a bicycle.

The teaching order in this Unit should not be altered too much, although some of the later topics could be taught in other sequences.

Assessment opportunities

Basic skills

11.1 Measuring forces

11.1 Extras 3: estimating forces

11.2 Choosing and drawing a graph for stretching a spring

Communicating and interpreting

11.3 Weight in the solar system

11.6 A lot of friction

11.9 Cars

Observing

11.4 Forces at work

11.5 Joints

11.7 Reducing friction

Planning investigations

11.6 Extras 1: Skateboards

11.10 Extras 1: The bounciness of a football

Investigating and making

11.2 Changing the strength of a spring

11.7 Parachuting

11.10 A ball launcher

11.1   Using force

Apparatus list

Pupils: 0–1N, 0–10N, 0–100N force meters
Teacher: Assorted rubber bands
              Sponges
              1kg masses
              Bathroom scales marked in newtons
              Graph paper

Video resources

Scientific Eye, 'Force and Friction'.

You might try

In 'Measuring forces' some work could be done on predicting and estimating forces to improve these two skills. Pupils would then be able to select the appropriate force meter. (Schools have many sensitive force meters ruined by pupils using them over and beyond their force limits.)

11.2   Springs

Apparatus list

Pupils: 50cm length of approx. 22 swg copper wire
              Stand and clamp
              10 × 10g masses on hanger
              10 × 100g masses on hanger
Teacher: Materials to make poster displays
              Assorted clothes pegs
              Assorted force meters (0–100N especially)
              Additional copper wire, 18 swg and 26 swg approx.
              Wire cutters

You might try

Pupils could investigate whether some wires are better for making springs than others. They could try: copper, nichrome, iron. Ask them: 'Does thickness matter?'

This would be an opportunity to talk about the 'elastic limit'. Children are fascinated by the impossibility of squashing a spring back to its original shape once it has passed its limit.

Children could make a collection of springs, and it is surprising how many kinds there are. Some are excellent for pupils to handle, e.g. a Slinky spring, or the long bouncy springs sold with a toy animal on the end. Some work on classifying is possible here.

Assessment criteria

Changing the strength of a spring (Investigating and making)

Checklist – the investigation included:

Identification of key variables:

To alter — the number of coils;
the width of the coils;
the size of the wire.

To measure — the 'springiness' of the spring.

Putting it into practice effectively:

Altered by — using different known numbers of coils;
using different measured widths of the coils;
using different gauges of wire.

Measured by — the extension for a given load, or the load for a given extension.

Controlled — the other variables not under investigation;
the method of loading.

Validity of results:

Scale — sensible numbers and widths of coils, and gauges of wires.
Suitable range of numbers, widths and wire gauges.

Accuracy — ± 10%, say, on dimensions of coils and extensions.

LEVEL 1	LEVEL 3
Identified the problem by making springs with different numbers of coils (for instance) and looking to see how springy they were.	Identified the problem by making two or more springs with sensible, and suitably different, numbers of turns. Measured their springiness by the extension for a given load (or equivalent), accurately enough to distinguish between them.

11.3 Force and weight

Apparatus list

Pupils: Assorted rubber bands
Drawing pins
Paper clips
Scrap wood, preferably about 2cm × 5cm × 30cm

Teacher: Assorted force meters

Video resources

Scientific Eye, 'Gravity'.

You might try

An exercise which is good fun, but makes children think carefully, is for them to prepare a report about a sports day held on one of the other planets in the solar system. This can be done as a comic strip, a newspaper article, etc.

Assessment criteria

Weight in the solar system (Communicating and interpreting)

Answers to questions:

1. Jupiter.
2. Mercury.
3. a. 10N.
    b. 4N.
    c. Jupiter.
4. 360N.
5. The Earth's moon.
6. No, because (for instance) Saturn is further than Jupiter but gravity is less.

LEVEL 1	LEVEL 3
Located single items of information given specific references – questions 1 and 2 in particular.	Located single items of information – questions 1 and 2. Interpreted the information in the table and brought other knowledge to bear – questions 3, 4, 5 and 6.

11.4   Forces at work

Apparatus list

Pupils: Scrap wood, preferably about 2cm × 5cm × 30cm
          10 × 100g masses
          1kg mass
          Metre rule
          Assorted elastic bands
          String
Teacher: Assorted force meters

Video resources

Scientific Eye, 'Force and Friction'.

You might try

Pupils could make a class mural of levers with pictures cut from old magazines, showing items such as kitchen equipment, doors, wheelbarrows, see-saws, bicycles, etc.

Assessment criteria

Forces at work (Observing)

LEVEL 1	LEVEL 3
Description of objects focuses only on their use.	Description uses relevant ideas to explain how the thing worked.

11.5   Levers in your body

Apparatus list

Pupils: Stand and clamp
              10 × 100g masses on hanger
              1kg mass
              Metre rule
              Assorted elastic bands
              String
              Worksheet 11.5 (Carrying loads)
Teacher: Model skeleton if available
              Assorted force meters

You might try

With the model arm, it is worth mentioning that muscles often work in pairs. Pupils could then consider why this is so. Do they need a pair of muscles on their model arm?

There is a good opportunity here to look at the way animals move and how they use levers in their bodies.

Assessment criteria

Joints (Observing)

LEVEL 1	LEVEL 3
Sketch and any description relates to position and use of joint.	Sketch and any description links ideas from examples of different sorts of joints to joints in body. Muscles included with an indication of how their position affects the direction of the movement of the joints when they are in use.

11.6 Stop that movement!

Apparatus list

Pupils: 2 × 1kg (or 20 × 100g) masses
            String
Teacher: Assorted force meters
            OHP transparencies and pens
            Bag of old shoes

Video resources

Technology and Design, 'Moving'.
Starting Science, 'Making Things Move' (also relevant to 11.9).

You might try

Some good work involving mathematics could be done on calculating stopping distances with regard to (a) speed, (b) surface, (c) new or worn tyres. (This links to 11.8.)

The study of tyres can be a good project connecting friction to other forces. For example: types of tyres (bicycle, tractor, earth movers); radial and cross-ply tyres; tread (patterns, racing 'slicks').

Assessment criteria

A lot of friction (Communicating and interpreting)

Answers to questions:

2. 60kg.
3. Friction between the rope and the edge of the cliff stopped him from being pulled over.
4. There is a lot of friction between the rope and the descendeur, so the force needed to control the lowering is reduced (or similar).
5. Because there is less friction between the rope and the descendeur.
6. Friction of rope on hands causes heat, which burns.

LEVEL 1	LEVEL 3
Located single items of information given specific references – questions 2 and 3 in particular.	Located single items of information – questions 2 and 3. Interpreted the information in the table and brought other knowledge to bear – questions 4, 5 and 6.

Extras 1: Skateboards (Planning investigations)

Checklist – the plan included:

Identification of key variables:
    To alter   – the type of oil.

To measure – which oil is best.

Putting it into practice effectively:

Altered by   – using the same quantities of the three types of oil.

Measured by – speed down a ramp, or distance travelled with known push (for instance).

Controlled   – the skateboard, the ramp or the push.

Validity of results:

Scale   – some suggestion as to distance over which test is to be made.

LEVEL I	LEVEL 3
Identified the problem by using the different types of oil and looking to see which type made the skateboard go fastest (or equivalent).	Identified the problem by using the three types of oil, in equal quantities, on the same or identical skateboards and measuring their speed down a slope (or equivalent) of suitable length.

11.7 Using friction

Apparatus list

Parachuting

Pupils: Materials to make parachute from (examples): _
             canopy: cloth, polythene, paper
             strings: thread, string
             payload: 2 x 10g masses
             Sellotape
             Worksheet 11.7 (Free fall)

Streamlining

Pupils: Lumps of Plasticine, approx. 20g
             Im x 2.5cm acrylic tube with bung at bottom
             Stopwatch or stopclock

Teacher: Wallpaper paste (to thicken water if needed)
             Electronic balance

You might try

Pupils could investigate streamlining bikes (this is a good link to 11.12). When the speed of a bicycle doubles, the friction (air resistance) gets four times bigger unless the rider somehow overcomes it. Pupils could study some modern track cycles, in particular the shape of the frame and handlebars and the 'solid' rear wheel, i.e. no spokes. They could also study a 'vector' cycle that has a very light, streamlined body around it. These cycles can easily travel at 60mph (95km/h).

Assessment criteria

Parachuting (Investigating and making)

LEVEL 1	LEVEL 3
The parachute was reasonably well constructed and worked.	The parachute was well built and tested. The results of the test were used in modifying the design and sensible choices of materials were made.

Reducing friction (Observing)

LEVEL 1	LEVEL 3
Sketch and description concentrate on the obvious features of shape, colour and size.	Sketch and description reflect an attempt to link the shape of the bird to the streamlining effect and its subsequent motion.

11.8 Speed

Apparatus list

How fast?

Pupils: Stopwatch or stopclock
Teacher: Tape measure, 10 or 20m
          Maggots or woodlice if available
          Clockwork toy car

Changing speed

Pupils: A4 card
          Brass fastener
          100g mass
          Sellotape
          Plasticine
          String
          Worksheet 11.8 (Stopping distances)

You might try

A dragster (see 1.3) shows rapid acceleration, high speed and relates back to friction (tyre grip) and braking (parachute). Pupils could improve on the dragster they made in 1.3 and give it special features to improve its performance.

11.9 Forces and movement

Apparatus list

Pupils: Assorted rubber bands
           Empty 250g margarine tub (or similar)
           Assorted force meters
           Stand and clamp
           Metre rules
           10 × 10g masses
Teacher: Tape measure, 10 or 20m

Video resources

Technology and Design, 'Moving'.
Starting Science, 'Making Things Move'.

You might try

Pupils could find out how huge structures were built thousands of years ago. (This involved different forces for different movements.) They could investigate the building of the pyramids, or Stonehenge:

1. Stones across land – rollers (or slide on ice)
2. Stones loaded on to boats – levers
3. Stones ferried across water – oars, sails, rafts
4. Stones moved up ramps – rollers
5. Stones cut to size – wedges

(This links to 11.11.)

Assessment criteria

Cars (Communicating and interpreting)

Answers to questions:

7. 1800cm^3.
8. Rover 820 and Sterling.
9. Rover Sterling.
● Table:

Name	Mass	Acceleration
Rover 216	925	10.9
Sierra 1.6L	980	12.0
Cavalier 1.6	1000	12.0

10. The heavier the car, for the same engine size, the lower the acceleration.
● Powerful engine, low mass, streamlined (and good brakes and steering).
● Advert shows ability to pick out important discriminating features.

LEVEL 1	LEVEL 3
Located single items of information given specific references – questions 5, 6 and 7 in particular.	Located single items of information – questions 5, 6 and 7. Identified the correct data for the table and interpreted it sensibly. Answers to questions 10 and 11 indicated an awareness of the important features for increased acceleration.

11.10 Bouncing forces

Apparatus list

What makes a ball bounce?

Pupils: Eye protection (EACH)
Bunsen burner, heatproof mat, tripod, gauze
Beaker 250cm^3
Tongs
Thermometer
Metre rule
Stand and clamp
Squash balls (a range of spot colours)

Teacher: Assortment of small balls: golf, table tennis, tennis, air flow, sponge, 'Supa-ball', cricket, hockey etc.

A ball launcher

Pupils: Stand and clamp
Assorted rubber bands
A4 card
Sellotape
Brass paper fasteners
Table-tennis ball
Thread
String
Egg box (empty!)
Cardboard tube (e.g. off kitchen paper roll)

You might try

A discussion on sport would be relevant, including questions such as:
1. How do footballers 'bend' free kicks?
2. How do cricketers spin or 'seam' a ball?
3. How and why do tennis and table-tennis players top-spin or undercut the ball?
4. How do baseball pitchers deliver an 'arm ball' or a 'fast ball'?
5. How do golfers 'soft-land' a ball on the green or get extra distance on a hard fairway by hitting shots that are low and fast?

Assessment criteria

A ball launcher (Investigating and making)

LEVEL 1	LEVEL 3
The ball launcher was sensible in theory but failed in practice due to poor design or construction.	The ball launcher was well built and had been developed during a series of tests in which the design had been sensibly modified. It was reasonably accurate and incorporated the requisite design features asked for.

Extras 1: The bounciness of a football (Planning investigations)

Checklist – the plan included:

Identification of key variables:
  To alter   – the amount of air in the ball.
  To measure   – the bounciness.

Putting it into practice effectively:
  Altered by   – using different counted numbers of pumpfuls of air (for instance).
  Measured by – the height of rebound from a fixed release height (or equivalent).
  Controlled   – the surface of bounce, the method of release.

Validity of results:
  Scale   – suggestion of sensible release height.

LEVEL 1	LEVEL 3
Identified the problem by suggesting ways of changing the amount of air in the ball and looking to see how it bounced.	Identified the problem by suggesting that the amount of air be changed by counting the numbers of pumpfuls and measuring the rebound height, on the same surface, from a fixed and sensible release height.

11.11 Changing the force – machines

Apparatus list

Pupils: A simple machine (e.g. lab. clamp, vice, nut cracker, car jack, egg whisk, door handle assembly, hoist, adjustable spanner, hand drill, bottle top remover). It is important to have a range of different machines.
1kg mass
String
Assorted rubber bands
Metre rule
Worksheet 11.11 (Where do cars get their go?)

Teacher: Assorted force meters
If available, a Lego-type gear construction kit

Video resources

Science – Start Here, 'Machines'.

You might try

You could point out the efficiency of machines. The more efficient the machine (i.e. the less work wasted), the better it is. For example, pulleys are 70–80% efficient, whereas some machines may be as low as 25% efficient.

11.12 Investigating bicycles

This may be done as a participative demonstration.

Apparatus list

Pupils: Worksheet 11.12A (Bike power)
Worksheet 11.12B (A bike quiz)

Teacher: Bicycle and bike pump
Assorted force meters, including 0–500N
Rope
String
Tape measure, 10 or 20m
Powdered chalk or talc

You might try

It may be useful to investigate the best type of rubber for the brake blocks (see also 1.9). Why is the best 'stopper' not the most sensible type to use for a bicycle?

You could also study topics such as pumps, pressure, a dynamo, strength of frame, friction. (See also 11.7 on streamlining.)

Unit 11 test

Mark scheme

1. a. 10 seconds.
    b. 13 seconds.
    c.

Material	Time to fall (s)
Plastic	20
Silk	13
Paper	10
Cotton	7

d. Change the weight, or area of canopy, or put holes in the canopy etc.

2. a. Bar chart with suitable scale (more than half the graph paper used), axes labelled, bars correctly plotted and labelled, titled.
    b. About 25 newtons.

3. 1 = B, 2 = A, 3 = C

4. a. 633.
    b. Blue Flame and Budweiser.
    c.

Name	Speed in m/s
Budweiser	331
Thrust 2	283
Blue Flame	278
Bluebird	192
Goldenrod	187

5. a. 45 (approx.)
    b. 28m/s.
    c. As the speed increases the stopping distance increases, but at higher speeds the stopping distance increases at a 'faster rate', or suitable version.
    d. About 140 metres.

6. a.

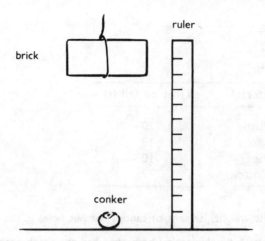

b. The bigger the conker, the higher the brick has to be in order to smash it.
c. The fourth conker: 28mm, 60cm.
d. For example, change the height of the brick in smaller steps, repeat the test with conkers of the same size.

7. a. 70cm.
b. 20cm.
c. Line 1 stretched 25cm compared to line 2 which only stretched 20cm (even though it was the longer one to start with).

8. Does the plan:
– identify the variable to alter: the type of tyre and the road conditions?
– suggest how this could be put into practice?
– identify the dependent variable: how good the tyres are?
– decide how this can be measured, e.g. by measuring the stopping distance from a fixed speed?
– mention some things to control: the type of car, the force on the brakes, for instance?

9. a. 10.15m/s.
b. About 10m/s faster.
c. The speed gets less for longer distances, due to tiring.

10. a. Twice.
b. Go faster (ratio 25:20), harder work.
c. $2\frac{1}{2}$ times as fast.

INVESTIGATIONS

Introduction

This Unit is different from the others. It is intended to provide a range of topics in which skills, knowledge and understanding can be applied. These topics include some important content areas not covered in other Units – for example, the Earth in the solar system, and electronics. These topics can be used as the basis for extended individual projects or for shorter class activities. The spreads are intended to:

– provide basic information on each topic
– act as signposts to richer sources of information
– stimulate further investigations
– form a balanced and wide range of contexts
– provide material that teachers can adapt to suit their own situation.

The topics can be approached in any order, and the Unit offers teachers an opportunity to class-teach a selection of themes or allocate them to interest groups or to groups that need extra practice at certain skills.

12.1 Out of this world

Apparatus list

Pupils: Display paper (assorted colours)
            Scissors
            Metre rules
            Pritt Sticks or glue
            Graph paper

Teacher: Slides of solar system, if available
            Slide projector, tennis ball and football to illustrate day/night and eclipses
            Globe if available

You might try

Astronomy could be linked to astrology: Do horoscopes have a scientific basis?

You could ask pupils about measuring 'age' on other planets: 'How old would you be if you had "Jupiter birthdays"?'

12.2 Down to Earth

Apparatus list

Pupils: Eye protection (EACH)
            Pestle and mortar
            Microscope and slide
            Filter funnel and paper
            Cotton wool
            Measuring cylinders, $250cm^3$ and $50cm^3$
            Test tubes and rack
            Tin trays (for drying and heating soil on)
            Tripod
            Gauze
            Heatproof mat
            Tongs
            Beaker $250cm^3$
            Gas jar with lid

Teacher: Dry sand
            Dry clay soil (powdered)
            Dry loam soil (powdered)
            Universal Indicator solution and colour charts
            Electronic balance
            Oven at 60°C

Worksheet 12.2 Seed composts

Pupils: Small plant pots or margarine tubs
            Trowel
Teacher: Seed (grass or peas)
            Seed compost
            Potting compost no. 1
            Potting compost no. 3
            Sticky labels
            Liquid fertiliser

Video resources

Science – Start Here, 'Plant Life'.

You might try

Pupils could do a moisture test on different types of soil to see how well they retain water. Small quantities of soil can be weighed, heated in crucibles or tobacco tins until the water evaporates, and re-weighed.

12.3 A place to live

Apparatus list

Looking at habitats

Pupils: Metre rule
Teacher: Suitable 'wild' area in school grounds
            10m tape is useful
            Keys to common flora and fauna are useful

Water communities

Pupils: 2 metre rules
            Stopwatch or stopclock
            Measuring cylinder 250cm^3
            Filter funnel and paper
            Universal Indicator solution and colour chart
            Test tubes
            Container for water samples
            Worksheet 12.3 (Pollution indicators)
Teacher: 10m tape is useful
            Electronic balance
            Portable oxygen meter/pH meter if available

Video resources

There is a series of 17 programmes entitled *A Place to Live*, and another series of 10 programmes entitled *Environments*.
Science – Start Here, 'Playground Visitors', 'Home Wanted'.

You might try

Woodlice still seem to make the best subjects for studying and are abundant all over the country.

An 'ant town' can easily be set up in the classroom, and pupils will then be able to observe the behaviour of ants at any time.

12.4 Catch the burglar!

Apparatus list

Fibres

Pupils: Eye protection (EACH)
Microscope and slide
Samples of wood, cotton, nylon fibres and any others
Tongs
Bunsen burner, heatproof mat
10g and 100g masses

Ink

Pupils: Filter paper
Scissors
Boiling tubes
Teacher: Black ink
Ink solvents (e.g. meths, propanone)

Fingerprinting

Pupils: Coated (glossy) paper
Rough paper
Carbon or aluminium powder
Fine paintbrush
Dark-coloured chalk (blue/purple work well)
Sellotape
Scissors

Video resources

Scientific Eye, 'Crimebusters'.

You might try

Most local education authorities have a school–police liaison scheme. A police officer may be invited into the school to do some fingerprinting with the pupils and also talk to them about other aspects of police work.

Pupils could extend this topic to include a footprint in the garden. They could investigate shoe patterns using plaster of Paris moulds.

12.5 Chemical detectives

Apparatus list

Pupils: Eye protection (EACH)
          Test tubes and rack
          Bunsen burner, heatproof mat
          Nichrome wire (for flame test)
          Worksheet 12.5 (Identifying rocks)

Teacher: Minerals (as available, or use appropriate chemical) e.g:
             calcite (calcium carbonate)
             gypsum (calcium sulphate)
             malachite (copper (II) carbonate)
             halite (sodium chloride)
             fluorite (calcium fluoride)
             cerussite (lead carbonate)
          'Household' chemicals e.g:
             eggshell (calcium carbonate)
             stomach powder (sodium hydrogen carbonate)
             limestone and chalk (calcium carbonate)
             salt (sodium chloride)
             washing soda (sodium carbonate)
             fertiliser (all sorts of NPK compounds)
          Reagents, preferably in sets of dropper bottles:
             1molar hydrochloric acid
             1molar nitric acid
             0.005molar silver nitrate (or alternative test for chloride ion)
             0.5molar barium chloride (POISON)
             lime water
             0.5molar sodium hydroxide
             0.5molar ammonium hydroxide

Worksheet 12.5 Identifying rocks

Pupils: Eye protection (EACH)
          Hydrochloric acid 1molar in dropper bottles
          Small iron nail
          Hand lens

Teacher: Samples of rocks (for example granite, sandstone, limestone, slate, marble, shale or mudstone)
          Any available reference material on rocks
          Hammer
          Craft knife

You might try

The first part of this spread would fit well into any topic on pollution, or it could be the starting point for work on pollution.

12.6 Zoos

Apparatus list

Pupils: Access to a zoo, or to small mammals
           Worksheet 12.6 (Human organisations)

You might try

Many zoos now have first-class educational services with talks, slides, videos, worksheets and so on.
   Discuss why safari parks are popular and how they compare to zoos.

12.7 Bread science

Apparatus list

Making bread

Pupils: Ingredients to make bread (plain flour, yeast, sugar, salt)
           Clean beaker and mixing bowl
           Access to hot oven (if they are to bake it)
Teacher: Electronic balance
           Baking trays
           Polythene bags and ties

Baking should not be done in the science laboratory, but in the home economics area.

Testing yeast

Pupils: Conical flask fitted with delivery tube
           Trough to collect gas over
           Test tubes
           Yeast
           Sugar
Teacher: Electronic balance

Clinker toffee

Pupils: Ingredients to make toffee (sugar and syrup)
           Sodium hydrogen carbonate
           Beaker 100cm^3
           Pan to cook toffee in (messy!)
Teacher: Electronic balance
           Lard
           Trays to set toffee on

This should not be made in the science laboratory.

Video resources

Scientific Eye, 'Plants for Food'.
Science – Start Here, 'Food'.
Science Workshop, 'Bread'.

You might try

Bread is an excelled subject for cross-curricular work. It could involve:
- humanities (communities, grain production)
- religious education (Bible stories, communion, unleavened bread)
- home economics
- mathematics (costing)
- multi-cultural education (differences in types of bread eaten in different societies)

12.8 Cleaning off grease

Apparatus list

Pupils: Goggles and gloves (EACH)
    Washing-up bowl
    Cloth (e.g. J-cloth)
    Scouring pad
    Greasy plates to test (can be made by greasing ovenproof plates then heating in an oven!)
    Beaker 100cm^3
    Measuring cylinder 100cm^3

Teacher: Soap solution
    Detergent
    Ammonia solution 0.5molar
    Paraffin (fuel)
    Range of commercial oven cleaners
    Universal Indicator paper
    Electronic balance

Safety is very important in this investigation.

Video resources

Scientific Eye, 'Getting Things Clean'.

12.9 Electronics

Apparatus list

Electronic light, Transistors

Pupils: Eye protection (EACH)
    Matrix board and pins
    Solder, soldering irons and holders
    LED and 1000 ohm (brown, black, red) resistors
    9V PP3 battery and clip
    BFY51, BC109 or similar transistor
    Single-core insulated wire
    Worksheet 12.9A (Soldering)

Printed circuits

Pupils: Circuit rub-off transfers or light-proof pen (black permanent OHP works)
OHPs to make circuit on (suggested size: about 5cm × 8cm)
UV light box for exposing circuits (sunlight is a workable alternative)
Photo-resist board for etching (suggested size: about 5cm × 8cm)
Etching solution (about 500g iron (III) chloride in 1 litre of solution).
CARE! A bubble etch tank is best for etching, but developing trays work too.
Developing trays
0.5molar sodium hydroxide
Alcohol (flammable – care!)
Components: at least LED, 1000 and 10 000 ohm resistors, LDR, thermistor, BC108/109 and BFY51 (or equivalent)
Transistors
Solder and single-strand wire
Soldering irons and holders
9V PP3 battery and clip, connecting wire.
Worksheet 12.9B (Testing a chip)

Worksheet 12.9C Some other circuits to make

Pupils: As for 'Printed circuits' (12.9 above) plus:
100 ohm resistor
10, 100 and 1000 microfarad capacitors
Piezo-electric buzzer

You might try

For the moisture detector, set children the problem of building a device (with a buzzer instead of LED) to tell a blind person when to stop pouring tea because the cup is full.

There are many simple electronics experiments for extending the work in this Unit. Pupils could try making: a timer switch, a burglar alarm, a fire alarm, a light detector.

12.10 Paper

Apparatus list

Wet strength

Pupils: Variety of tissues/kitchen/toilet paper
10g masses and hangers
Sellotape and string
Newton meters 0–1 and 0–10N
Microscope and slide

Paper strength

Pupils: Complete newspaper
            String
            Scissors
            House brick
            Metre rule

Card strength

Pupils: A4 sheets of card
            A4 sheets of corrugated card
            Sellotape
            100g and 1kg masses

Board strength

Pupils: Newspaper (lots)
            Scissors
            Flour or wallpaper paste
            Metre rule
Teacher: 2 house bricks

Worksheet 12.10   Making paper

Pupils: Old newspapers
            Large bowl
            Wooden spoon
            Fine-mesh sheet fixed to a wooden frame
            2 or 3 clean cotton cloths
Teacher: Electric iron
            Kettle
            Liquidiser

Video resources

Science Workshop, 'Paper'.
Search, 'Search Goes Full Circle – Recycling of Materials'.
Science – Start Here, 'Paperchase'.

You might try

Children are usually interested in pictures or a video of how paper is made by hand. Better still, it may be possible for children to attend an actual demonstration of this if there is a suitable place locally.

Children enjoy 'Fu Pong'. Fu Pong says his toilet paper is softer, stronger and more absorbent than any other toilet paper. Are all his claims true? (Select one type of toilet paper to be 'Fu Pong' and give a good selection of others to be tested.)

END-OF-COURSE TESTS

Basic skills practical test

Apparatus list

The instruments should either be easy for pupils to describe – the 25N meter, say – or, preferably be labelled A, B etc. at each station.

1. Range of forcemeters – 1, 10, 25, 50 newtons plus any others available, magnetic door catch fastened to bits of wood or with string attached to fix hook of newton meter.

2. 0–50°C, 0–110°C, 0–250°C thermometers plus digital if available.

3. Range of force meters, kitchen scales, bathroom scales, fishing-type spring balance, lever arm balance plus any others available and familiar. Plastic bag with suitable collection of objects to give total weight appropriate to instruments available.

4. 1.5V and 6V batteries, voltmeters reading to say 5 and 10V, suitably protected against overload.

5. 15 and 30cm rulers, metre rule, tape measure.

6. 15 and 30cm rulers, metre rule, tape measure, pencil.

7. As wide a range of measuring cylinders and graduated beakers as possible, kitchen jug(s), yoghurt pot. (Supply of water needed.)

8. As wide a range of measuring cylinders and graduated beakers as possible, kitchen jug(s), small bucket or paint container or similar. (Supply of water needed.)

9. Stopwatch, stopclock, wristwatch with sweep second hand or digital type. Toy car and length of hardboard (say 1m × 30cm) to make ramp.

10. Range of indicators, beaker with a small quantity of vinegar, test tubes in a rack.

Ideas for mark schemes

The answers given here are typical values only. The ranges for accuracy suggested here can be changed to suit the ability, age and experience of the group – the ones included here are examples only.

Marking may be carried out in a number of ways. One such is to give 1 mark for the choice of instrument. Then allocate 3 marks to a value within the range given (or whatever range is chosen in individual circumstances), 2 to one within twice that range and 1 to any value up to 5 times the range. This would give a total of 4 marks per question, and 40 for the complete test.

1. Sensible choice of instrument. Force measured to ± 10%, or 1 scale division, say.

2. Sensible choice of instrument. Temperature to within I scale division.

3. Sensible choice of instrument. Weight to within I scale division.

4. Sensible choice of instrument. Voltage to within I scale division.

5. Sensible choice of instrument. Width to within Icm.

6. Sensible choice of instrument. Width to within Imm.

7. Sensible choice of instrument. Volume to 10%.

8. Sensible choice of instrument. Volume to 10%.

9. Sensible choice of instrument. Time to 5s.

10. Sensible choice of instrument. pH to to within I of correct value.

Basic skills written test

Mark scheme

1. a.

Type of liquid	Number of drops
Fiery Liquid	58
Moonlight	70
Longlife	20

b.

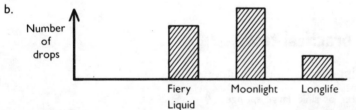

c. Moonlight.

2.

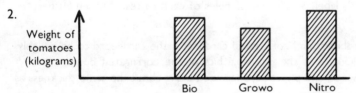

3.

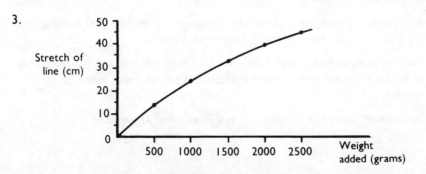

Communicating and interpreting

Ideas for mark scheme

1. One mark can be allocated to each major point in the report.

2. a. Moulds in a bed of sand.
   b. Cast or pig iron.
   c. 1200°C.
   d. Heat strongly and burn off the carbon.
   e. Bellows and tall chimney.
   f. Suitable paraphrase of parts of last two paragraphs.

3. a. 8 min.
   b. 12 min.
   c. Hot – dissolves quicker whether stirred or not.
   d. Stirring makes less difference than the temperature of the water, supported by suitable selection of data.
   e. Small pieces, in hot water, and stirred.

4. a. 28cm.
   b. The red spots.
   c. 8cm (approx.)
   d. None (or almost none).
   e. Bounciness of all balls increases with temperature, the increase gets less as temperature increases, the difference between balls gets less as temperature increases.

Observing practical test

Apparatus list

1. Bowl of water or sink, large sponge.

2. Samples of knitting wools of different sorts – acrylic, wool, etc. – with manufacturer's label. Smaller cut samples of each to test. Bunsen burner, mat, tongs.

3. Pieces of cardboard and corrugated cardboard, the cardboard to be roughly the same thickness as the individual bits of the corrugated board.
   Pieces of wood and plywood, the wood being about the same thickness as the plies.

4. Good colour photograph, series of photographs, slides or video material of any animal, preferably one that is reasonably familiar.

5. Clear glass mains bulb, torch bulb – both with central contact, Indicator bulb or similar from car with two central contacts or otherwise more complicated.

6. Selection of teeth from herbivores and omnivores, as available.

7. Selection of samples of 'fibre glass' type and vermiculite roof insulation, foam pipe lagging, felt pipe lagging, bubble plastic, duster type material, aluminium foil.

8. Two mirrors in holders set as shown in sketch.

9. Suitable dilute bench acid and alkali, marble chips, goggles, suitable containers for experiment, teat pipettes.

10. Selection of: nutcrackers, eggwhisk, crowbar or jemmy, scissors, or other similar.

Ideas for mark scheme

1. a. Floats high in water.
   b. Bubbles.
   c. Floats low in water.
   d. Air expelled, so more dense (or words to that effect – 'heavier'), so floats lower.

2. a. Notices different amount of smoke, ash, colour of ash, etc.
   b. Links appearance to information on label, e.g. man-made or artificial.

3. a. Corrugations give rigidity in one direction, so a box is more rigid than one made from ordinary card.
   b. Wood bendy along grain but strong across it, plywood made up of crossed layers so strong both ways.

4. Paragraph includes sensible scientific observations of, say, down on chest keeps bird warm, or shape of fish makes it glide through water, etc.

5. a. Description includes such things as identification of connectors, which may be spot at bottom and screw base, filament, etc. It may also include comments that are not visible, such as that the filament is connected to the two external connections. On our definition of observation, this is to be commended!
   b. Similarities such as filament, number of connections, glass bulb.

6. Description might include link to feeding habits, etc.

7. a. Comment on air trapped inside lagging making it a good insulator, or words to that effect.
   b. Comment on material, or thickness or other appropriate feature.

8. Laterally inverted in one mirror (back to front), right way round in two. Suggestions that lateral inversion in one mirror is doubled in two, therefore back to the original.

9. a., b., c. Notes taken of reaction, or lack of it. Pupils should be looking for fizzing etc. not the colour of the material or other irrelevant feature.
   d. Links observations to action of acid on limestone, gas given off, etc.

10. Paragraph describes key features of 'machine', pivot, lever, how lever makes machine useful and so on.

Planning investigations

Ideas for mark scheme

I. Fertilisers

Checklist – the plan included:

Identification of key variables:
    To alter   – the type of fertiliser.
    To measure   – which is 'best'

Putting it into practice effectively:
    Altered by   – using known quantities of the fertilisers.
    Measured by   – the growth of a number of plants: increase in height, say.
    Controlled   – conditions of heat, light, soil, watering, etc.

Validity of results:
    Scale   – some suggestion about number of plants needed.

2. Parachute

Checklist – the plan included:

Identification of key variables:
    To alter   – the area of the parachute.
    To measure   – the speed of fall.

Putting it into practice effectively:
    Altered by   – using known areas.
    Measured by   – time to fall a given distance.
    Controlled   – weight of 'man', conditions in room.

Validity of results:
    Accuracy   – use of stopclock mentioned.

3. Soils

Checklist – the plan included:

Identification of key variables:
    To alter   – the amount of lime in the soil.
    To measure   – acidity.

Putting it into practice effectively:
    Altered by   – using known proportions of soil and lime, by weight or by volume.
    Measured by   – pH paper or similar, in water from soil.
Validity of results:
    Accuracy   – suggestion as to instrument used to weigh soil.

4. Washing

Checklist – the plan included:

Identification of key variables:
To alter	– the strength of the wind; the temperature.
To measure	– how well clothes dry.

Putting it into practice effectively:
Altered by	– using different temperatures (choice of day, or use of heater).
	– with a draught, again by choice of day or using hair drier.
Measured by	– the feel of the clothes, or perhaps by weight change.
Controlled	– the size and material of the cloth, initial wetness.

Validity of results:
Scale	– suggestion as to use of large range of temperatures and wind speeds.

Investigating practical test

Apparatus list

For each station:

Kitchen towels

Three or more types of kitchen roll
Samples of dirt, jam, oil, etc.
Supply of water
Selection of measuring cylinders and beakers
Three funnels
Large tray to hold the equipment
Kitchen scales

Toy car

Wind-up toy car (these can be purchased very cheaply from toy shops)
Metre rule
30cm ruler
String
Chalk
Cloth

Soggy lawns

Sand – approx. 500ml
Soil – approx. 500ml
2 beakers – 400ml
12 test tubes

Test-tube rack
Filter funnel (10cm diameter)
10 filter papers
Stopclock
Measuring cylinders – 1 × 500ml, 1 × 250ml
Large spatula
A balance may be required by pupils who choose to mix by weight

Mark scheme

Kitchen towels

Identification of key variables:

To alter   – the type of towel.
To measure   – which is 'best'.

Put into practice effectively:

Altered by   – using the three towels.
Measured by   – the cleanliness after mopping up spills, or how much water
will mop up, or other appropriate factor.
Controlled by   – the area of the paper used; the method of use.

Validity:

Scale   – sensibly-sized piece of towel (not $1cm^2$!)
Accuracy   – as appropriate to the test.
Conclusion   – matches data obtained.

Toy car

Identification of key variables:

To alter   – the number of winds.
To measure   – distance travelled.

Put into practice effectively:

Altered by   – counting the number of complete winds.
Measured by   – distance travelled using suitable instrument.
Controlled by – method of release, surface.

Validity:

Scale   – suitable range of number of turns.
Accuracy   – within say ± 1cm; repeats where necessary.
Conclusion   – matches data obtained.

Soggy lawns

Identification of key variables:

To alter	– amount of sand.
To measure	– time for water to drain.

Put into practice effectively:

Altered by	– changed proportions sand:soil.
Measured by	– rate of drainage, e.g. time for specified volume of water to drain.
Controlled by	– volume of water; fresh mixture each time.

Validity:

Scale	– 3 or more mixtures used; > 20ml water drained.
Accuracy	– ± 2cm
Conclusion	– matches data obtained.

1 WHAT IS SCIENCE?

1.2A Planning an investigation

This worksheet will help you to answer the question:

Does a big candle burn for longer than a small candle in a beaker?

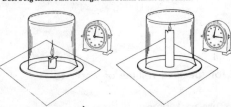

First, you have to decide what to alter in your experiment. Second, you must decide what to measure. To help you decide, answer these questions:

1. What can I alter in this investigation?
2. How many values or sizes shall I use?
3. What will I measure each time?

You now know what the investigation is about:
– using different-size candles,
– using at least four different sizes,
– measuring the time each one burns for.

A fair test

Imagine doing the candle experiment in a laboratory. You time the first candle. Then you use a bigger candle. But you pick up a bigger container as well. Would the experiment still be fair? You have to be very careful to keep it fair.

4. What should you be sure not to alter in this experiment?
5. How will you stop these things changing?

Measuring

Finally, you have to decide *how* to measure the time.
6. How will you do this?

Five decisions

Each time you do an experiment, decide:
– what to alter
– how to alter it
– what to measure
– how to measure it
– what must *not* be altered!

Get your teacher's approval for your plan.

1

1 WHAT IS SCIENCE?

1.2B Volume

The volume of something is how much space it takes up.

This is what one cubic centimetre (1 cm³) can look like:

This block has a volume of 8 cubic centimetres: 2 cm × 2 cm × 2 cm makes 8 cm³.

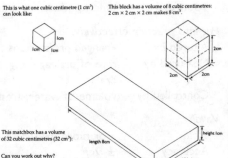

This matchbox has a volume of 32 cubic centimetres (32 cm³):

length 8cm   width 4cm   height 1cm

Can you work out why?

- Below are some volumes for you to work out. Use the table for your results.
- Choose two objects of your own to finish the table.

Object	Width	Height	Length	Volume
A cereal box				
A paperback book				
A packet of tea or teabags				
A sandwich box				
A brick				
_____				
_____				

2

1 WHAT IS SCIENCE?

1.10A Using a thermometer

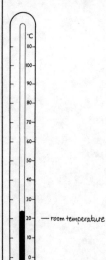

°C

— room temperature

- Mark on the thermometer these temperatures. You may have to guess some of them – use your common sense!
  – a room (this has been done for you)
  – iced water
  – your skin
  – the middle of a fridge
  – boiling water
  – a hot bath
  – cold water
  – hot soup you can just drink
  – a freezer (tricky!)
  – a very hot day

- Cut out the thermometer and your labels and stick them in your book.

1. Why could you not use this thermometer in your oven?

2. How does a thermometer work? These questions may help:
   (a) What is inside the thermometer?
   (b) Why does this substance go up when it gets hot?
   (c) Why is the thermometer case made of glass?

3. Find out other ways of measuring temperature.

4. When a doctor says 'You've got a temperature', what does s/he really mean?

3

1 WHAT IS SCIENCE?

1.10B Cooling kettles

John and Mary wanted to find out how quickly the water in their electric kettle cooled down after the kettle had been switched off. They put some water in the kettle and boiled it. They agreed they should measure the temperature every five minutes. This is what they wrote down:

start   finish
95, 72, 64, 50, 40, 33, 27, 23, 20

This is not a very good way of writing down the results.

Communicating
- Put these results into a table. Remember to make sure that your table is labelled, so that someone else could understand it.

- Now use the information in the table to draw a line graph. You must decide what to plot along the bottom axis and what to plot upwards. The one along the bottom (the *x* axis) is the thing you decide on before you start taking readings – the time between readings. The axis going upwards (the *y* axis) is the thing you measure – the temperature. Choose a scale and draw and label the axes. Plot the points and draw a smooth curve.

Here are some questions about the graph:

1. What was the temperature of the water after 5 minutes?
2. What was the temperature of the water after 23 minutes?
3. At what time was the temperature of the water 45°C?

4. What do you think the temperature would have been if they had carried on making measurements for 50 minutes?

- Their next-door neighbour had a plastic kettle. John thought the water in it would cool down more slowly. Mary thought it would cool faster. What do you think?

5. Can you explain why you think that?

Communicating
- Sketch on your graph in a different colour what you think the curve would have looked like for the plastic kettle.

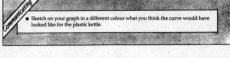

4

1 WHAT IS SCIENCE?
1.10c Lids and cups

If you buy a cup of hot tea or soup from a café, you may get a plastic cup or a polystyrene one.

Sometimes you get a lid on, sometimes you don't.

What keeps it hot?

Investigating
- Your job is to find out whether it is the *lid* or the *material* that is most important for keeping soup hot.

  You can use any of the apparatus listed:
  - cups
  - lids
  - electric kettle or a Bunsen, tripod and gauze
  - thermometers
  - beakers
  - measuring cylinders
  - funnels
  - clock

  Get your teacher's approval before you start.
- You must write your work up carefully!

2 WATER
2.1 Library skills

Water
- Study the diagram and then fill in the missing words in the passage.

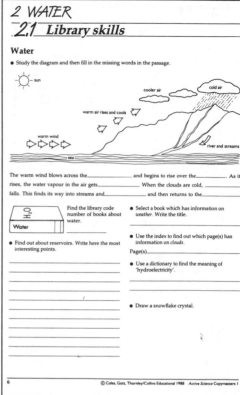

The warm wind blows across the_____ and begins to rise over the_____. As it

rises, the water vapour in the air gets_____ When the clouds are cold,_____

falls. This finds its way into streams and_____ and then returns to the_____.

Water — Find the library code number of books about water.

- Find out about reservoirs. Write here the most interesting points.

_____

- Select a book which has information on *weather*. Write the title.

_____

- Use the index to find out which page(s) has information on *clouds*.

Page(s)_____

- Use a dictionary to find the meaning of 'hydroelectricity'.

_____

- Draw a snowflake crystal.

2 WATER
2.2 House drains

Liquid waste
Houses produce two sorts of liquid waste: waste water from sinks, basins and baths, and toilet waste (called soil waste). This diagram shows how the waste reaches the main sewer:

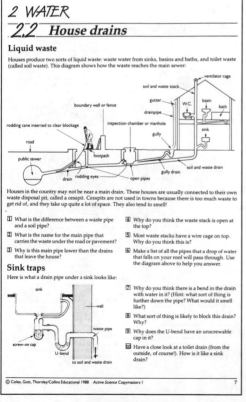

Houses in the country may not be near a main drain. These houses are usually connected to their own waste disposal pit, called a cesspit. Cesspits are not used in towns because there is too much waste to get rid of, and they take up quite a lot of space. They also tend to smell!

1. What is the difference between a waste pipe and a soil pipe?
2. What is the name for the main pipe that carries the waste under the road or pavement?
3. Why is this main pipe lower than the drains that leave the house?

Sink traps
Here is what a drain pipe under a sink looks like:

4. Why do you think the waste stack is open at the top?
5. Most waste stacks have a wire cage on top. Why do you think this is?
6. Make a list of all the pipes that a drop of water that falls on your roof will pass through. Use the diagram above to help you answer.
7. Why do you think there is a bend in the drain with water in it? (Hint: what sort of thing is further down the pipe? What would it smell like?)
8. What sort of thing is likely to block this drain? Why?
9. Why does the U-bend have an unscrewable cap in it?
10. Have a close look at a toilet drain (from the outside, of course!). How is it like a sink drain?

2 WATER
2.3 How much water do you use?

Every one of us uses more water than we drink.

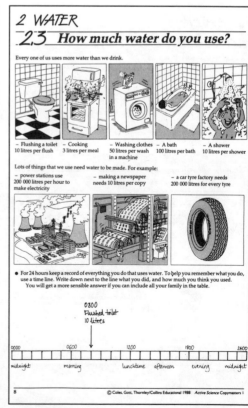

- Flushing a toilet 10 litres per flush
- Cooking 3 litres per meal
- Washing clothes 50 litres per wash in a machine
- A bath 100 litres per bath
- A shower 10 litres per shower

Lots of things that we use water for need to be made. For example:
- power stations use 200 000 litres per hour to make electricity
- making a newspaper needs 10 litres per copy
- a car tyre factory needs 200 000 litres for every tyre

- For 24 hours keep a record of everything you do that uses water. To help you remember what you do, use a time line. Write down next to the line what you did, and how much you think you used. You will get a more sensible answer if you can include all your family in the table.

0800
Flushed toilet
10 litres

0000	0600	1200	1800	2400
midnight	morning	lunchtime	afternoon	evening	midnight

2 WATER
2.4 Key to small water organisms

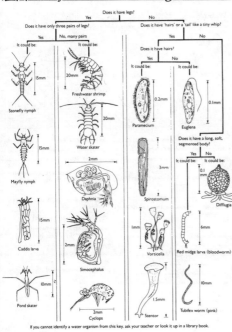

If you cannot identify a water organism from this key, ask your teacher or look it up in a library book.

© Coles, Gott, Thornley/Collins Educational 1988   *Active Science Copymasters I*   9

---

2 WATER
2.6 How well does sugar dissolve?

Investigating

You have to do an investigation to answer one of these questions:
– Does sugar dissolve more quickly in warm water or in cold water?
– Does stirring make sugar dissolve more quickly?
– Does sugar dissolve more quickly if you use more water?

Your teacher will tell you which question to investigate.

● Decide what you are going to do:
– what you will alter
– what you will measure
– what you will keep the same
– what equipment you will need (you can choose from the items below)

test tubes and rack	hot water supply	measuring cylinders
spatula	beakers	stirring rods
thermometer	stop clock/watch	sugar

● Get your teacher's approval and carry out your experiment.
● Put a date in your book, and a title that describes your experiment.
● Write up your results neatly. Make sure you have written about all the changes.

1 What did you decide to alter in your experiment?
2 How did you alter it?
3 How did you judge the rate that the sugar dissolved?
4 What instruments did you use to measure the rate of dissolving?
5 What did you NOT alter in your experiment (to make sure it was a fair test)?
6 What did your results tell you?
7 If you did the experiment again, what would you do differently to make it better?

10   © Coles, Gott, Thornley/Collins Educational 1988   *Active Science Copymasters I*

---

2 WATER
2.9 Sketch graphs

You have drawn graphs from tables of data.

Sometimes it is useful to *sketch* a graph. A sketch graph is a graph without numbers on the axes. Here is an example:

[graph: Amount of air (y-axis) against Distance from Earth (x-axis), decreasing curve]

The amount of air in the atmosphere gets less and less as you go further from the earth. This graph shows this.

● Now try the examples below. Talk to your friend and try to imagine what would happen in each of the examples.
● Draw your sketch graphs on separate pieces of paper. Be ready to tell the class why you drew them like you did.

1 You are in a car travelling at a steady speed along the motorway. What would a graph of **speed** against **time** look like?

3 When the water flows out of your cold-water tank, the level falls. What would a graph of the **height** of the water against **time** look like?

These examples are harder:

4 What would the graph for number 2 look like if the beaker was cone-shaped, like this?

2 A beaker is being filled from a tap at a steady rate. What would a graph of **height** against **time** look like?

5 Suppose you fell out of a helicopter. What would a graph of your speed against time look like?

© Coles, Gott, Thornley/Collins Educational 1988   *Active Science Copymasters I*   11

---

3 AIR
3.2 Weather maps

Weather maps give a picture of what is happening to the air. They are used by *meteorologists* to say what the weather will be like. The map below shows the weather for 18 January 1953.

The lines drawn across the map are called *isobars*. Isobars join places where the air pressure is the same.

Air pressure is given in millibars. The closer the lines (isobars) are together, the stronger the wind.

Arrows show the wind direction.

[weather map of British Isles with isobars and a LOW pressure area]

The wind blows round and round a low-pressure area – like the water going down a plug-hole.

Cold front, bringing cold air behind it.
The symbol for a warm front is:
It brings warm air behind it.

Weather forecasts

● Watch the weather maps for a week. You can see them on the TV news, or in most newspapers. What weather would you expect to get if:
(a) the isobars are close together?
(b) the isobars are a long way apart?
(c) a cold front passes over?
(d) a warm front passes over?
(e) the wind is from the north?
(f) the wind is from the west?

● Make a collection of a week's weather maps and forecasts. Stick them in order in your book. Write down under each one what the weather was like that day.
● Give the forecaster a mark out of ten for each forecast. Can you think of a fair way of doing this?
● Look at the weather pattern for the week. Write a short description of the week's weather, and what caused it.

12   © Coles, Gott, Thornley/Collins Educational 1988   *Active Science Copymasters I*

3 AIR

3.7A Observing burning

Substances to test

a very little cooking oil
paper
a nail
coal

a synthetic material
a crisp
flakes of paint
wood

a marble chip
a match-head
aluminium foil
grass
wool

Safety checklist

☐ Eye protection?
☐ Table protection? ►

☐ Small amounts used?
☐ Dish held safely?

☐ Any fumes?
☐ Care with hot equipment?

Try to make sure that the tests are fair. You should heat each substance in the same way for the same length of time.

Writing up

15/8/98	Burning			
Substance tested	Easy to light?	Flames?	Fumes?	Ash?

Putting the substances in groups

Makes flames	Makes ash

Makes fumes	Easy to light

© Coles, Gott, Thornley/Collins Educational 1988 Active Science Copymasters 1   13

---

3 AIR

3.7B Find the kidnappers

'Here's the ransom note,' said Detective Inspector Lagney, passing the scruffy piece of paper over to Casey of the Forensic Department. 'We think it was written on one of these sorts of paper. If you can find out which one, we'll be half way to nailing the gang.'

'Who's been kidnapped?' Casey asked.

'I can't tell you that – but she works in a school in your area. You'd better get a move on – and don't make any mistakes!'

How are you going to test the paper? Here are some clues to start you off.

● Burn a piece of paper – any sort will do, but only a small piece! What do you notice about:
– the way it burns?
– how long it burns for?
– what sort of flame and smoke it produces?
– how much smoke?
– what sort of ash it leaves behind?

● Make a list of the things you noticed.
● Now design a fair test so that you can compare the way different sorts of paper burn. Make up a blank table to fill in when you test other pieces of paper.
● Now test your test. Try out five different sorts of paper. Make a record of your results. Does your test show up differences between the different sorts of paper? If it doesn't, you will need to think again about your test!

● And now for the crunch. Can you identify which type of paper the ransom note was written on?
● Write a report on your tests for Det. Insp. Lagney. It should look like a police report. Remember that you will have to stand up in court and give evidence – how sure are you about your findings?

14   © Coles, Gott, Thornley/Collins Educational 1988 Active Science Copymasters 1

---

4 MATERIALS

4.1 Talking about materials

Describing word	A material which is like this	Opposite word	A material which is like this
Strong	steel	weak	paper
Elastic			
Tough			
Flexible			
Rot-proof			
Insulating			
See-through			
Light (in weight)			
Waterproof			
Runny			
Squashy			
Heat-resistant			
Cheap			
Safe			
Hard			
Hard-wearing			
Sticky			
_____			
_____			
_____			
_____			
_____			

(Add five words of your own.)

● Think of a material that could be described by as many of the words in the *first* list as possible:_____

Which words describe it?:_____

● Think of a material that is described by as many of the words in the *last* list as possible_____

© Coles, Gott, Thornley/Collins Educational 1988 Active Science Copymasters 1   15

---

4 MATERIALS

4.4 Solids, liquids and gases

Particles

Why are solids, liquids and gases like they are? To start with, you will have to imagine that everything is made of tiny particles. The particles are called atoms and molecules. They are so small that it would take about two million atoms end-to-end to cross the full stop at the end of this sentence.

Next, you must imagine that the particles are always moving. Sometimes they move slowly, sometimes they move quickly. The hotter they are, the faster they move. But even if you make them very cold, they do not stop completely.

If you can imagine both these things, then you can try the next experiment.

Looking at melting and boiling

● Warm each of these substances on a tin tray. Use a small flame. There is no need to get any of them too hot.

Substances:
– ice
– solder (stop heating when it has melted)
– wax (stop heating when it has melted)

● For each one write down:
– what it is like to start with
– what you see when it is heated
– what it is like when it has cooled down

● Whilst you are watching, try to think what is happening to the atoms or molecules that the substance is made of.

What happens to the particles?

This diagram shows you what we think happens to the particles in a substance when it is heated or cooled. You may like to add it to your experiment notes.

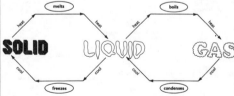

EXTRAS

1 Imagine you are a particle of wax. Describe what happens to you as you are warmed up.

2 Imagine you are a particle of nitrogen in the air. Describe what happens to you as you are cooled down in a refrigeration plant. The lowest temperature you reach is −210°C, which is the freezing point of nitrogen.

16   © Coles, Gott, Thornley/Collins Educational 1988 Active Science Copymasters 1

4 MATERIALS
4.5 Making a concrete mixture

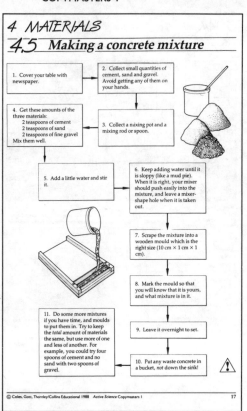

1. Cover your table with newspaper.

2. Collect small quantities of cement, sand and gravel. Avoid getting any of them on your hands.

4. Get these amounts of the three materials:
2 teaspoons of cement
2 teaspoons of sand
2 teaspoons of fine gravel
Mix them well.

3. Collect a mixing pot and a mixing rod or spoon.

5. Add a little water and stir it.

6. Keep adding water until it is sloppy (like a mud pie). When it is right, your mixer should push easily into the mixture, and leave a mixer-shape hole when it is taken out.

7. Scrape the mixture into a wooden mould which is the right size (10 cm × 1 cm × 1 cm).

8. Mark the mould so that you will know that it is yours, and what mixture is in it.

11. Do some more mixtures if you have time, and moulds to put them in. Try to keep the *total* amount of materials the same, but use more of one and less of another. For example, you could try four spoons of cement and no sand with two spoons of gravel.

9. Leave it overnight to set.

10. Put any waste concrete in a bucket, *not* down the sink!

© Coles, Gott, Thornley/Collins Educational 1988 *Active Science* Copymasters I   17

---

4 MATERIALS
4.6 Strong straw structures

The problem

Can you make a structure from 20 straws that will support a brick?
You may be able to do this without any help. But you should know how to break the problem up. Here is one method.

Thinking

How are thin materials used in structures? Can you think of any other examples?

The parts of the problem

1. How to join the straws?

glue   pipe cleaner or wire

Plasticine or clay   pin joint

● Carry out experiments to find out the best way of joining two straws. The joint must be strong, and it must not weaken the straw.

2. Make a strong straw square
● Use four 10 cm straws to make a strong square with good joints. Can you find a way of using one or two more straws to make it much stronger?

3. Make a 20-straw structure
● Use the methods you learnt in parts 1 and 2 above. The structure has to support as much weight as possible 10 cm off the ground.

Testing

● Decide on a fair way of testing how strong your model is, then carry out the test. Did it hold a brick?

Results

● Write up your results. Include:
  – a sketch of your design
  – how you tested it
  – where your design was weakest
  – how you could strengthen it

Look back at the original problem. Did you manage to solve it?

More problems

● Use the problem-solving system to tackle this problem: What is the tallest structure you can make from 20 straws? This time it does not have to be strong, but it must be stable.
● Write a report showing how you tackled the problem, and what your solution was.
● Finally, have a go at this problem: Can you make a structure from a single newspaper that stands on the floor and reaches to the ceiling?

18   © Coles, Gott, Thornley/Collins Educational 1988 *Active Science* Copymasters I

---

4 MATERIALS
4.8 Key for identifying plastics

This key is not guaranteed to give the right answers! There are many plastics that are not included in it. Also, the plastics may be specially treated or mixed together, so they do not behave as you might expect.

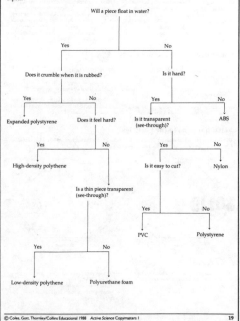

Will a piece float in water?

Yes → Does it crumble when it is rubbed?
- Yes → Expanded polystyrene
- No → Does it feel hard?
  - Yes → High-density polythene
  - No → Is a thin piece transparent (see-through)?
    - Yes → PVC → Yes → Low-density polythene
    - No → Polystyrene → No → Polyurethane foam

No → Is it hard?
- Yes → Is it transparent (see-through)?
  - Yes → Is it easy to cut?
    - Yes → PVC
    - No → Nylon
  - No → ABS
- No → ABS

© Coles, Gott, Thornley/Collins Educational 1988 *Active Science* Copymasters I   19

---

5 LIFE
5.3A How to use a microscope to look at cells

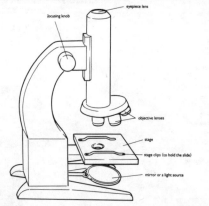

eyepiece lens
focusing knob
objective lenses
stage
stage clips (to hold the slide)
mirror or a light source

― Basic skill ―
How to use a microscope

● Set it up with the light on (if it has a plug), or facing the light (if it has a mirror).
● Turn the objective so the smallest lens is facing the stage.
● Put your cells on the microscope slide (see worksheet 5.3B).
● Put the slide on the stage, with the cells above the lit hole.
● Use the focusing knob to make the slide look sharp. Check you are focused on the slide by moving it slightly whilst you look through the eyepiece. If the slide is in focus, you will see it move. Watch out for air bubbles – they look like big round circles and are NOT what you are looking for!
● If you want to use a higher-power objective, swing the objective lens to the next size lens. You will not have to alter the focus very much to get the cells sharp. (If you do, start again with the smallest lens.)
● When you have finished, wash up your slide. Leave your microscope clean and tidy.

20   © Coles, Gott, Thornley/Collins Educational 1988 *Active Science* Copymasters I

5 LIFE
5.3B How to make a plant cell slide

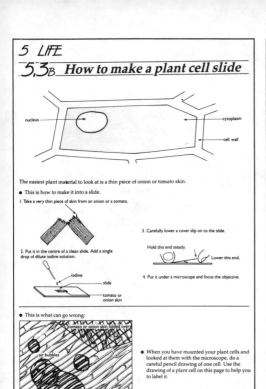

The easiest plant material to look at is a thin piece of onion or tomato skin.

● This is how to make it into a slide.

1. Take a very thin piece of skin from an onion or a tomato.

2. Put it in the centre of a clean slide. Add a single drop of dilute iodine solution.

3. Carefully lower a cover slip on to the slide.

Hold this end steady.

Lower this end.

4. Put it under a microscope and focus the objective.

● This is what can go wrong:

● When you have mounted your plant cells and looked at them with the microscope, do a careful pencil drawing of one cell. Use the drawing of a plant cell on this page to help you to label it.

© Coles, Gott, Thornley/Collins Educational 1988 *Active Science* Copymasters 1   21

5 LIFE
5.5 Growing cuttings

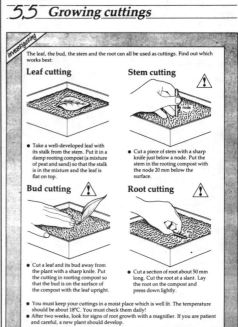

The leaf, the bud, the stem and the root can all be used as cuttings. Find out which works best:

Leaf cutting

● Take a well-developed leaf with its stalk from the stem. Put it in a damp rooting compost (a mixture of peat and sand) so that the stalk is in the mixture and the leaf is flat on top.

Stem cutting

● Cut a piece of stem with a sharp knife just below a node. Put the stem in the rooting compost with the node 20 mm below the surface.

Bud cutting

● Cut a leaf and its bud away from the plant with a sharp knife. Put the cutting in rooting compost so that the bud is on the surface of the compost with the leaf upright.

Root cutting

● Cut a section of root about 50 mm long. Cut the root at a slant. Lay the root on the compost and press down lightly.

● You must keep your cuttings in a moist place which is well lit. The temperature should be about 18°C. You must check them daily!
● After two weeks, look for signs of root growth with a magnifier. If you are patient and careful, a new plant should develop.

22   © Coles, Gott, Thornley/Collins Educational 1988 *Active Science* Copymasters 1

5 LIFE
5.9 The menstrual cycle

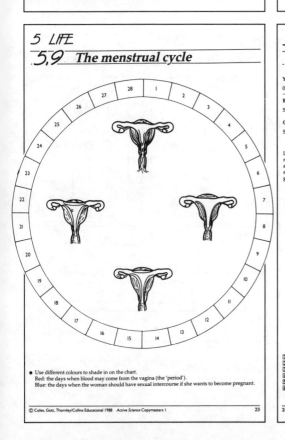

● Use different colours to shade in on the chart.
Red: the days when blood may come from the vagina (the 'period').
Blue: the days when the woman should have sexual intercourse if she wants to become pregnant.

© Coles, Gott, Thornley/Collins Educational 1988 *Active Science* Copymasters 1   23

5 LIFE
5.11 Growing taller

Years	0	1	2	3	4	5	6	7	8	9	10	11	12	13	14	15	16	17	18
Boys/cm	57	77	89	98	105	112	118	124	129	134	139	144	149	154	159	164	168	174	179
Girls/cm	56	76	87	96	104	111	117	123	128	133	138	145	151	156	161	164	168	169	169

Look at the development chart above. Use it to make a line graph of the average height of boys and girls at different ages. You should use the same graph for both, but use one colour for the girls and another for the boys.

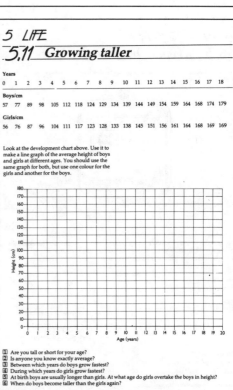

1. Are you tall or short for your age?
2. Is anyone you know exactly average?
3. Between which years do boys grow fastest?
4. During which years do girls grow fastest?
5. At birth boys are usually longer than girls. At what age do girls overtake the boys in height?
6. When do boys become taller than the girls again?

24   © Coles, Gott, Thornley/Collins Educational 1988 *Active Science* Copymasters 1

6 ELECTRICITY

6.1 Steady as you go

How steady is your hand? Could you follow a line through a maze without going off the track?
- Make an electrical maze like this one. You will need a piece of card, some cooking foil, glue, wires, a battery and a bulb or a buzzer.

Making the maze

- Cut two strips of foil and stick them down on to a piece of card. You could do it like this, but perhaps you can think of a better maze.

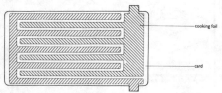

cooking foil

card

The circuit

Make the circuit below.
The cooking foil conducts electricity. The circuit is not complete unless a conductor makes a bridge across the two strips of foil.

START

FINISH

Testing steady hands

- Trace the maze from start to finish with the edge of a small coin. If you bridge the gap at any time, you must stop and start again. Who can get from start to finish in the quickest time?

6 ELECTRICITY

6.2 Electrician's diagrams

Component

Symbol

Basic skill

See if you can make each circuit using only the electrician's diagram.
- Cover over the drawing, then make the circuit. Use the drawing if you get stuck.
- Find out what happens if bulb X in the diagram is unscrewed.
- Write down your results.
- Try to do all the circuits without using the drawings at all.

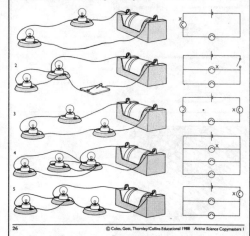

1

2

3

4

5

6 ELECTRICITY

6.3 Keeping track of electricity

How much electricity does your family use in 24 hours? How much does it cost?
The Electricity Board measures what you use with a meter.

The electricity is measured in kilowatt hours. On your electricity bill these are usually just called 'units'. When you use 1000 watts of electricity at home for an hour, your meter will go up 1 unit.

- Keep a record on here of how much electricity you use:

Record kept by_____

From (time)_____ to (time)_____

Electricity meter reading *now*:_____   A modern meter is easy to read, but you may find:
                                                     – that you have an older meter (ask an adult to help you).
                                                     – that you have two meters (read them both, and add up the amount of electricity measured by both. Find out why you have two meters as well!)

Electricity meter reading at end:_____

Units of electricity used:_____

Cost of electricity per unit:_____   (If you can, get this from your parents' bill. If not, assume 5p per unit).

Total cost of electricity for 24 hours:_____

6 ELECTRICITY

6.4 How an electric bell works

Circuit completed: electricity flows   Circuit broken: electricity does not flow

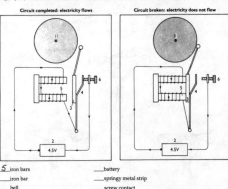

5 iron bars   ___battery
___iron bar   ___springy metal strip
___bell   ___screw contact

This bell has six numbered parts. Fit the words to the parts. The first one is done for you.
Now read the passage below. Fit the words into the gaps so that everything makes sense.

The electricity from the ____*battery*____ can only flow in

this circuit when the_____touches the_____

When this happens, the_____become magnetic because

they have the circuit wire coiled around them. This electromagnet

then attracts the_____, which moves towards its poles.

That movement makes the hammer strike the bell.

That movement also breaks the circuit and switches off the electromagnet. In your own words, describe what happens next to make the bell go on ringing.

_____

_____

_____

_____

6 ELECTRICITY
6.7A Wiring a plug

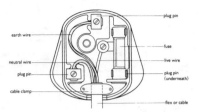

- plug pin
- earth wire
- fuse
- neutral wire
- live wire
- plug pin
- plug pin (underneath)
- cable clamp
- flex or cable

Follow these instructions, then get your partner to mark your work.

Basic skill

- Carefully cut away 5 cm from the outer cover of the flex.
- Push the flex under the cable clamp.
- Screw the clamp on the outer cover of the flex.
- Cut the wires so that they just fit right through the holes in the plug pins.
- Remove the insulation from the ends of the wires.
- Fix the wires into the plug pins and screw down.
- Check each connection is tight, and that there are no bits of wire loose.
- Check the fuse is right. Imagine that your plug is connected to a table lamp.
- Screw the plug cover on.

- Give your finished plug to your partner.
This is how to mark it:

Score

5 if the plug is screwed together tightly.
10 if the fuse is correct for a table lamp.
5 if the fuse is in the plug properly.
5 if the cable clamp is done up tight on the outside cover of the cable.

Then mark each pin of the plug:

5 per pin if there are no strands of wire poking out of the pin.
5 per pin if you cannot get the wire out of the pin without undoing the screw.
15 per pin if the right wire is connected to the pin.

Add up the marks. The maximum total is 100.

- Undo the plug, take the wire out and cut off the end. Then let your partner wire it. You can mark it when she or he has finished.

6 ELECTRICITY
6.7B Wiring a table lamp

Choose the flex

Use this table to decide what type of flex to use:

Appliance	Typical cable wattage	Number of cores	Flex type
Iron	1200	3	Rubber/textile braided (unkinkable)
Toaster	1400	3	Rubber insulated textile braided
Room heater	1400 2000 3000	3 3 3	
Vacuum cleaner	400 to 1000	2 or 3†	Ordinary duty PVC
Lawnmower	700 to 1400	2 or 3†	Ordinary duty PVC
Kettle	1200 1500 2400 3000	3 3 3 3	Ordinary duty PVC. Recommend buy complete with connector
Extension lead	1000 3000*	3	Ordinary duty PVC *When fully uncoiled.
Immersion heater Storage heater	3000*	3	85°C rubber insulated high temperature cord
Clock	720	usually 2	Parallel twin PVC, length not to exceed 2m
Slow cooker Deep fat fryer	1500	2 or 3†	Ordinary duty PVC
Hair dryer Refrigerator Food mixer	1400	2 or 3†	Light duty PVC
Table lamp	720	2 or 3†	Light duty PVC. Length not to exceed 2m, if it does exceed 2m, use 720W cable.

† Where 2 or 3 cores are shown above replace as the maker intended.

Basic skill

Wire up the lamp socket

- Unscrew the lamp socket.
- Work out how the electricity flows to the bulb.
- Connect the cable to the socket.

Wire up the plug

- Connect up the other end of the cable to the plug.

Choose the right fuse

- Read about the right fuse for the job in the Extras on 6.5. Use this information to choose the right fuse for the lamp. Fit it into the plug.

Safety check

- Get your teacher to check your work.

6 ELECTRICITY
6.8 Building up electricity

Where will electricity build up?

You can build electricity up on a plastic comb or a polythene strip. All you have to do is to rub it hard with a cloth. Here are three ways to detect the electricity:

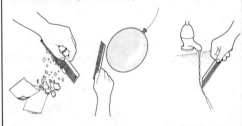

- Use one or more of these methods to find out what other things you can store electricity on. You should try metals, plastics, wood, rubber, fabrics like nylon or cotton, and anything else that might work.
- Here is one way to record your results:

17.3.99   Which objects will electricity build up on?

Object tested	Was the paper attracted?	Was the balloon attracted?	Did the water move?	Did electricity build up?
Plastic comb	Yes	Yes	Yes	Yes

- Look carefully at all the objects that electricity will build up on. Do they have anything in common? If they do, write it down:

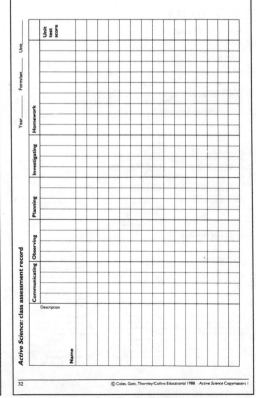

Unit 1 WHAT IS SCIENCE?

How well did I do?

My name_____ My form_____

Basic skills

If you think you have done well at any of these skills, tick the box and ask your teacher to check:

I have successfully:
used a measuring cylinder (1.2)
used a Bunsen burner safely (1.5)
completed a line graph for a pendulum (1.6)
estimated quantities (1.8)

used weighing scales (1.8)
measured small quantities (1.8)
used a thermometer (1.10) and worksheet 1.10A

Observing

Tick one box for each:

1.4 Mosquitoes, ants and bees

I could pick out some differences between the animals.

I tried to pick out the important similarities and differences between the animals to see why they had been put into different orders.

1.5 Sorting the substances

I sorted the substances into two groups.

I sorted the substances into two groups depending on whether things had been permanently changed by being heated.

Planning investigations

Tick one box for each:

1.2 Testing other candles

My plan was to:
use different candles and watch how long they burned.

use different candles, put them under the same container, and use a stopclock to time how long they burned.

1.9 Take a brake

My plan was to:
use different types of brake block and find out how well they stopped a bike.

use different blocks and measure how far the same bike, with the same rider and going at the same speed, went before it stopped after the brakes had been put on with the same force.

Investigating and making

Tick one box for each:

1.3 Changing speed

I tried to find how fast the dragster went after I twisted the elastic band. I did this twice. The second time I twisted the elastic band more times than before.

I twisted the elastic band by two different amounts. I measured the speed over a distance of at least one metre using a stopclock. I kept other things, like the surface and the sort of rubber band, the same to make the test fair.

1.10C Lids and cups

I used two of the same sort of cups – one with a lid and one without. Then I used two different sorts of cups. I tried to find out which was the best.

I used two cups – one with a lid and one without. Then I used two different types of cup. I put the same amount of a hot liquid in each of them. I used a stopwatch and thermometer to measure how quickly the liquid cooled down.

© Coles, Gott, Thornley/Collins Educational 1988 *Active Science Copymasters 1*   33

Unit 1

Communicating and interpreting

Tick one box for each:

1.3 Designing a winner

I could do the first three questions where I had to pick out bits of information from the passage.

I could do most of the questions including those where I had to put together several bits of information from the passage.

1.9 Buying a bike

I could do the first two questions where I had to pick out bits of information from the table.

I could do most of the questions including those where I had to pick out several bits of information from the passage. I made a sensible choice of bike to buy. I knew which were the important things in making my decision.

1.10B Cooling kettles

I could do the table and some of the questions. I finished the graph when I had been shown how to start it.

I could do the table, the graph and most of the questions. I drew a sensible sketch graph.

Did I get involved in the work?

Tick any boxes you think you did well at:

I talked well about scientific things.
I wrote well about scientific things.
I discussed problems my friends.
I discussed problems with my teacher.
I worked well with my group in practicals.

I have been curious to find out about things.
I have been quick to settle down.
I have been good at finishing things off.
I have been helpful in lessons.
I have been good at making notes in my book.

What did I learn?

The most important things I have learned from this unit are:	The things I had most difficulty with were:

Unit test

My mark was_____ I think this is:
good for me. ☐   about what I expected. ☐   not so good for me. ☐

Teacher's comments:

Unit 2 WATER

How well did I do?

My name_____ My form_____

Basic skills

If you think you have done well at any of these skills, tick the box and ask your teacher to check:

I have successfully:
used a microscope (2.1)
drawn a bar chart of rainfall figures (2.3)
followed instructions for setting up glassware (2.3)

used a top-pan balance (2.4)
followed instructions and drawn a line graph for boiling water and melting ice (2.9)

Communicating and interpreting

Tick one box for each:

2.5 Clean water and disease

I could do the first three questions where I had to pick out bits of information from the passage.

I could do all the questions, including those where I had to use information from the passage to draw diagrams or suggest solutions.

2.6 Using water to dissolve things

My report had most of the information. I recorded my results and sorted at least four things into 'dissolvers' and 'non-dissolvers'.

My report had all the information needed, in the correct order. I presented my results neatly in a table. I used the results to decide whether things were 'dissolvers', 'non-dissolvers' or some other group.

2.12 Dried food

I could do the first few questions where I had to pick out information from the table.

I could do most of the questions. I could think of sensible reasons for my answers and I made a long list of foods from our kitchen.

Investigating and making

Tick one box for each:

2.2 Making a roof

My idea for the roof was OK, but it didn't work very well.

My idea was OK and I made it well. It was strong and kept things dry. I worked out a way of checking how good it was.

2.5 Can I drink it?

I used two different sorts of water and at least one test to see if the water was clean.

I used two or more sorts of water and several tests to see if the water was clean. I used the same volumes of water to make it a fair test. I made sure all the glassware was clean before starting on another test.

2.6 How well does sugar dissolve?

I used two temperatures or volumes of water (or I stirred one and not the other) and watched to see when the sugar had all dissolved.

I used two temperatures (or volumes of water or I stirred one and not the other) and timed how long it took to dissolve. I used a sensible amount of water and sugar and I used the same amounts for each test.

© Coles, Gott, Thornley/Collins Educational 1988 *Active Science Copymasters 1*   35

Unit 2

Observing

Tick one box:

2.4 Living things in water

My drawings had the main parts of the animals which I thought were important. Before I decided what to draw, I thought about where the animal lived, how it moved and what it might eat. I put a scale on my diagram to show how big things were.

Planning investigations

Tick one box for each:

2.8 What is the best way to dry a cloth?

My plan was to:
try cloths flat and crumpled (or hot and cold, or in a draught or not) and see which dried best.

try cloths flat and crumpled (or hot and cold, or in a draught or not) and weigh them before and after, to see which dried best. I would keep other things the same. I would use the same-sized pieces of cloth.

2.12 How much water is there in fresh food?

My plan was to:
use two different foods, dry them and see how their weight changed.

use two or more different foods, dry them and measure their weight. I would dry them and measure their weight again. To check that they had dried out completely I would heat them again to make sure they didn't lose any more weight. I would use enough food to make sure I could measure the loss in weight accurately.

Did I get involved in the work?

Tick any boxes you think you did well at:

I talked well about scientific things.
I wrote well about scientific things.
I discussed problems with my friends.
I discussed problems with my teacher.
I worked well with my group in practicals.

I have been curious to find out about things.
I have been quick to settle down.
I have been good at finishing things off.
I have been helpful in lessons.
I have been good at making notes in my book.

What did I learn?

The most important things I have learned from this unit are:	The things I had most difficulty with were:

Unit test

My mark was_____ I think this is: good for me. ☐   about what I expected. ☐   not so good for me. ☐

Teacher's comments:

Unit 3 AIR

How well did I do?

My name_____ My form_____

Basic skills

If you think you have done well at any of these skills, tick the box and ask your teacher to check:

I have successfully:
used a top-pan balance (3.1) ☐
tested for carbon dioxide (3.7) ☐

drawn a bar chart about breathing (3.9) ☐
drawn a line graph about how long air lasts (3.11) ☐

Communicating and interpreting

Tick one box for each:

3.3 Uses of air

We collected some information about our question and put it onto a poster. ☐ ○
☐ ◐
Our poster explained how the thing worked. We picked photographs or diagrams that helped our explanation. ☐ ●

3.10 How do fire-fighters ventilate a fire?

I could do the first two or three questions where I had to find bits of information from the passage. ☐ ○
☐ ◐
I could do most of the questions, including those where I had to put together ideas from the passage with what I knew already or could work out. ☐ ●

Observing

Tick one box for each:

3.2 Taking air away

My drawing or description showed a can which had been crushed. ☐ ○
☐ ◐
My drawing or description showed a can which had been crushed. I explained on my drawing or in my description that air pressure had crushed the can inwards in all directions. ☐ ●

3.5 Finding out about air

I noticed some things for all the experiments. ☐ ○
☐ ◐
I already had some idea of what air was. I looked for things in the experiments to make my ideas clearer. ☐ ●

3.7 Observing burning

I noticed things like the colour of the flame and how much smoke there was. ☐ ○
☐ ◐
I looked for important things about the flame which I could use to sort the materials into different types. ☐ ●

Planning investigations

Tick one box:

3.4 Testing the propeller

My plan was OK, but it might not have worked in practice. ☐ ○
☐ ◐
My plan was OK. It would probably have worked in practice. I would have got some measurements for the force of the propeller or the speed of the air. ☐ ●

© Coles, Gott, Thornley/Collins Educational 1988 *Active Science* Copymasters 1   37

Unit 3

Investigating and making

Tick one box for each:

3.1 Measuring the speed of air

My idea was OK, but it didn't work very well. ☐ ○
☐ ◐
My idea was OK and I made it well. It worked for a lot of different wind speeds. ☐ ●

3.9 Extras

I tested two people at home to see if their breathing rates were different. ☐ ○
☐ ◐
I tested at least two people, one young and one old, and measured the number of breaths they took in a minute (or longer) when they were sitting down. ☐ ●

3.12 Flying machines

I made my plane and tried different things to see if it went further. ☐ ○
☐ ◐
I made my plane and then changed things on it one at a time. I measured how far it went by averaging several flights. I made sure I set it off the same way each time. I kept other things the same to make it a fair test. ☐ ●

Did I get involved in the work?

Tick any boxes you think you did well at:

I talked well about scientific things. ☐
I wrote well about scientific things. ☐
I discussed problems with my friends. ☐
I discussed problems with my teacher. ☐
I worked well with my group in practicals. ☐

I have been curious to find out about things. ☐
I have been quick to settle down. ☐
I have been good at finishing things off. ☐
I have been helpful in lessons. ☐
I have been good at making notes in my book. ☐

What did I learn?

The most important things I have learned from this unit are:	The things I had most difficulty with were:

Unit test

My mark was_____ I think this is:

good for me. ☐   about what I expected. ☐   not so good for me. ☐

Teacher's comments:

38   © Coles, Gott, Thornley/Collins Educational 1988 *Active Science* Copymasters 1

PRACTICAL TEST

In this test you will be doing some simple experiments. You will have a few minutes for each question. The number of the question is the same as the number on the card by the experiment. When the teacher tells you to move on, go to the next question. So if you are on question 3, go to question 4 when you are told to move. And so on.

Write your answers on a separate answer sheet. Don't forget to put your name on it.

1 What is the length of line A **to the nearest millimetre?**
What is the length of line B **to the nearest centimetre?**

2 Cut 12.6 cm of tape from the roll in front of you and stick it on to your answer sheet.

3 Put 73 cm³ of sand from the beaker into the measuring cylinder. Then put the sand on to the scales and note down its mass. Put the sand back into the beaker when you have finished.

4 Use the forcemeter and the ruler to find the force needed to stretch the elastic band to make it 9 cm longer.

5 What is the volume of the coloured water in the beaker?
Now put 1.8 cm³ of the coloured water from the beaker into the syringe. When you have done it, put your hand up for your teacher to check. When it has been checked, put the water back into the beaker ready for the next person.

6 What is the volume of the water in the big measuring cylinder?
What is the volume of the water in the small measuring cylinder?

7 This question asks you to make a number of measurements of temperature. For each one, write down the temperature you have measured.
(a) room temperature
(b) the temperature of the palm of your hand
(c) the temperature of the water from the cold tap

8 Set up the apparatus shown in the diagram below.

(a) Now set the pendulum swinging and find out how long it takes to make ten complete swings. Write your answer down.
(b) Now write down the time for **one** swing. Make sure you show how you did it.
When you have finished, take the apparatus apart ready for the next person to use.

9 This question is about reading stop clocks. **Do not touch the stop clocks.**
(a) What does the electronic stop clock read?
(b) What does the clock-work stop clock read?

10 In this question you have to make an estimate (your best guess) of the answer. For each one write down what you think the measurement is. Don't forget to put **units**.
(a) the length of the match
(b) the length of the laboratory, from front to back
(c) the mass of the Bunsen burner
(d) the area of the top of the test tube
(e) the mass of the stool
(f) the volume of the test tube
(g) the volume of the laboratory sink

11 This question is about using a Bunsen burner to heat something safely. **Don't forget to use goggles and be very careful.**
Light the Bunsen and adjust it to give a small blue flame. Put a small quantity of water in the test tube – about a fifth full – and heat it gently until the water boils.
Pour the water away and put the test tube back into the test tube rack. Turn off the Bunsen.

12 The diagram on the right shows some apparatus set up for an experiment. Your job is to choose the correct pieces of apparatus and set up the apparatus to match the diagram.
You can choose any of the apparatus you like. You may not need to use it all.

When you have finished, put your hand up for your teacher to check the apparatus. When it has been checked, take it apart, ready for the next person. Make sure the apparatus is left exactly as you found it.

13 The kitchen roll in front of you is said by the manufacturers to be very good at soaking up water. Use the apparatus in front of you to find out how much water one sheet of the paper will soak up. (You may not need to use all the apparatus – think before you start!) Write your answer down and say how you measured the water.

14 In front of you is a pile of paper and a ruler. Your job is to find the thickness of a single sheet of paper as accurately as you can.
Write your results down. Show how you worked out your answer.

15 Can you find the volume of the ball of Plasticine? You can make the Plasticine into any shape you like.
Write your answer down and say how you worked it out.
Roll the Plasticine back into a ball.

16 In front of you is a steel spring. When you hang weights on the spring, it stretches. Your job is to make some measurements of the extension of how far the spring stretches when different weights are hung on it. Make enough measurements to draw a graph, but you do not need to draw the graph.
Put your results into a table. Make sure you label your table.

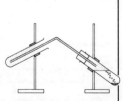

© Coles, Gott, Thornley/Collins Educational 1988 *Active Science* Copymasters 1   45

46   © Coles, Gott, Thornley/Collins Educational 1988 *Active Science* Copymasters 1

Panel 1 (page 47)

Practical test

Reading instrument scales test

On pages 47–48 there are drawings of different measuring instruments. Your job is to write down (on a separate piece of paper) the reading on each of the instruments. Don't forget to put the units.

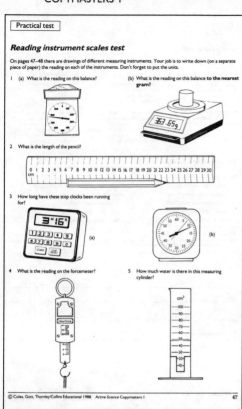

1 (a) What is the reading on this balance?

(b) What is the reading on this balance **to the nearest gram?**

2 What is the length of the pencil?

3 How long have these stop clocks been running for?

(a)

(b)

4 What is the reading on the forcemeter?

5 How much water is there in this measuring cylinder?

Panel 2 (page 48)

Practical test

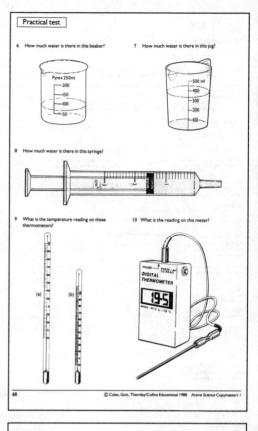

6 How much water is there in this beaker?

7 How much water is there in this jug?

8 How much water is there in this syringe?

9 What is the temperature reading on these thermometers?

(a)   (b)

10 What is the reading on this meter?

Panel 3 (page 49)

Test

You will need your *Active Science 1* book.

1 This pie chart is about the cost of your water services.

Where every pound goes
- 45p Sewage services
- 1p Land drainage
- Environmental services
- 18p Water resources
- 34p Water supply

(a) How much of every pound is spent on water resources?

(b) Which service costs most?

(c) The cost of environmental services has been left off the chart. About how much do you think these services cost?

2 Jane and Sarah had four different sorts of material. They decided to make a skirt out of one of them. Before they started, they wanted to know:
Do any of the materials shrink?
Do they fade in the wash?
Do they crease easily?

They carried out some tests on small pieces of each material. This is what they found out.

Material A didn't shrink or fade, but it was quite creased.
Material B didn't shrink or fade. It was only creased a bit.
Material C didn't shrink, but it faded a bit and was quite creased.
Material D didn't fade, but it shrunk a lot and was very creased.

(a) Do a table that shows this information. It might start like this:

Material	Did it shrink?
A	No
B	
C	

(b) Which material would you choose for the skirt? Why?

3 This question is about the photographs of water animals in section 2.4. You will need to look back at them.

(a) Look carefully at the picture of a **pond skater**. Imagine you are writing about it in a nature book. Write a few sentences describing the important things about it.

(b) Now look at the photographs of the **pond skater** and the **mosquito larva.** Make a list of things which are different about these two animals.

Panel 4 (page 50)

4 You are shipwrecked on a desert island. You find some murky-looking water. What tests would you do on the water before you could be reasonably sure that it was safe to drink?

5 This question is about the design of a roof that you have looked at in section 2.2 (not the roof you built yourself). Look back at the diagram of the roof in that section. Write a guide called: **'The important things to remember in building a roof'.** Make sure that it is clear to someone who does not know about roofs.

6 If you put a sweet into water, it will slowly disappear (dissolve).

(a) Write down three things that might make the sweet dissolve more quickly.

(b) Pick one of those things and write a plan for an experiment you could do to find out whether your idea was correct.

7 Gillian lives in Newtown. Her dentist says that she is lucky because their water supply has fluoride in it. He says that this helps to prevent tooth decay. John lives in Oldtown, where the water has no fluoride in it.
   The dentist told them about a survey of 1000 children which was done to see if they had any bad teeth. The two bar charts show the results.

(a) How many children in Oldtown had **1 tooth** affected by decay?

(b) How many children in Newtown had **no teeth** affected by decay?

(c) Look at the bars for children with no teeth affected by decay in both of the towns. Which town had most children with no bad teeth?

(d) Do you think the dentist is right when he says that fluoride helps to prevent decay? Explain your answer.

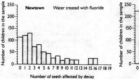

Newtown — Water treated with fluoride
Number of children in the sample
Number of teeth affected by decay

Oldtown — No fluoride in the water
Number of children in the sample
Number of teeth affected by decay

Unit 2

8 Peter and Jane were doing an experiment to find out which of two washing powders was best for removing grease and dirt from a piece of material.
   They took four pieces of material. They smeared two of the pieces with dirt and the other two with grease.

dirt

dirt

grease

grease

They took four beakers of hot water and put the washing powders in them like this:

(a) Where should they put the four pieces of material? Copy the table and fill it in. One example is done for you.

Beaker	Greasy or dirty
1	dirty
2	
3	
4	

(b) Write down the things they should keep the same to make it a fair test. You should be able to think of at least five things.

9 The writing below is about the treatment of sewage. Read it carefully and then answer the questions.

Preliminary treatment

Sewage arriving at the works carries paper, rags, sticks, coarse grit and other objects. If these are not removed, they will choke pipelines, damage pumps and interfere with the operation of the valves. The first step in the treatment, therefore, is to remove these objects by passing the sewage through **screens.** Here the objects are removed and disposed of separately.
   Besides these large objects, rainwater carries grit and sand from the roads into the sewers. Unless grit and sand are removed, they cause blockages and excessive wear in pumps and machinery. The process involves passing sewage through channels slowly enough for the heavy grit to fall to the bottom, yet fast enough for the light organic solids to **remain in suspension.**

(a) What things in the sewage could choke pipelines?
(b) What do you think a screen is?
(c) What is carried by the rainwater into the sewers?
(d) What do you think to 'remain in suspension' means?

51

Unit 2

10 This question is about water supplied by the Water Boards in England and Wales. Don't be put off by the tables of figures!

Table 1   Average household bills 1979–83

Year	Average bill (£)
1979	21
1980	27
1981	30
1982	33
1983	35

Table 2   Water supplied 1979–83

Year	Quantity of water supplied (millions of litres a day)
1979	11 900
1980	12 500
1981	12 300
1982	12 300
1983	12 500

Table 3   Water resources 1983

Region	Average annual rainfall (mm)
North-West	1200
Northumbrian	900
Severn–Trent	800
Yorkshire	850
Anglian	600
Thames	700
Southern	800
Wessex	850
South-West	1200
Welsh	1350

Table 4   Reservoirs in each region 1983

Region	Number of reservoirs
North-West	44
Northumbrian	19
Severn–Trent	20
Yorkshire	42
Anglian	11
Thames	20
Southern	5
Wessex	6
South-West	13
Welsh	31

Table 5   Water supplied 1983

Region	Quantity of water supplied (millions of litres a day)
North-West	2500
Northumbrian	650
Severn–Trent	1900
Yorkshire	1350
Anglian	1050
Thames	2500
Southern	650
Wessex	350
South-West	400
Welsh	1100

(a) Which table will tell you about the average household bill for water in 1983?

(b) Look at the table which tells you about the average annual rainfall in the different regions of the country for 1983. Which region had the highest annual rainfall?

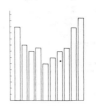

(c) Look at the bar chart. It is a chart for one of the tables above, but the labels have been left off. Which table does this chart show?

(d) Draw a bar chart on a piece of graph paper to show the average household bills between 1979 and 1983.

52

Unit 3   AIR

Test

You will need your *Active Science 1* book.

1 Look at this diagram carefully as you answer the questions.

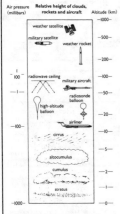

Air pressure (millibars)   Relative height of clouds, rockets and aircraft

(a) About how **high** can a radiosonde balloon reach?

(b) What **types** of clouds might an airliner have to fly through on its way to its cruising height?

(c) At what **height** is the air pressure about 1 mb?

(d) What is the **air pressure** at the height that an airliner flies at?

(e) What do you think would happen if somebody made a hole in the side of the airliner? Explain why you think that.

2 Footballs and netballs are blown up with a pump. The squashy air inside them makes them bounce well.

   Suppose you had to find out how the bounciness of a football or a netball depended on how much it had been blown up. Write down a plan for an experiment. You can use some or all of the equipment shown in the diagram below.

tyre pressure gauge

pressure gauge

3 Look back at the passage about the discovery of oxygen in section 3.6.

(a) Which gas was once called 'inflammable air'?

(b) What did Priestley use to provide heat for his experiment?

(c) What experiments did Priestley do that told him the gas he had produced was different from air?

(d) Who do you think discovered oxygen? Was it Priestley or Lavoisier? Say how you decided.

53

Unit 3

4 The map and the table show the midday temperatures and the weather conditions in some cities around the world on a day in late October.

City	Weather	°C
Algiers	sunny	23
Belgrade	fair	14
Berlin	sunny	7
Bordeaux	cloudy	16
Dublin	cloudy	7
Helsinki	cloudy	4
Luxembourg	foggy	1
London	sunny	9
Madrid	rain	13
Moscow	cloudy	2
Munich	sunny	15
Oslo	fair	4
Paris	cloudy	11
Rome	sunny	18
Stockholm	sunny	4

(a) Which city had the highest temperature?
(b) Which had the lowest?
(c) How many cities were sunny?
(d) Look at the temperatures of the cities on the map. What pattern can you see?
(e) One of the cities does not fit the pattern. Which city is it? Is the temperature higher or lower than you would expect?
   Can you think of a possible reason for the difference? You might need to look at the table as well as the map.

5 The instructions below are about selecting the correct sort of fire extinguisher to put out a fire. If you pick the wrong one, the fire could get worse!

Classification of fires

Class A   Ordinary combustibles, e.g. wood, paper, cloth, rubber, plastics.
Class B   Flammable liquid fires, e.g. cooking fat, oil, paraffin, petrol, methylated spirits.
Class C   Electrical fires.
Class D   Metal fires, e.g. sodium, magnesium.

Choice of extinguisher

Class A   Water
Class B   Fire blanket, carbon dioxide extinguisher, foam extinguisher, powder extinguisher. **(Never use water.)**
Class C   Carbon dioxide. **(Never use water or foam, and always switch off the electricity supply before you tackle the fire.)**
Class D   Dry powder.

Suppose you set the chip pan on fire.
(a) What class of fire is this?
(b) What sorts of extinguisher could you use!
(c) What sort of extinguisher should you **never** use?

54

Unit 3

6 This is a weather map for Great Britain.

warm front
cold front
wind direction

(a) Find London on the map. What direction do you think the wind was blowing from – north, east, south or west?
(b) Now find Edinburgh and Manchester. Which of the three cities (London, Edinburgh or Manchester) was the windiest? Which was least windy?
(c) What are the lines on the map called?
(d) What do they tell you?

7 Paul and Yasmin were doing an experiment to find out how much air weighs. This is what they did:

– They weighed an empty plastic Coke bottle. It weighed 73.2 grams.
– They connected the bottle to a pump. They put it behind a safety screen and sucked all the air out.
– They weighed it again. It weighed 71.6 grams.

(a) How much did the air weigh?
(b) The bottle was labelled '2 litres'. How much does 1 litre of air weigh?
(c) They checked their answer in a book. The book said that 1 litre of air weighs just over 1 gram. Can you think of any reasons why their answer was different from the one in the book?

8 When Paul and Yasmin did the experiment in Question 7, the bottle collapsed. You may have seen the same thing happen to a tin can.

(a) Sketch a tin that collapsed when the air was sucked out of it. Draw arrows on your sketch to show which way you think the forces must have been pushing on the can.

(b) Air is made up of tiny particles that are too small to see. The three diagrams below show the can:

– before the air is taken out.

– after some of the air has been taken out, but before the can has collapsed.

– after the can has collapsed.

The particles of air on the outside of the can have been put in for you. Copy the three diagrams and put in the particles on the **inside** of the can.

(c) Use your drawing to help you explain why the can collapses.

Unit 3

9 The graph below shows two things. One line shows the amount of rainfall during one month. The other line shows the amount of cloud cover.

Is graph A the one of rainfall? Or is it the graph of cloud cover? Explain why you think that.

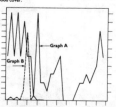

Graph A
Graph B

Submarine and custard

"Let's see what you can do, then, Number 1," said the captain of the submarine to his second-in-command. "Bring her up to the surface."

"Aye, aye, captain," said Cool Joe, putting down his half-finished dish of custard. "**Blow forrard tanks.**"

There was a hiss of compressed air as the water was forced out of the tanks at the front of the boat.

The boat angled sharply upwards, catching the captain by surprise. He tripped over his own feet and fell face down on to the deck.

Cool Joe was busy shouting orders. "**Blow aft tanks, flood forrard.**"

This time the air rushed into the tanks at the back of the boat, while water sloshed greedily into the front ones.

The boat shuddered and started to return to an even keel. And then to angle the other way. The captain, still on the deck, holding his head and muttering to himself, saw the dish of cold custard slide off the table above him.

"Which idiot left this . . . glug glug glug?" he gurgled.

Cool Joe was beginning to lose his cool. "Flood aft tanks – no, blow them, left hand down a bit, put the handbrake on," he shouted, his voice rising as fast as the back of the submarine.

10 Cool Joe hasn't quite got it right, has he?

(a) Explain to him why the boat behaved as it did after each instruction that is shown in very dark print.

(b) Suppose you are the captain. What would you say to bring the boat to the surface?

Unit 4 MATERIALS

Test

You will need your *Active Science I* book and worksheet 4.8.

1 Here is a list of things. Your job is to sort them out into solids, liquids and gases.

wood	glass
cricket ball	smoke
air	fog
exhaust fumes from a car	jelly
water	ice cream
vinegar	your breath
salt	treacle

Do a table like the one below and put them into the correct column. The table is started for you.

Solids	Liquids	Gases
wood		

2 For this question you will need worksheet 4.8. Use the key in the worksheet to identify this plastic:

The material: sinks in water
is hard
is transparent
is difficult to cut

3 Each of the sentences below has the name of a gas missing. Write down the names of the missing gases.

(a) _____ is used as a fuel in rockets.
(b) When animals died and rotted millions of years ago, _____ was formed.
(c) All animals need _____ to stay alive.
(d) _____ is used by plants to make carbohydrate (food).

4 Look back in your text book to section 4.6 – the one with photographs of four bridges.
Pick one of the bridges and write it down as a title. Write a few sentences about the bridge you have chosen. Say why it is built the way it is.

5 The different parts of a pram are made out of different materials.

Which material would you use for:
(a) the hood? Why?   (c) the frame? Why?
(b) the tyres? Why?   (d) the springs? Why?

```
                              nylon      group
                  synthetic── polyester    I
                  │           acrylic
        artificial┤
FIBRES──┤         regenerated── viscose    2
        │
        │         ┌ wool
        └ animal──┤              3
        natural   └ silk

                  plant────── cotton       4
```

6 Look at the chart and answer these questions.
(a) Which fibres come from animals?
(b) Make a list of the artificial fibres.
(c) Linen is a natural fibre made from a plant. Which group does it belong to on the chart – group 1, 2, 3 or 4?

7 Julie is going away on a camping holiday. It might be very cold. She has to decide which sort of sleeping bag to take.
Her family has two sleeping bags. She decides to do an investigation to see which would keep her warmest.
What should she do? Write a plan for the investigation.

Unit 4

Table I Properties of fibres

Name of fibre	Other names used	Price range	Water absorbency*	Durability†	Other advantages and disadvantages
Cotton		medium	high	medium	Feels comfortable, absorbs perspiration.
Wool		high	high	high	Feels comfortable and looks attractive. Very warm when knitted.
Silk		very high	high	high	Looks and feels attractive.
Viscose	Rayon, Sarille, Modal	low	medium	low	
Acetate	Dicel	low	medium	low	
Triacetate	Tricel	medium	medium	low	
Nylon	Bri-nylon, polyamide	medium	low	high	Stretches, dries quickly, strong.
Polyester	Terylene	medium	low	high	
Acrylic	Courtelle, Acrilan, Mostacrylic, Orlon	medium	low	medium	Warm when knitted.

*High water absorbency means the fibre attracts water. It can absorb quite a lot of water before it feels wet.
†High durability means the fibre is hard-wearing.

8 Look at the table. It gives you some information about different sorts of fibres. Use the table to help you decide which material to use for each of these jobs. For each one say why you decided on your choice.

(a) a tea-towel for drying dishes
(b) a blouse or a shirt for going to a party
(c) a hard-wearing jumper for working in the garden

9 Ashok and Jane were buying cups of coffee from a stall at the fair. They noticed that at one stall the cups were plastic and at another polystyrene. Both stalls gave them a lid to keep their coffee warm.
They decided to do an investigation like one they had done at school. They wanted to find out:
– whether the *type of material* was most important for keeping things warm,
– or whether it was the *lid* that mattered most.
At home, they filled four cups with hot coffee. They measured the temperature and waited for ten minutes. Then they measured the temperature again. These are their results:

	Temp. at start (°C)	Temp. after 10 mins (°C)	Change in temp. (°C)
Polystyrene cup without lid	80	64	16
Polystyrene cup with lid	80	72	8
Plastic cup without lid	80	60	20
Plastic cup with lid	80	68	12

(a) Which cup was the best for keeping coffee warm?
(b) Which cup was the worst?
(c) What makes most difference? Is it the material of the cup? Or is it whether there is a lid on or not? Explain your answer carefully.

Sink or swim

Janice Bond looked over the side of the hot-air balloon. She was 100 feet above the Pacific Ocean. And she was losing height. The sharks were watching. Janice could see the coast, but she knew she wasn't going to make it. She reckoned that the wind would take 40 minutes to blow her onto the land.

Janice felt in her pocket for her top-secret manual on how to steer a hot-air balloon. It said she would have to:

– throw out 50 kilograms of weight every ten minutes to stay just above the sea, or
– turn on the gas heater that heated the air in the balloon, or
– panic.

10 (a) How would throwing out the weight help?
(b) How would using the heater help?

But Janice still had a problem. She had thrown everything out already. All she had left to throw out was herself and the gas canister for heating the air. The gas canister weighed 150 kg and would burn for thirty minutes.

(c) Can she escape? Explain how she might save herself.

Unit 5 LIFE

Test

You will need your *Active Science 1* book.

1 Find out from the textbook what each of these things is.
(a) a cocoon
(b) an aphid
(c) a spore

Write a sentence in your own words to describe each one. You may need to look in the reference section or the glossary to find out.

2 Manufacturers make different sorts of fertiliser for growing different things.

A friend of yours works for a market gardener. She wants to compare three sorts of fertiliser – Growup, Growgreat and Growbest.

She set up this investigation:

Growup

Growgreat

Growbest   water

– She moistened four filter papers, one with each of the fertilisers and one with water.
– She put some cress seeds on the filter papers.
– Then she left them.

(a) What should she measure to decide which was the best fertiliser?
(b) Why did she use a lot of cress seeds – why not just use one?
(c) Why did she use plain water on one of the filter papers?

3 Look at the photograph of an elephant in the reference section. Imagine you had to describe the important things about an elephant over the phone to someone who had never seen one before. Write down what you would say.

4 This question is about the classification diagram at the beginning of the reference section. Use it to answer these questions.

(a) What are amphibia like?
(b) What group are amphibia in?
(c) What is the scientific name for plants which have leaves and stems but no roots?
(d) What things come under the group called ARTHROPODS?
(e) Which group are *you* in?

5 Here is a list of different things. Your job is to put them into as many groups as you like. The things in each group should have something in common. Give a title to each group.

goldfish   ant   sparrow   cod
bee   stone   bear   shrimp
monkey   snake   matchstick potato
magpie   carrot   deer   car
lettuce   robin   man

6

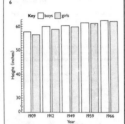

Key □ boys □ girls

The bar charts show the **average heights** of children aged 13½ at different times since 1900.

(a) How tall, on average, were girls in 1909?
(b) How tall, on average, were boys in 1959?
(c) How much taller were girls in 1966 compared to 1909?
(d) Write one sentence describing the patterns in the two bar charts.
(e) Can you think of any reasons that could explain the pattern? Write down as many as you can.

Unit 5

7 Below are some statements about cells. Part A of the statements does not match part B – they are jumbled up. Rewrite them so that they match up correctly.

Part A	Part B
A cell wall or membrane	is where a cell makes and stores chemicals.
Cytoplasm	controls what the cell does.
The nucleus	holds the cell together.
Tissue	contains information to allow cells to divide.
A chromosome	is a lot of cells joined together.

8 The table shows how long people could expect to live for if they were born in 1960.

Country	How long people can expect to live for (in years)
Denmark	72
Italy	70
Argentina	60
Mexico	57
Canada	71
India	42
Brazil	53

(a) Draw a bar chart for this table.

(b) Write a sentence describing the pattern. Why do you think the pattern is like this?

9 You can use your textbook to help you answer this question.

(a) Plants can make new plants by making seeds. Gardeners often collect or buy seeds if they want new plants. Write a sentence about how plants make seeds.

(b) Gardeners can also make new plants from cuttings. How are plants grown from cuttings different from those grown from seeds?

(c) Write down as many advantages as you can think of for making new plants by taking cuttings.

Now write down any disadvantages you can think of.

10 A conker is the seed of a horse chestnut tree. Do you play conkers?

Some people say that new conkers are better than old ones. Others say that they are best when they are about a week old. Other people pickle them in vinegar – they reckon that makes them good ones. Perhaps you have tried roasting them in the oven – that's supposed to make them good as well.

Suppose you wanted to enter a conker competition with a big prize for the winner. You wanted to check these ideas out so that you had the best conker.

Write a plan for an investigation that you could do to find out what makes the best conker for the competition.

Unit 6 ELECTRICITY

Test

You will need graph paper.

1 Here are some sketches of electrical circuits.

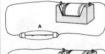

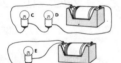

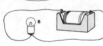

(a) Write down the letters of the bulbs which will light.
(b) Pick one of the circuits which you think won't work. Explain why you think that.
(c) Now draw the circuit, but change it so that it will work.

2 In a series circuit the components are joined **end to end**. In a parallel circuit they are joined **side by side**. Look at these diagrams:

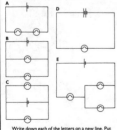

Write down each of the letters on a new line. Put alongside them: SERIES, or PARALLEL, or MIXTURE of series and parallel.

3 The diagram below is of a press switch. Various parts of the switch are labelled.

Your job is to decide which of the list of materials you would use to make each of the labelled parts. You have these materials:

Part A	B	C	D
plastic	plastic	plastic	plastic
wood	wood	wood	wood
steel	steel	steel	steel
brass	brass	brass	brass

(a) Copy this table and fill it in:

Part	Material
A	
B	
C	
D	

(b) Explain your choices.

Unit 6

4 Electricians use circuit diagrams instead of sketches. Draw the electricians' diagrams for these circuits.

(a)

(b)

(c)

5

(a) The advert for 'Infinity' light bulbs can't be checked scientifically. Why not?
(b) Write a plan for an experiment to check the claims of the makers of 'Everlasting' light bulbs.

6 Read the passage and then answer the question.

Power cut!

If all your lights go out, or if all the electrical appliances stop, first check that the neighbours, too, have no electricity. At night the street lights may indicate whether the whole of the road is without electricity.

If yours is the only house without electricity, the fault must be in your house. If only one or two appliances stop working, then you may have blown one of the fuses where the mains come into the house. Check first whether it is the supply to the plugs or to the lights. Get a torch and find the mains fuses – they may be under the stairs.

SWITCH OFF the main switch. Remove the fuse box cover. You should find a list telling you which fuses are for which circuit. Find the fuses that are labelled with the circuit that is not working. Replace the fuse and the fusebox cover and try the circuit.

If you are not sure what to do, call in an electrician. Never take chances with electricity – it could kill you.

Suppose you work out that it is the lighting circuit which is not working. Write yourself a list of instructions telling you what to do. Look at the passage again – carefully – before you start.

Unit 6

7 Use the tables to answer the questions.

Table 1

Typical appliances	Wattage up to
Table lamps, food mixers, hairdriers	720 W
Refrigerators, vacuum cleaners, electric drills, irons, televisions	1440 W
Kettles, fan heaters	3240 W
Storage heaters, immersion heaters	3840 W

Table 2

Typical appliances	Type of flex
Electric clocks	Parallel twin PVC
Refrigerators, televisions, hairdriers, table lamps, food mixers	Light duty PVC
Vacuum cleaners, washing machines	Ordinary duty PVC
Frypans, plate warmers	Rubber (60°C)
Room heaters, fan heaters, toasters	Rubber-insulated cores with loose textile braid
Irons	Ruber/textile braided
Immersion heaters, storage heaters	80 °C rubber high-temperature cords

Table 3

Wattage up to	Fuse
720 W	3 amp
3240 W	13 amp

(a) What type of flex should be used for an electric clock?
(b) What fuse should be used for an appliance with a wattage of 500?
(c) What fuse would you use for
 – a table lamp?
 – a vacuum cleaner?
(d) What type of flex should you use for an electric iron? Why do you think this type is used?

8 Jim and Anne bought a big electric boiler to use for heating water for washing clothes in their caravan. They needed to know how long it would take to get the water to different temperatures.
They filled the boiler with cold water and borrowed a thermometer to check its temperature. Here are their results.

Time from switching on (minutes)	Temperature (°C)
0	10
1	14
2	30
3	45
4	59
5	72
6	84
7	93
8	98
9	100
10	100

(a) They decided the best thing to do was to plot a graph. Use the graph paper to plot a line graph for this table.
(b) The labels on their first batch of washing said 60 °C. How long should they heat the water for?
(c) Their next batch was at 60°C as well. But they only needed half a boiler full of water. About how long should they heat it for this time?

9 Jane asked Jill to test her arm with two blunt pins to see how sensitive the nerves in her arm were.
First of all Jill drew a pattern of dots on Jane's arm like this:

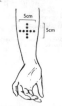

Then she gently pressed the two pins onto Jane's arms at different distances apart. She asked Jane if she could feel one or two pins. Here are the results she wrote down:

Table 1 Along Jane's arm

Distance apart along arm (cm)	Could Jane tell if there were two pins?
0.5	No
1	No
1.5	No
2	Sometimes
2.5	Sometimes
3	Yes
3.5	Yes
5	Yes

Table 2 Across Jane's arm

Distance apart across arm (cm)	Could Jane tell if there were two pins?
0.5	No
1	Sometimes
1.5	Sometimes
2	Yes
2.5	Yes
3	Yes
3.5	Yes
5	Yes

(a) How far apart must the two pins be across Jane's arm before she can tell for sure that there are two and not one?
(b) Look at the pattern of results in the two tables.
(c) Write a sentence or two about how sensitive Jane's arm is.
(c) Can you think of any reasons why the results should be different along her arm from across it?

10 Some cars have an electronic circuit which makes a light flash on the dashboard if either of the front seat passengers have not fastened their seat belts.

(a) Which of these sensors could be used to check whether the driver's seat belt is fastened?

a pressure switch
a light sensor
an ordinary press switch
a sound sensor
a temperature sensor

How would it work?

(b) What sort of sensor could detect whether there was someone sitting in the passenger seat? How would that work?
(c) Any electronic circuit has an output device. What output is being used in this circuit?

7 HEALTH
7.1 Energy in food

Food (1 helping)	Energy (kJ)	Protein (g)	Carbohydrate (g)	Fat (g)
Grapefruit (half)	92	1	5	0
Sugar (spoonful)	188	0	12	0
Breakfast cereals (with milk)				
Corn Flakes	1403	10	60	8
Weetabix	1274	12	49	9
Rice Krispies	1274	9	53	9
Porridge	728	7	18	9
Cooked breakfast				
Bacon (rasher)	1132	6	0	27
Kipper	922	19	0	16
Boiled egg	376	7	0	7
Fried egg	504	7	0	10
Buttered toast	393	2	16	3
Preserves (for one slice of bread or toast)				
Honey	172	0	11	0
Jam or marmalade	155	0	10	0
Golden syrup	176	0	11	0
Drinks (one cup or glass)				
Tea with milk	54	1	1	0
Coffee with milk	72	1	2	2
Drinking chocolate (made with milk)	636	7	15	8
Milk	539	6	10	8
Sugar (teaspoon)	94	0	6	0
Fruit juice (pure)	394	2	23	0
Snacks				
Buttered bap or 1 slice buttered bread	393	2	16	3
Ham (slice)	250	2	0	6
Cheese (slice)	245	4	0	5
Fish finger	342	6	9	3
Sausage	439	3	3	9
Meat pattie	558	5	10	6
Beefburger	660	5	5	13
Fishcake	510	9	14	5
Meat samosa	512	5	16	6
Sardine	224	4	0	4
Tomato soup	400	2	14	5
Meat				
Pork chop	3762	32	0	86
Lamb chop	1596	15	0	34
Fried liver	1156	30	4	16
Steak	1014	29	0	14
Beef curry	1250	26	1	22
Roast lamb	1190	25	0	20
Roast pork	1344	25	0	23
Roast beef	1050	27	0	15

Food (1 helping)	Energy (kJ)	Protein (g)	Carbohydrate (g)	Fat (g)
Meat pie	2166	23	28	36
Chicken (quarter)	1542	59	0	15
Fish				
Fried cod	834	20	8	10
Poached fish	492	27	0	1
Tinned salmon	557	20	0	6
Vegetables (cooked)				
Chips	1405	6	53	13
Boiled potatoes	331	1	20	0
Roast potatoes	515	3	27	2
Baked beans	385	6	17	0
Garden peas	102	3	4	0
Mushy peas	201	4	9	0
Sprouts	67	2	2	0
Cabbage	34	1	1	0
Carrots	96	1	5	0
Cauliflower	101	3	3	0
Vegetable stir fry	500	5	20	10
Rice, pasta and dough				
Rice	854	4	49	1
Spaghetti	864	6	48	1
Chapati	1500	19	20	0
Yoghurt				
Natural	335	5	8	4
Fruit	460	5	19	3
Fresh fruit				
Apple	220	0	14	0
Orange	252	1	14	0
Banana	540	2	33	0
Puddings, cakes and sweets				
Fresh raspberries	105	1	6	0
Fresh strawberries	109	1	6	0
Tinned apricots	444	1	28	0
Tinned peaches	369	1	23	0
Tinned pineapple	318	0	20	0
Single cream	225	1	1	5
Custard	867	6	31	8
Ice cream	805	4	20	11
Currant bun	1374	8	59	9
Fruit cake	3084	9	110	32
Plain cake	2703	11	75	36
Jam tart	1638	3	64	14
Rice pudding	595	4	16	8
Chocolate bar (100g)	2422	9	55	38

7 HEALTH
7.2A Energy cost of activities

Under each picture you can see how much energy is needed to do the activity for an hour. The figures are for someone of average weight. If you are overweight, you need more energy.

Sleeping: 200kJ/h

Reading or watching TV: 350kJ/h

Darts or snooker: 450kJ/h

Light work: 600kJ/h (e.g. mending a bike or teaching)

Gardening: 900 kJ/h

Walking: 1000kJ/h

Manual work (e.g. carrying heavy weights): 1250kJ/h

Gentle jogging or cycling: 1500kJ/h

Swimming: 1800kJ/h

Hockey, football or running: 2200kJ/h

7 HEALTH
7.2B Square meals

A square meal contains four types of food:
1. ....
2. ....
3. ....
4. ....

Complete the following tables to make each snack into a square meal. Then use worksheet 7.1 to work out the energy value (in kJ) of each meal.

Food	Food type	Energy value
Soup		
Bread roll		
Ham		
	Total	

Food	Food type	Energy value
Cheese		
Cream crackers		
Apple juice		
	Total	

Food	Food type	Energy value
Soup		
Scrambled egg		
Ham		
	Total	

Food	Food type	Energy value
Burger		
Bap		
Coffee with milk		
	Total	

Food	Food type	Energy value
Ham omelette		
	.	
A banana split		
Cup of tea		
	Total	

Food	Food type	Energy value
Salad		100
Bread and butter		
Orange squash		
	Total	

3

7 HEALTH
7.4 The digestive system

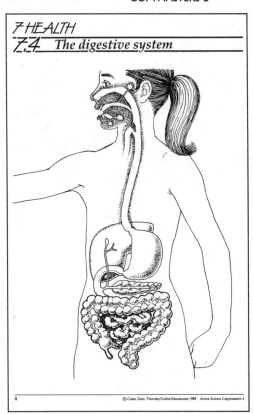

4

7 HEALTH
7.5 A tooth chart

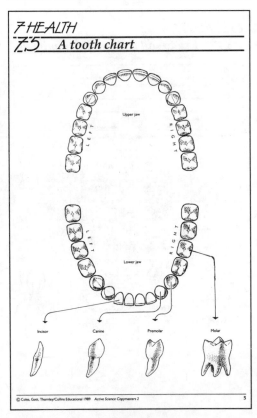

5

7 HEALTH
7.6 Height and weight

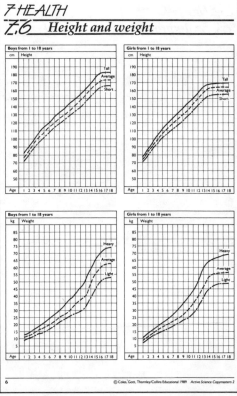

6

7 HEALTH
7.8 What would you do?

Here are some of the things that you could do to help. Look through them all and sort out the ones you would do. Put them in order.

1. Run to the nearest phone booth.
2. Check if the casualty is breathing.
3. Keep the casualty warm and quiet.
4. Check if the casualty has a pulse.
5. Make sure someone is controlling the traffic.
6. Check for fractured bones.
7. Comfort the casualty.
8. Check for severe bleeding.
9. Get someone to dial 999 and ask for an ambulance.
10. Look for signs of blockage of the casualty's airway.
11. Ask casualty for name and address (if he or she is conscious).
12. Get someone to keep onlookers away.
13. Move the casualty to a safe place.
14. Control severe bleeding by using pressure pads.
15. Find out how long the ambulance will take.
16. Place the casualty in the recovery position.
17. See if casualty is carrying a donor card.
18. Dial 999 and ask for an ambulance.
19. Give artificial ventilation if necessary.
20. Decide which is the most serious injury.
21. Pump the heart.
22. Make sure the road is clear for the ambulance.
23. Take name and address of the van driver.
24. Wait for help to arrive.
25. Find out if any passers-by know first aid.

© Coles, Gott, Thornley/Collins Educational 1989   Active Science Copymasters 2   7

8 ENERGY
8.3A Making oil into useful fuels

😊 ⚠️

Set up the apparatus as shown. Make sure that:
– you have eye protection,
– the bung is in tightly,
– the clamp is at the top of the tube,
– your Bunsen is on a low blue flame.

● Warm the crude oil *gently*. When the temperature reaches 80°C, stop heating.
● Let any liquid run into test tube A.
● Move test tube B under the glass tube. Heat again, gently, until the temperature reaches 120°C.
● Again, stop heating and let any vapour run into the test tube.
● Move on to tube C and repeat the process up to 160°C.
● Finally, heat the crude oil up to 200°C, using tube D to collect the vapour.

Do not heat the oil over 200°C.

● Use your samples (called fractions) to fill in the table.
● To test ease of lighting, put a few drops of the liquid on a piece of heatproof paper in a tin tray and use a spill to light it.

ceramic wool soaked with crude oil

A B C D

	Colour	Runniness (viscosity)	Smell	How easy is it to light?	How smoky is the flame?
Original crude oil					
Tube A (20–80°C)					
Tube B (80–120°C)					
Tube C (120–160°C)					
Tube D (160–200°C)					
Residue (what's left in the big tube)					

8   © Coles, Gott, Thornley/Collins Educational 1989   Active Science Copymasters 2

8 ENERGY
8.3B Improving wood as a fuel

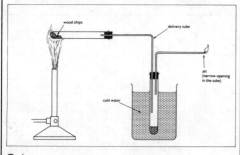

wood chips
delivery tube
jet (narrow opening in the tube)
cold water

😊 ⚠️

● Heat the wood chips gently for two minutes, then gradually increase the heat. Heat all round the wood chips, not just in one place.
● When smoke comes from the jet, try to light it.
● Stop heating after ten minutes.
● Write a report on your investigation whilst the wood cools.
● When the wood is cool, find out if you have made charcoal.
● Try to find out what is in the other test tube.

© Coles, Gott, Thornley/Collins Educational 1989   Active Science Copymasters 2   9

8 ENERGY
8.7 Key to soil and leaf litter animals

Observing

● Look closely at a compost heap or some leaf litter. Use this key to identify any animals.

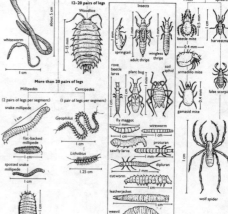

10   © Coles, Gott, Thornley/Collins Educational 1989   Active Science Copymasters 2

8 ENERGY
8.10 Energy sources

- Make a list of all of the energy sources which are shown in the picture.

1 Which one is most important for supplying the country with energy?

- Put the other sources in order of how important they are for supplying energy, with the most important first. You may have to discuss this with your friends.

2 Which energy source is the cheapest to use?
3 Which sources will never get used up?
4 Some fuels are called non-renewable. Can you guess which ones these are?

5 Imagine you could be transported forward in time by 50 years. Which energy sources do you think will be more important then?

9 SENSES
9.2A   Making a pinhole camera

Basic skill

You will need
aluminium foil (about 5cm × 5cm)
large nail
pin
empty tin (with a base about 120mm square).
No lid is required.

hammer
greaseproof paper (tracing paper)
black sugar paper
Sellotape

How to make the camera
Follow these instructions:
1. Draw a line with a pencil across the closed end of the tin.
2. Draw another line across the bottom of the tin so that it crosses your first line at right angles.
3. Use the hammer and nail to punch a hole in the tin at the place the two lines cross over. ⚠
4. Tape the aluminium foil over the hole.

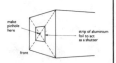
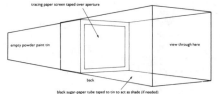

5. Use the pin to make a very small hole in the aluminium foil. This should be in the middle of the hole in the tin.
6. Tape the greaseproof paper over the open end of the tin.
7. Point the end of the tin with the hole in it at a window at least 5 metres away. Look at the greaseproof paper end. Can you see an image of the window?

Improving the image
- Experiment with the size of the hole at the front of the camera.
- Make a shade out of black sugar paper to surround the viewing end.
- Try making several small pinholes. What happens?

9 SENSES
9.2B Taking and developing photographs

Improving the pinhole camera
Put a fresh piece of foil over the front of your camera. Make a new small hole in it. Cover the hole with light-proof tape. Practise taking the tape off and putting it back without moving the camera in any way. The light-proof strip makes a shutter.

For taking a photograph, you need to fix some light-sensitive paper to the back of your camera in place of the greaseproof paper. This must be done in low red light (safe light) which will not spoil the light-sensitive paper. Blu-tack is good for holding the paper in. When you have done this, cover the back of the camera with a light-proof layer of black sugar paper.

Taking a photograph
Decide what you are going to photograph. Something in sunlight, at least 5 metres away, is best. Put your camera on a firm object (like a low wall). Hold the camera steady, then remove the tape over the hole for 5 seconds and then replace it.

Developing the picture
To make your picture visible you need to soak your photograph in some special chemicals. This must also be done in low red light. The stages are:
1. Make sure there is no white light in the room.
2. Remove the sensitive paper from the camera.
3. Put it in the developer solution for about a minute.
4. Remove it from the developer and very quickly wash it in water.
5. Put it in fixer solution. Leave it for at least 2 minutes.
6. Wash it under a running tap for about 30 seconds.
7. Hang it on a line to dry.

Some guidelines for better photographs
- Keep the paper out of any white light. The camera and the room you are working in must be light-proof.
- If your photo is too dark, leave it in developer solution for a shorter time. Or remove the tape for 3 seconds (instead of 5), or try a smaller pinhole.
- If your photo is too light, leave it in developer solution for a longer time. Or remove the tape for 10 seconds instead of 5.
- If your picture is not clear, practise making it better with the greaseproof screen instead of the light-sensitive paper. You may have to change the time you let light into the camera or use a smaller pinhole.

9 SENSES
9.2C A modern camera

Modern cameras have many features that make it easy to take good photographs. In this diagram, each feature has been labelled with a letter.

- Study the table below and fill in the gaps. The first one is done for you.

Feature	What it does	Letter
Shutter button	Opens the shutter to let in a small amount of light.	E
Self-timer		F
	Focus light on the film.	B
Zoom control		L
Rewind lever		A
Focusing ring	Lets you control the focus by hand.	
Counter window		I
Light detector for the flash		J
Film speed setting		G
	Lets you control the size of the aperture by hand.	D
Viewfinder		H
Automatic focus windows	Detect a sharp image.	
Flash unit		M

9 SENSES
9.4 Dissecting an animal eye

The eye you will be dissecting has come from an abattoir. This is a place where farm animals are killed humanely before being sold to butchers' shops. Some people do not feel comfortable dissecting an eye. If you feel like this, discuss it with your teacher.

- Have a close look at the eye before you cut it. Can you find all of the parts that are labelled in this diagram?

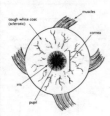

- Behind the iris you will see a little ball of jelly resting in a bed of softer jelly. The little ball of jelly is the lens. Pick it out of its bed. Hold the lens over some writing and look through it. What do you notice?

- Wash out the hollow eyeball. If you look inside, you will be able to see the beautifully coloured retina. This is the lining of the inside of the eye and is made up of thousands of nerve endings.

- All of these nerve fibres come together and leave through a tube at the back of the eye. Can you find the place they come out? This is the optic nerve and it carries information about the light entering the eye to the brain.

⚠ The outside of the eye is tough, and you will need sharp tools to cut through it. You will need to be extra careful when you use them.

- Hold the eye above an enamel dish or glass bowl and make a small cut next to the pupil. Continue to cut around the pupil. A clear, watery liquid (the aqueous humour) will run out into the dish.
  You will probably have removed the iris with the cornea. The iris will look black, with the muscles looking like the spokes of a wheel.

- If you scrape around the edge of the iris, you can remove it from the cornea. Wash it and turn it over. You may be able to see its colour.

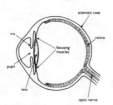

- Look at the diagram of the eye and see if you have found all of the parts.

- Make a list of each part of the eye and next to each part write a few words about the job it does to help a person see.

15

9 SENSES
9.9A Learning

One reason why the human race is so successful is because humans learn quickly.

How quickly can you learn to copy a shape in a mirror?

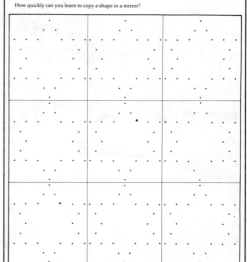

- Number each attempt that you make, and write down how long it took you.
- After ten tries, decide if you have learnt or not.
- Repeat the activity in a week's time. Has your brain remembered what it learnt?

16

9 SENSES
9.9B Reading and remembering

Remembering things that you have read can be a problem. Some young people were asked how well they remembered things when they revised for a test.

"I get to the end of the page and I can't remember what was at the beginning." **Jamie**

"When I read I only remember what I'm interested in." **Alex**

"People with photographic memories are really lucky. For me it's a hard slog to remember things." **Annie**

"I forget what I'm supposed to be reading the work for. My mind wanders." **Tabinder**

"About a day is all I can remember it for." **Liz**

"I can easily remember things in pictures or graphs, but writing – no chance." **Jo**

Do you agree with any of their comments?

SQ3R

How well do you remember things you've read? There is a method, called SQ3R, that will help you to study.
S Survey
First read through the whole passage you wish to learn.
Q Question
Make up a question and keep it in your mind when you read.
R Read
Read the passage through carefully. Remember your question.
R Review
Has your question been answered? Are there parts of the message you need to read again?
R Recall
Can you remember the important information in the passage?
- Try the SQ3R method on the passage opposite. Your question could be: How do people get better at thinking as they get older?

Think about it!
Thinking gets more complicated as we get older. Scientists agree that thinking develops in stages. Each stage builds on the one before it.
We can show this using numbers. Count these smiley faces:

If you got to seven, you can count! Perhaps this is the first stage in understanding numbers.
Now decide which of these rows has more faces in it:

Most five-year-olds would not agree with you! They would say there are more grumpy faces. Young children can count to seven, but they don't really understand numbers yet. They get length muddled up with counting. But by the time they are eight, most of them will agree there are the same number of faces in each row.
Gradually we learn about length, area, volume and weight. But even adults find these ideas difficult. Ask an adult what the volume of a room is if the floor area is 5m by 8m and the height 2m!
Some people are good at linking basic ideas to understand harder ones, such as density. They won't be tricked by this question: Which is heavier, a tonne of coal or a tonne of feathers?

17

10 SUBSTANCES
10.4A Gardening 1

A new garden

Mr and Mrs Antonelli have just moved into their new house at 11 Indigo Drive. There are seven main garden areas. Each of these has a thick layer of topsoil on it, but this soil has come from different places. Your job will be to help Mr and Mrs Antonelli plan their new garden so that it looks good and the plants grow well in the right type of soil.

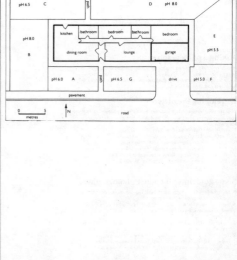

18

10 SUBSTANCES
10.4A Gardening 2

Planting things in the right place

Some plants prefer acid soils and some like alkaline soils. Mr and Mrs Antonelli have a gardening book with information on the best soil pH for different plants:

Plant	pH	Plant	pH
Anemone	7.5	Lavender	8.5
Bilberry	6.5	Lily	5.5
Broom	8.5	Lily of the valley	7.5
Buddleia	8.5	Magnolia	5.5
Cabbage	6.5	Mallow	8.0
Camellia	5.0	Phlox	8.5
Cedar	8.0	Potato	5.5
Delphinium	7.5	Raspberry	6.5
Forsythia	8.0	Rhododendron	5.0
Geranium	7.5	Rose	8.0
Grass	6.5	Rosemary	8.5
Heather	6.0	Turnip	6.0

Mr and Mrs Antonelli would like to have these areas in their garden:

 vegetable plot

 lawn

flower beds, especially roses

fruit

 evergreen trees

shrubs

- Use reference books to help you put the plants in the different categories (vegetables, flowers, etc.). You don't need to include all the plants from the table.
- Then make a plan for Mr and Mrs Antonelli, showing where they could have their garden areas.
   First imagine that you live at 11 Indigo Drive and think about where you would like the different areas. Perhaps you could have a lawn at the front or a vegetable garden near the kitchen.
   When you have decided, draw your garden layout on the plan. In the space below the plan, explain your decisions.

10 SUBSTANCES
10.4B Neutralising

Vinegar

- Too much fizzy drink or vinegar can cause indigestion. How much stomach powder is needed to neutralise an overdose (say 5cm') of vinegar?

Acid soils

- Acid soils will not grow roses well. Measure how acid a sample of soil is by shaking it up with some pure water, then testing it with Universal Indicator paper. The soil may make the water too murky to test. If so, add some Universal Indicator solution and let the tube stand for an hour, or centrifuge it.
- Take a second sample of soil, but add some lime to it before shaking it. Test it again.

Toothpastes

- Measure how alkaline some toothpastes are.
- Find out how much toothpaste is needed to neutralise one acid drop.

10 SUBSTANCES
10.7 Using acid to make copper

Malachite is the name of an ore of copper. Malachite can be reacted with other chemicals to make it into pure copper metal.

- Try making some copper by following these instructions.

You will need:
- small glass beaker
- stirring rod
- 6 volt d.c. power pack
- three electrical leads and a 1.25V bulb
- measuring cylinder
- two carbon rods
- powdered malachite (this may be called copper(II) carbonate)
- sulphuric acid (1 molar)

Dissolving the malachite

1. Put some malachite powder in a test tube (¼ tube is about right).

2. Put about 50cm' of dilute sulphuric acid in your beaker.

3. Add a little malachite to the sulphuric acid and stir gently. Repeat this until your test tube is empty.

4. Connect up the carbon rods and the power pack. Make sure the electricity flows in your circuit and the bulb lights.

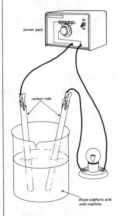

power pack

carbon rods

dilute sulphuric acid with malachite

malachite powder

dilute sulphuric acid

5. Watch the carbon rods carefully. Make a note of any changes you see.

6. After 10 minutes, switch off the electricity and disconnect the circuit.

7. Remove the carbon rods and wash them gently under a running tap.

8. If you can, scrape off a sample of copper from one of the rods. This is the copper you made from copper ore.

10 SUBSTANCES
10.11 What causes hardness in water?

Map 1 How hard your water is

Map 2 Where limestone and chalk are found

You will need to use an atlas map of the British Isles.

Map 1 above shows you how hard water is in different areas.
1. Name three towns with very hard water.
2. Say how hard the water is in: (a) Glasgow, (b) Chester, (c) Ipswich, (d) Basingstoke.

Map 2 above shows you where limestone and chalk are found.
3. Name three towns that are in limestone areas.
4. Name the type of rock around: (a) Dover, (b) Bristol, (c) Lancaster.
5. Put a piece of tracing paper over Map 2. Trace the outline of the British Isles and shade in the limestone and chalk areas.
6. Put your traced map over Map 1. Explain what you think the two maps show.

Rainwater

The diagram shows how the rain dissolves limestone and chalk rocks.
- Think of a way to prove that limestone and chalk do make water hard. What will you need for your investigation? How will you keep the tests fair? (Remember that rainwater is slightly acid anyway.)
- Make a flow diagram of your plan.
- After your teacher has checked your plan, you might be able to carry it out.

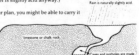

Rain is naturally slightly acid.

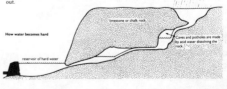

How water becomes hard

limestone or chalk rock

Caves and potholes are made by acid water dissolving the rock.

reservoir of hard water

11 FORCES
11.5   Carrying loads

We all have to carry loads around.

Problem 1   What is the best method of carrying a load? Experiment with a set of books:

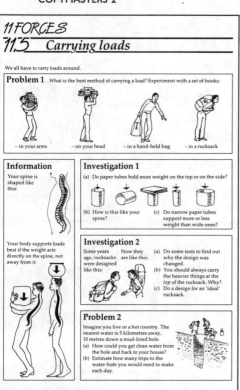

– in your arms   – on your head   – in a hand-held bag   – in a rucksack

Information
Your spine is shaped like this:

Your body supports loads best if the weight acts directly on the spine, not away from it:

Investigation 1
(a) Do paper tubes hold more weight on the top or on the side?

(b) How is this like your spine?

(c) Do narrow paper tubes support more or less weight than wide ones?

Investigation 2
Some years ago, rucksacks were designed like this:

Now they are like this:

(a) Do some tests to find out why the design was changed.

(b) You should always carry the heavier things at the *top* of the rucksack. Why?

(c) Do a design for an 'ideal' rucksack.

Problem 2
Imagine you live in a hot country. The nearest water is 5 kilometres away, 10 metres down a mud-lined hole.
(a) How could you get clean water from the hole and back to your house?
(b) Estimate how many trips to the water-hole you would need to make each day.

23

---

11 FORCES
11.7   Free fall

● Cut out the free fallers in the diagram.

● Try these tests:
1. Drop a free faller face down from the highest point you can reach. Look carefully as the paper falls. Write down a few words which describe the way the shape falls.
2. Free fallers get their bodies into a special star shape (see Pupil Book, p.112). Look at the picture of a free faller. Bend the arms and legs of your model so that they are in the same positions as the free fallers' star. Drop the model again and write down what happens this time.
3. Drop your model with the face upwards. What happens this time?
4. Make your free faller model do left- and right-hand turns by bending legs, arms, elbows and knees.
5. Can you make your model 'forward roll'?

● As the paper figure falls, it rubs against the air. Explain how this air resistance makes it possible for free fallers to control their flight. Discuss it in a group.

  Perhaps you will get a chance to try out your ideas on another group.

24

---

11 FORCES
11.8   Stopping distances

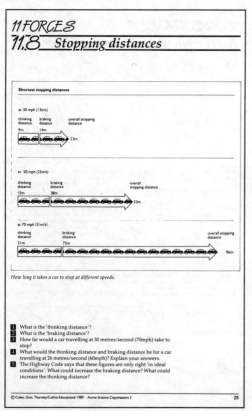

Shortest stopping distances

at 30 mph (13m/s)

thinking distance   braking distance   overall stopping distance
9m   14m   23m

at 50 mph (22m/s)

thinking distance   braking distance   overall stopping distance
15m   38m   53m

at 70 mph (31m/s)

thinking distance   braking distance   overall stopping distance
21m   75m   96m

How long it takes a car to stop at different speeds.

1 What is the 'thinking distance'?
2 What is the 'braking distance'?
3 How far would a car travelling at 30 metres/second (70mph) take to stop?
4 What would the thinking distance and braking distance be for a car travelling at 26 metres/second (60mph)? Explain your answers.
5 The Highway Code says that these figures are only right 'in ideal conditions'. What could increase the braking distance? What could increase the thinking distance?

25

---

11 FORCES
11.11   Where do cars get their go? 1

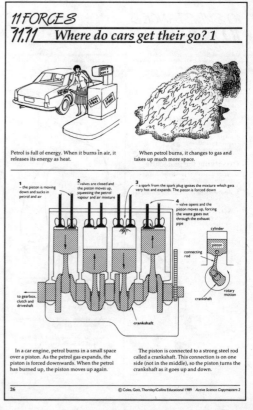

Petrol is full of energy. When it burns in air, it releases its energy as heat.

When petrol burns, it changes to gas and takes up much more space.

1 – the piston is moving down and sucks in petrol and air

2 – valves are closed and the piston moves up, squeezing the petrol vapour and air mixture

3 a spark from the spark plug ignites the mixture which gets very hot and expands. The piston is forced down

4 – valve opens and the piston moves up, forcing the waste gases out through the exhaust pipe

cylinder
piston
connecting rod
rotary motion
crankshaft

to gearbox, clutch and driveshaft

crankshaft

In a car engine, petrol burns in a small space over a piston. As the petrol gas expands, the piston is forced downwards. When the petrol has burned up, the piston moves up again.

The piston is connected to a strong steel rod called a crankshaft. This connection is on one side (not in the middle), so the piston turns the crankshaft as it goes up and down.

26

11 FORCES
11.11 Where do cars get their go? 2

The turning crankshaft is connected to the car's gearbox.

The gearbox is connected to a propeller shaft (prop shaft).

The prop shaft is connected to the four wheels through a differential gear. This gear lets the wheels turn a smaller or larger distance when the car goes round corners.

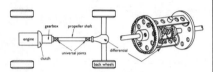

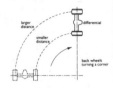

Not all the energy from the petrol goes into making the car move. About half the energy 'escapes' as other forms of energy.

- Make a list of other forms of energy produced by a moving car.
- When petrol burns, it changes. Make a list of the ways it changes.

1 The piston fits the cylinder exactly. Why is this important?

2 What gear would a driver use to:
(a) climb a steep hill?
(b) go fast on a motorway?
(c) go into a parking space backwards?

3 A clutch is a device which fits between the crankshaft and the gearbox. What does it do?

4 What does a 'differential' do?

- Find out what a universal joint is. Can you guess?
- Draw a flowchart of where the energy in petrol goes before it reaches the wheels and pushes the car along.

© Coles, Gott, Thornley/Collins Educational 1989   Active Science Copymasters 2   27

---

11 FORCES
11.12A Bike power

⚠ ● You are going to measure the pull of a bike in different gears. You will need a strong newton meter (0–500 newtons), a rope and a partner to help you. You will need to be very careful.

- Tie the rope securely to a post or strong tree.
- Tie the other end to the handle of the newton meter.
- Fix the hook of the newton meter round the frame just under the saddle.
- Take up the slack in the rope.
- Whilst your friend steadies you and reads the meter, try to ride forwards. Do this in each gear in turn.
- Write your results down in a table.

Gear	Force
1	
2	
3	
4	
5	
6	
7	
8	
9	
10	

1 Is there a pattern in your results?

28   © Coles, Gott, Thornley/Collins Educational 1989   Active Science Copymasters 2

---

11 FORCES
11.12B A bike quiz

1. How many pedal cycles are there in Britain?
(a) 5 thousand,
(b) 15 million,
(c) 50 million.

2. When a bike saddle is the right height, distance x should be:
(a) your inside leg measurement,
(b) so that you can just touch the pedal,
(c) your inside leg and a bit more.

3. What is the most dangerous feature of this bike?

(a) no bell,
(b) no steering,
(c) no pedals,
(d) hard wheels.

4. Why can you go faster on a bike in the racing position than sitting up?
(a) less air resistance,
(b) easier to breathe,
(c) better balanced,
(d) more force on pedals.

5. You may ride a pedal cycle:
(a) on a motorway,
(b) on a footpath,
(c) on a dual carriageway,
(d) past this sign?

6. The fastest a person has ever gone on a bike is:
(a) 62mph,
(b) 45mph,
(c) 85mph,
(d) 101mph.

7. To measure the speed of a bike you would use:
(a) a watch and a calculator,
(b) a tape measure and a calculator,
(c) a watch and a newton meter,
(d) a watch and a tape measure.

True or false?

8. Bikes have been around since 1600.

9. You must have two brakes on a bike.

10. You must have a bell or horn on your bike.

© Coles, Gott, Thornley/Collins Educational 1989   Active Science Copymasters 2   29

---

12 INVESTIGATIONS
12.2 Seed composts

Plants grow well in compost. The chemicals needed by the growing plant are ready and waiting in the rotted plants. Many gardeners buy their compost in bags from a garden centre. There are many types that do different jobs; three are listed below. The figures show how much loam, peat and sand is used to make a kilogram of compost. A little fertiliser and chalk is then added.

	Seed compost	Potting compost number 1	Potting compost number 3
Loam	500g	600g	600g
Peat	250g	250g	250g
Sand	250g	150g	150g
Fertiliser	4g	10g	30g
Chalk	2g	2g	2g

1. How does the seed compost differ from the other two? Why?
2. What would you use potting compost number 3 for? Why?

Growing things

- Find out how well grass seed grows in each of these three types of compost. Compare it with your garden soil.
- Find out what difference fertiliser makes to growing seeds. Make a sandy soil from a mixture of sand and soil. Set up some margarine tubs with the mixture in. Add different amounts of fertiliser to each tub (between 0 and 10 grams should be plenty). Sow some seeds in each tub.

3. How will you decide which seeds are growing best?
4. How will you water them?
5. How will you present the results?

30   © Coles, Gott, Thornley/Collins Educational 1989   Active Science Copymasters 2

12 INVESTIGATIONS
12.3 Pollution indicators

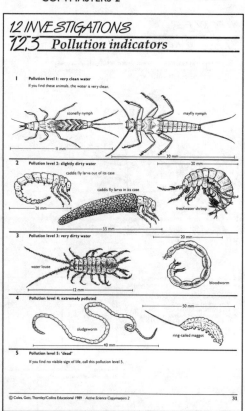

1 **Pollution level 1: very clean water**
If you find these animals, the water is very clean.

stonefly nymph — mayfly nymph

11 mm — 30 mm

2 **Pollution level 2: slightly dirty water**

caddis fly larva out of its case — 20 mm

caddis fly larva in its case

freshwater shrimp

26 mm — 55 mm

3 **Pollution level 3: very dirty water**

water louse — 20 mm

bloodworm

12 mm

4 **Pollution level 4: extremely polluted**

50 mm

sludgeworm

ring-tailed maggot

40 mm

5 **Pollution level 5: 'dead'**
If you find no visible sign of life, call this pollution level 5.

© Coles, Gott, Thornley/Collins Educational 1989   *Active Science Copymasters 2*   31

12 INVESTIGATIONS
12.5 Identifying rocks

Special instructions	Observation	Answer	
1 Test with a drop of hydrochloric acid.	Fizzes. Does not fizz.	Try step 2. Try step 4.	Sedimentary
2 Examine with a hand lens. Press with fingernails.	Hard, in beds or layers. Not hard, in beds or layers.	Limestone. Try step 3.	
3 Look closely.	Soft, white, fine-grained. Made of small spheres.	Chalk. Oolite.	
4 Examine with a hand lens.	Interlocking crystals randomly arranged. Crystals banded, or no crystals and layered.	Try step 5. Try step 8.	Igneous
5 Look closely.	Crystals visible to the naked eye. Crystals not visible to the naked eye.	Try step 6. Try step 7.	Plutonic Volcanic
6 Look closely.	Light minerals mainly, glassy quartz, common. Dark minerals mainly, glassy quartz, rare.	Granite. Gabbro.	
7 Look closely.	Dark in colour. Light in colour.	Basalt. Rhyolite.	
8 Look closely.	Interlocking or banded crystals. No crystals and layered.	Try step 9. Try step 10.	Meta-morphic
9 Look closely.	Thin bands; splits, giving wavy surface. Coarse bands, does not split easily.	Schist. Gneiss.	
10 Look closely.	Particles easily seen. Particles not visible to naked eye.	Try step 11. Try step 13.	Sedimentary
11 Look closely.	Particle size less than 2mm. Particle size more than 2mm.	Sandstone. Try step 12.	
12 Look closely.	Particles angular. Particles rounded.	Breccia. Conglomerate.	
13 Test by tapping with a hammer.	Soft. Not soft.	Clay. Try step 14.	
14 Try to break a piece off.	Breaks. Does not break.	Shale. Try step 15.	
15 Try to scratch glass with the rock.	Scratches glass. Does not scratch glass.	Try step 16. Try step 17.	
16 Look closely.	Surface carved. Rectangular shape.	Flint. Chert.	
17 Look closely.	Dark layers. Dark, not in layers.	Coal. Peat.	

32   © Coles, Gott, Thornley/Collins Educational 1989   *Active Science Copymasters 2*

12 INVESTIGATIONS
12.6 Animals living in groups

Many animals, like humans, live in groups. These groups have to be organised so that everyone knows their job in a group. Your school is one example of a human group. Can you answer these questions about it?

1 How is it organised?
2 Who tells who what to do?
3 What rules does it have?
4 What happens to anyone who breaks the rules?

Who's the boss?

Packs of dogs and flocks of chickens have a 'pecking order'. Each animal knows its place. Some members of its group are stronger and more powerful, while others are weaker. This order comes about in all sorts of ways, but often through a series of fights. If a new cock is put in with a group of chickens, the 'boss cock' will attack it to show who's on top of the pecking order. If the new bird loses, another cock may attack to try to get above the new cock in the pecking order.

● Look at these dogs. They have been drawn so that you can work out their position in the group. Decide by looking at the group where the dogs come in the 'pecking order'.

● Discuss these questions:
5 Do groups of humans have pecking orders?
6 What sort of things could be important in deciding a pecking order in humans?

© Coles, Gott, Thornley/Collins Educational 1989   *Active Science Copymasters 2*   33

12 INVESTIGATIONS
12.9A Soldering

1. Clean the tip of the soldering iron on a damp sponge.

2. Run a little solder on to the clean tip of the iron.

Soldering on etched circuits

3. Push the component wire through the drill hole.

resistor — plastic side — copper side

4. Hold the iron so that it touches the pin and the wire. Count to three slowly.

5. Run the solder on to the copper *and* the component.

solder

6. Let the solder set, then cut off any spare wire. Check that the joint looks soldered.

Soldering on a matrix board

3. Wrap the wire around the pin.

4. Hold the iron on the copper track and the component. Count to three slowly.

solder — wire — matrix board — matrix board pin

5. Run the solder on to the pin *and* the wire.

6. Let the solder set, then cut off any spare wire. Check that the solder has run into the joint properly.

34   © Coles, Gott, Thornley/Collins Educational 1989   *Active Science Copymasters 2*

12 INVESTIGATIONS
12.9B Testing a chip

1. This circuit uses a small chip called a 555.

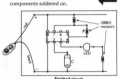
Circuit diagram

2. On chip circuits, the pins are not necessarily shown in the correct order. This chip circuit has been redesigned so that it can be etched.

Construction diagram

4. The circuit is etched and the components soldered on.

Finished circuit

3. The design is traced on to acetate film, with the lettering on the reverse side.

Circuit transparency to make the etched circuit

• Try different resistors and capacitors (at R and C) as shown in the table. Watch the LED and fill in the LED column.
• When you have done this with the LED, take

out the LED and the resistor next to it. Solder a piezo-electric buzzer between the two points marked X. Use it to fill in the buzzer column.

Resistor (R)	Capacitor (C)	LED (on or off)	Buzzer sound (yes or no)
1000 ohms	100 microfarads		
10000 ohms	100 microfarads		
100 ohms	100 microfarads		
1000 ohms	10 microfarads		
1000 ohms	1000 microfarads		

How it works

The 555 is a 'clock' chip. It produces pulses from pin 3. The speed of the pulses depends on the resistor at R and the capacitor at C. With a big capacitor and resistor you get slow pulses. You can see these with an LED. With smaller values you get fast pulses. You cannot see them with an LED. But they are too fast. But they are just right for a buzzer.

© Coles, Gott, Thornley/Collins Educational 1989 Active Science Copymasters 2   35

12 INVESTIGATIONS
12.9C Some other circuits to make

Flashing lights

You can make this circuit on a matrix board or by etching.

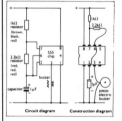

• Connect the + and − to a 4.5V or 9V battery. If the circuit doesn't work, check that:
  – the battery is the right way round,
  – the LEDs are the right way round,
  – the two capacitors are the right way round,
  – the two transistors are the right way round.
• Try putting in different resistors for the two centre 10kΩ ones (1kΩ or 100kΩ).
• Try putting in different capacitors (100μF).

A chip timer

This timer is in two parts: a buzzer and a time delay.

• First make the chip buzzer.

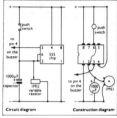
Circuit diagram   Construction diagram

• Then make the time delay.

Circuit diagram   Construction diagram

• Test the buzzer. It should buzz when the + and − are connected to a 9V battery.
• Connect pin 3 of the time delay to pin 3 of the buzzer.
• Connect together the + power line on the two circuits.
• Connect together the − line on both circuits.
• Connect the + and − terminals to a battery. A small 9V battery is best, but 4.5V will do.
• Press the push switch (and let it go) to start timing.

• Twist the variable resistor. The buzzer should sound.
• Now set the variable resistor about halfway round.
• Press the push switch and let it go. The buzzer should go off after 5-10 minutes. With practice, you can set the resistor to time eggs for boiling.
• If it does not work, check for short circuits (where solder has joined to tracks by mistake) and dry joints (where a wire is not soldered).

36   © Coles, Gott, Thornley/Collins Educational 1989 Active Science Copymasters 2

12 INVESTIGATIONS
12.10 Making paper 1

You can recycle waste newspapers to make fresh paper. You will need:
– an old newspaper
– a bowl
– hot water from a kettle ⚠
– a wooden spoon
– a fine-mesh sheet fixed on to a wooden frame (this will be your sieve)
– clean cotton cloths
– an electric iron ⚠
– a liquidiser
– wallpaper paste powder (optional)

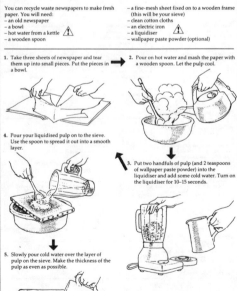

1. Take three sheets of newspaper and tear them up into small pieces. Put the pieces in a bowl.

2. Pour on hot water and mash the paper with a wooden spoon. Let the pulp cool.

3. Put two handfuls of pulp (and 2 teaspoons of wallpaper paste powder) into the liquidiser and add some cold water. Turn on the liquidiser for 10–15 seconds.

4. Pour your liquidised pulp on to the sieve. Use the spoon to spread it out into a smooth layer.

5. Slowly pour cold water over the layer of pulp on the sieve. Make the thickness of the pulp as even as possible.

© Coles, Gott, Thornley/Collins Educational 1989 Active Science Copymasters 2   37

12 INVESTIGATIONS
12.10 Making paper 2

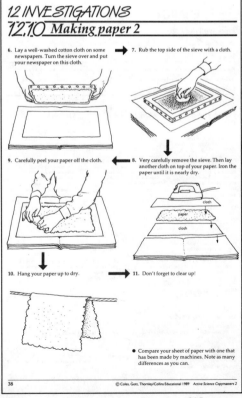

6. Lay a well-washed cotton cloth on some newspapers. Turn the sieve over and put your newspaper on this cloth.

7. Rub the top side of the sieve with a cloth.

8. Very carefully remove the sieve. Then lay another cloth on top of your paper. Iron the paper until it is nearly dry.

9. Carefully peel your paper off the cloth.

10. Hang your paper up to dry.

11. Don't forget to clear up!

• Compare your sheet of paper with one that has been made by machines. Note as many differences as you can.

38   © Coles, Gott, Thornley/Collins Educational 1989 Active Science Copymasters 2

Unit 7 HEALTH

How well did I do?

My name _____   My form _____

Basic skills

If you think you have been successful at any of these skills, tick the box and ask your teacher to check:

I have successfully:

tested for protein, glucose, starch and fat (7.1) ☐
drawn a bar chart on energy use (7.2) ☐
tested milk for sourness with Resazurin (7.3) ☐
drawn a bar or pie chart or a line graph about illnesses (7.8) ☐

Communicating and interpreting

Tick one box for each:

7.4 Where the food goes

I drew a flowchart showing the main things that happened to the food. ☐ ○

I drew a flowchart that showed what happened at each stage. I labelled each box. I wrote about what happened at each stage and how long it took. ☐ ●

7.8 Sickness and health

Which activity I did _____

Write a sentence saying how well you think you did.
_____
_____

Observing

Tick one box for each:

7.4 Ways of preserving food

I looked at the food at home and made a list of foods that last a long time. ☐ ○

I looked at the food at home that lasts a long time. I worked out what had been done to the food to make it last. ☐ ●

7.5 Teeth

I looked at the teeth and described what they do. ☐ ○

I looked at the teeth. I thought about what the animals eat. I described how the shape of the teeth helps the animals eat. ☐ ●

Planning investigations

Tick one box for each:

7.2 Water in living things

My plan was to use bits of meat and plant and find out how much water there was in them. ☐ ○

My plan was to use the same amount of fresh meat and plant. I would dry them to get all the water out. I would weigh them before and after drying. ☐ ●

7.6 Comparing toothbrushes

My plan was to use the two toothbrushes and see how well they cleaned my teeth. ☐ ○

My plan was to use the two brushes with the same amount of toothpaste. I would brush my teeth for the same length of time with the two brushes. I would do it at the same time but on different days. I would use disclosing tablets to see how clean my teeth were. ☐ ●

Unit 7

Investigating and making

Tick one box for each:

7.3 Extras I: Food preferences of birds

I put different foods out and looked to see which type the birds liked best. ☐ ○

I put out equal amounts of different foods. I counted how many birds went to each one. (Or I weighed how much food had been eaten.) ☐ ●

7.5 Saliva at work

I used saliva at different temperatures and tested to see how well it worked. I tried to find out if chewing or the type of food made any difference. ☐ ○

I used saliva at two or more temperatures with the same amount of the same type of food. I tested the food after a sensible length of time. I used the glucose test I had been shown. I did the same sort of experiment to see if chewing or the type of food made any difference. ☐ ●

7.8 Testing the model leg

My model leg was OK, but it didn't work very well. I tried to change it to make it work better. ☐ ○

I made my model leg well. I changed the position of the muscle to see if I could make it work better. I used the results to decide on the best design for making the ball go a long way or go high. ☐ ●

Did I get involved in the work?

Tick any boxes you think you did well at:

I talked well about scientific things. ☐	I have been curious to find out about things. ☐
I wrote well about scientific things. ☐	I have been quick to settle down. ☐
I discussed problems with my friends. ☐	I have been good at finishing things off. ☐
I discussed problems with my teacher. ☐	I have been helpful in lessons. ☐
I worked well with my group in practicals. ☐	I have been good at making notes in my book. ☐

What did I learn?

The most important things I have learned from this unit are:	The things I had most difficulty with were:

Unit test

My mark was _____   I think this is:

good for me. ☐   about what I expected. ☐   not so good for me. ☐

Teacher's comments:

Unit 8 ENERGY

How well did I do?

My name _____   My form _____

Basic skills

If you think you have been successful at any of these skills, tick the box and ask your teacher to check:

I have successfully: drawn a pie chart of energy usage (8.5) ☐   tested leaves for starch (8.6) ☐

Communicating and interpreting

Tick one box for each:

8.4 Making fuels into electricity

I wrote about how electricity is made. I used the information in the book and from my teacher. ☐ ○

I wrote about how electricity is made and about its good and bad points. I used information from several sources. I tried to make it interesting for young children by including diagrams and drawings. ☐ ●

8.8 Is cost everything?

I decided which stove would be the best for each place. ☐ ○

I thought about what would be needed for each journey before I decided which stove would be best. I wrote about how I had decided on my choice. ☐ ●

8.11 Five-minute special

My group made a tape that had some information in about the good and bad things about a nuclear power station. ☐ ○

My group made a tape which had information from many places in it. We made it interesting. We tried to include arguments in favour and against the power station. We tried to make it fair. ☐ ●

Observing

Tick one box for each:

8.7 Identifying small animals

I could identify some common animals. I could decide which groups to put others in. ☐ ○

I could identify most of the animals. I decided which group to put each of them in. Then I looked at them more closely to decide which animal it was in the group. ☐ ●

8.9 Saving money at home

I looked around at home and made a list of some ways of saving heat. ☐ ○

I thought about the different ways heat could escape from our home. I looked around to see where heat would escape most easily and if we had done anything to try to stop it. ☐ ●

Planning investigations

Tick one box for each:

8.6 Extras I: Geranium plants and starch

My plan was to: put the plants in different-coloured light and looked to see how they grew. ☐ ○

put the plants in different-coloured light. I would make the light the same brightness. I would leave the plants for several days and then measure how much starch there was in the leaves. ☐ ●

8.8 Which is cheapest?

My plan was to: use each stove and see how fast it heated the water. ☐ ○

use both stoves to heat the same amounts of water. I would time how long they took to make the water boil. ☐ ●

Unit 8

Investigating and making

Tick one box for each:

8.2 Comparing fuels

I used both sorts of fuel and tried to find out which heated things best. ☐ ○

I heated the same amount of water with different fuels for the same length of time (or until the water boiled). I used the same amount of fuel in each test. I measured how hot the water became, or how long it took to boil. ☐ ●

8.7 Making a good compost heap

I made two compost heaps. I put accelerator on one heap and not on the other. I looked to see what happened. ☐ ○

I made two identical compost heaps. I put accelerator on one and followed the instructions on the packet. I left the heaps for several weeks and then looked to see how rotten the plants were and how many little animals there were in them. ☐ ●

8.10 A solar heater

The design for my solar heater was OK, but it didn't work very well. ☐ ○

My design was good and it worked well. I used ideas from the pictures in the book. I worked out a way of testing to see how well the heater worked and compared it with other people's. ☐ ●

Did I get involved in the work?

Tick any boxes you think you did well at:

I talked well about scientific things. ☐	I have been curious to find out about things. ☐
I wrote well about scientific things. ☐	I have been quick to settle down. ☐
I discussed problems with my friends. ☐	I have been good at finishing things off. ☐
I discussed problems with my teacher. ☐	I have been helpful in lessons. ☐
I worked well with my group in practicals. ☐	I have been good at making notes in my book. ☐

What did I learn?

The most important things I have learned from this unit are:	The things I had most difficulty with were:

Unit test

My mark was _____   I think this is:

good for me. ☐   about what I expected. ☐   not so good for me. ☐

Teacher's comments:

Unit 9 SENSES

How well did I do?

My name_____ My form_____

Basic skills

If you think you have been successful at any of these skills, tick the box and ask your teacher to check:

I have successfully: made a pinhole camera – following instructions ☐   used a microscope (9.3) ☐
(worksheet 9.2B)

Communicating and interpreting

Tick one box for each:

9.2 A shadow theatre

I wrote about one of my experiments and included some data. ☐ ○

I wrote about all my experiments. I included data in tables and wrote about what the data told me. I summarised all my results at the end so that I knew what I had found out. ☐ ●

9.10 Images

We designed a logo that created an image. We showed it to other groups, but they didn't think the image was right. ☐ ○

We thought about the image we wanted, then we designed our logo. Other groups thought that it gave the right sort of image. ☐ ●

Observing

Tick one box for each:

9.2 Extras I: Coloured objects in street lights

I noticed that the colours of the objects were different in the street light. ☐ ○

I noticed that some objects seemed to change colour in one sort of street light. Other objects seemed to change colour in a different coloured light. I tried to see if there was any connection between the colour of the object in ordinary light and what happened to it in the street light. ☐ ●

9.3 Extras 3: Looking at things in water

I noticed that things seemed to look different in water. ☐ ○

I noticed that things looked different where they entered the water. The pencil seemed to bend at the surface. I decided this was something to do with the fact that light rays bend when they go into water or glass. ☐ ●

Investigating and making

Tick one box for each:

9.4 Far vision

I asked somebody to read different-sized print at different distances and found out how far away they could still read it. ☐ ○

I asked several people to read several sizes of writing, from small to large. I measured how far away the people were when they just couldn't read it any more in the same lighting conditions. ☐ ●

9.6 Musical instruments

I made an instrument that would play different sounds. ☐ ○

I made an instrument on which I could play a tune. I used ideas in the book to help me start, but I changed things to match the apparatus I could find. I made a sounding board to make the sound louder. ☐ ●

9.7 Imitating touch

I made something for picking up eggs, but it would have broken a lot of them. ☐ ○

I made something that was based on the ideas in the book. I made it so that I could change the force on the egg to stop it breaking. ☐ ●

Unit 9

Planning investigations

Tick one box for each:

9.4 Extras 4: Can adults see further than children?

My plan was to:

ask an old person and a young one to look at something a long way off. ☐ ○

measure how far away several old people and several young people could read a book. I thought I would need more than one person because people's eyes are different even when the people are the same age. ☐ ●

9.5 A sound detector

My plan was to:

pass sound through the different materials and see which stopped it most. ☐ ○

pass the same sound through same-sized pieces of the different materials and measure the height of the trace on the oscilloscope screen for each one. ☐ ●

9.7 Tasting tea

My plan was to:

see if one person could tell the difference between tea that had milk in first and tea that had it in afterwards. ☐ ○

see if several people could tell the difference in the taste of tea if milk was put in first or second. I would use the same quantities of tea and milk and make sure the tea was the same strength. ☐ ●

Did I get involved in the work?

Tick any boxes you think you did well at:

I talked well about scientific things. ☐
I wrote well about scientific things. ☐
I discussed problems with my friends. ☐
I discussed problems with my teacher. ☐
I worked well with my group in practicals. ☐

I have been curious to find out about things. ☐
I have been quick to settle down. ☐
I have been good at finishing things off. ☐
I have been helpful in lessons. ☐
I have been good at making notes in my book. ☐

What did I learn?

The most important things I have learned from this unit are:	The things I had most difficulty with were:

Unit test

My mark was _____   I think this is:
good for me. ☐   about what I expected. ☐   not so good for me. ☐

Teacher's comments:

Unit 7 HEALTH

The first three questions are about information in the reference section for this Unit.

1 This question is about fighting illness (Reference 3, page 26).

Look at the graph of death rate from diphtheria in England and Wales.

(a) When was the death rate from diphtheria at its highest?

(b) When did the national immunisation campaign begin?

(c) Describe what the graph shows about the effect of the campaign.

2 This question is about the effect of smoking on health (Reference 4, page 27).

(a) What percentage of 12-year-old boys in the survey smoke?

(b) What percentage of women had never smoked when they were asked in 1982?

3 For this question you will need to find out where the information is in the reference section before you can answer the questions.

(a) How many deaths were caused by accidents at work every year?

(b) How many people over 65 years old died in fires at home in 1986?

(c) Look at the information about people of different ages who die from falling at home.

What pattern can you see in the information?

Can you suggest any reasons for this pattern?

The rest of the test does not refer to the reference section.

4 Jim, Fred, Sara and Winston were having their lunch. This is what they had.

JIM   sausage and chips
         cup of tea

FRED   fish and chips
         stewed apple and custard
         milk

SARA   glass of water
         egg and chips
         sponge pudding and custard

WINSTON a pork chop, mashed potatoes and cabbage
         peaches and ice cream
         Coke

(a) Who was having a 'square' meal?

(b) Why do you think that?

5 These labels are from some popular breakfast cereals.

(a) Which cereal contains most iron?

(b) Which vitamins are in all of the cereals?

(c) Make a table to show the energy (in kJ) for each of the cereals.

Kellogg's Country Store

Typical Nutritional Composition per 100g			
Energy	346kcal (1470kJ)	Available Carbohydrate	67.5g
Protein (N × 6.25)	11.4g	Vitamins:	
Fat	5.3g	Niacin	8.1mg
Dietary Fibre	5.6g	Riboflavin (B₂)	0.9mg
		Thiamin (B₁)	0.7mg
		Iron	9.6mg

Kellogg's Frosties

Typical Nutritional Composition per 100g	
Energy	355kcal (1515kJ)
Protein (N × 6.25)	5.3g
Niacin	16.0mg
Vitamin B₆	1.8mg
Riboflavin (B₂)	1.5mg
Thiamin (B₁)	1.0mg
Folic Acid	250µg
Vitamin D	2.8µg
Vitamin B₁₂	1.7µg
Iron	6.7mg

Kellogg's Ricicles

Typical Nutritional Composition per 100g	
Energy	354kcal (1510kJ)
Protein (N × 5.95)	4.3g
Niacin	16.0mg
Vitamin B₆	1.8mg
Riboflavin (B₂)	1.5mg
Thiamin (B₁)	1.0mg
Folic Acid	250µg
Vitamin D	2.8µg
Vitamin B₁₂	1.7µg
Iron	6.7mg

Kellogg's Rice Krispies

Typical Nutritional Composition per 100g	
Energy	351kcal (1500kJ)
Protein (N × 5.95)	6.2g
Niacin	16.0mg
Vitamin B₆	1.8mg
Riboflavin (B₂)	1.5mg
Thiamin (B₁)	1.0mg
Folic Acid	250µg
Vitamin D	2.8µg
Vitamin B₁₂	1.7µg
Iron	6.7mg

Kellogg's Crunchy Nut Flakes

Typical Nutritional Composition per 100g	
Energy	378kcal (1605kJ)
Protein (N × 6.25)	7.4g
Niacin	16.0mg
Vitamin B₆	1.8mg
Riboflavin (B₂)	1.5mg
Thiamin (B₁)	1.0mg
Folic Acid	250µg
Vitamin D	2.8µg
Vitamin B₁₂	1.7µg
Iron	6.7mg

Weetabix

An average serving of two Weetabix (37.5g) provides at least one sixth of the daily recommended requirements for the average adult of the vitamins listed and iron.

Typical Nutritional Composition per 100g			
Fat	2.0g	Dietary Fibre	12.9g
Protein	10.5g	Vitamins:	
Available		Niacin	10.0mg
Carbohydrate	66.8g	Riboflavin (B₂)	1.0mg
Energy	1400kJ	Thiamin (B₁)	0.7mg
	335kcal	Iron	6.0mg

Unit 7

6 John and Nasrin did some fitness tests at school.

They devised their own test to see how fit everybody's arm muscles were.

They asked some people in their class to lie flat on the ground, face up. Then they gave each person an identical weight and told them to throw it as far as possible. But they told people not to move their shoulders from the floor.

Here are their results:

Name	Distance (metres)
John	6
Maria	5
Nargis	4.5
Alexander	8
Nico	4
Sarah	4
Ali	6.5
Edward	6
Diana	3
Carl	6
Jim	7
Debbie	3.5
Fatima	3

(a) Make two tables to show this information (one for the boys and one for the girls).

(b) What do you think the results of this investigation show?

7 The information below is from a leaflet about protecting children from dangerous diseases.

Preventing disease

Children should be given a series of injections or other treatments at different ages and for different diseases. Between 2½ and 6 months of age, babies can be immunised against diphtheria, tetanus and whooping cough. An oral vaccine (one that you take by mouth rather than by injection) against polio is given at the same time. These treatments need to be boosted by a second dose between 4 and 8 months and a third at 10 to 14 months. A fourth boost is given at the age of 5 years (except for whooping cough).

Protection against measles is normally given when babies are between 1 and 2 years old. The remaining injections, against tuberculosis and, for girls, German measles, are usually made available during the first two years at secondary school.

Make up a timetable for the various treatments to remind you when they should be given.

8 Gordon played hockey for the school team. He was quite good at dribbling, but he couldn't hit the ball very hard.

A friend said that Gordon might be able to hit the ball harder with a heavier hockey stick.

Gordon decided to try a heavier stick.

Write a plan for an investigation that Gordon could do to help him decide whether a heavier stick was better, and how much better.

Unit 7

9 This is part of a leaflet about minor illnesses.

Vomiting

Vomiting may be caused by a virus infection of the stomach, by eating too much, and by drinking too much. It usually stops within 24 hours, but in some cases may be followed by diarrhoea.

Some children vomit when they have a temperature, which may be caused by tonsillitis or an ear infection.

Treatment:
Eat nothing.
Drink small quantities of water every two hours. As the stomach settles take semi-solid food such as dry biscuits, bread or breakfast cereals) before gradually returning to a normal diet.

When to see the doctor:
If vomiting is accompanied by continuous stomach pain
If vomiting lasts for more than 24 hours
If a vomiting child has a temperature of more than 38°C or 100°F
If the patient or parent is unduly anxious

(a) What are the three main causes of vomiting (sickness)?

(b) How long does it usually last?

(c) What should you do if you are sick?

(d) When should you consult a doctor about vomiting?

10 Julia is a journalist. She travelled to Austria, Mexico, Chile and Jordan to get a story for her newspaper. When she got back home, she began to feel ill.

(a) You are Julia's doctor. You think she may have caught malaria on her travels. Look at the table on the right. An r means somebody could catch the disease in that country. Could Julia have caught malaria? If so, where?

Now look at page 52.

(b) How can people catch malaria?

(c) What precautions should Julia have taken to avoid catching malaria?

Your health protection checklist

This alphabetical list shows for each country in the world:

r = You could catch the disease in that country.

Country	Cholera	Malaria	Typhoid	Polio	Yellow fever
Afghanistan	r	r	r	*
Albania			r	r	
Algeria	r	r	r	r	
Angola	r	r	r	r	Except children under 1 year old
Antilles, Neth.			r	r	
Argentina	r	r	r		
Australia				r	
Austria				r	
Azores				r	
Bahamas			r	r	*
Bahrain	r		r	r	*
Bangladesh	r	r	r	r	*
Barbados			r	r	*
Belgium				r	
Belize			r	r	r
Benin	r	r	r	r	Except children under 1 year old
Bermuda				r	
Bhutan	r	r	r	r	*
Bolivia	r	r	r	r	If going to Santa Cruz de la Sierra
Botswana	r	r	r	r	*
Brazil			r	r	*
Brunei	r		r	r	*
Canada				r	
Canal Zone, Panama			r	r	*
Canary Islands				r	
Cape Verde Islands	r		r	r	*
Cayman Islands			r	r	*
Central African Republic	r	r	r	r	Except children under 1 year old
Chad	r	r	r	r	*
Chile			r	r	
China			r	r	*
Colombia		r	r	r	*
Comoros	r	r	r		
Jamaica			r	r	*
Japan			r	r	
Jordan	r		r	r	
Kampuchea	r		r	r	
Kenya	r	r	r	r	*
Kiribati			r	r	*
Korea (North)	r		r	r	
Korea (South)	r		r	r	
Kuwait	r		r	r	
Mauritius		r	r	r	*
Mexico		r	r	r	*
Monaco				r	
Mongolia			r	r	
Montserrat			r	r	*
Morocco	r	r	r	r	*
Mozambique	r	r	r	r	*
Namibia			r	r	*
Nauru			r	r	*
Nepal	r	r	r	r	*
[...]					

*A certificate may be required if you have passed through a country where yellow fever is present.

Malaria warning!

You can get malaria, if bitten by an infected mosquito, in many parts of Africa, Asia, Central and South America.

So here's what to do if you visit a malarial country – or even stopover there:

● Ask your doctor about anti-malarial tablets
● Take the tablets before, during and after your visit
● Continue taking them for a month after you return
● Avoid mosquito bites

Keep arms and legs covered when outdoors after sunset. Sleep in screened accommodation or use mosquito nets. Use insect repellants and knock-down sprays.

Following this advice could prevent serious illness – particularly in children.

Diseases and precautions

	Risk areas	How caught	Vaccination	Vaccination certificate needed?	Revaccination	Other precautions
Cholera	Asia, Asia, Middle East especially in conditions of poor hygiene and sanitation.	Contaminated food or water.	Usually 2 injections by your doctor.	Some countries may require evidence of vaccination within previous 6 months if there have been any cholera outbreaks in countries through which you have travelled. Check before you go.	Every 6 months until you return.	Vaccination does not guarantee full protection, so take scrupulous care over food and drink.
Infectious hepatitis	Most parts of the world, in conditions of poor hygiene and sanitation.	Contaminated food or water or contact with an infected person.	Get advice from your doctor.	No.		Take scrupulous care over food, drink and hygiene.
Malaria	Africa, Asia, Central and South America.	Bite from infected mosquito.	None, but anti-malarial tablets are available.			
Polio	Everywhere except Australia, New Zealand, Europe, North America.	Direct contact with an infected person; rarely by contaminated water or food.	3 doses of drops in your doctor, taken at 4–8 week intervals.	No.	May be needed after 10 years. Ask your doctor.	Take scrupulous care over food and drink.
Rabies	Many parts of the world.	Bite or scratch from infected animal.				
Tetanus	Places where medical facilities not readily available.	Open injury.	Get advice from your doctor.	No.		Wash any wound thoroughly.
Typhoid	Outside Australia, New Zealand, Europe, North America in conditions of poor hygiene and sanitation.	Contaminated food, water or milk.	2 injections from your doctor, at an interval of 4–6 weeks. If you have to go abroad urgently, the interval can be reduced to 10 days.	No.	Usually after 3 years (one injection only).	Take scrupulous care over food and drink.
Yellow fever	Africa, South America.	Bite from infected mosquito.	1 injection at a Yellow Fever Vaccination Centre at least 10 days before you go abroad. To make an appointment for vaccination telephone your nearest centre.	Yes – see checklist. Other countries may ask for a certificate if you have passed through a country where yellow fever is present. Check before you go.	After 10 years.	Avoid mosquito bites, as for malaria.

N.B. Smallpox has been eradicated worldwide and there is no requirement for the vaccination of travellers.

Unit 8 ENERGY

1 The table shows the amount of energy in some vegetables.

Vegetable (100g)	Energy content (kilojoules)
Baked beans	300
Carrots	100
Tomatoes	60
Lettuce	40

Draw a bar chart to show this information.

2 The chart shows how an average British family uses energy.

heating the house
cooking
food
transport
heating water
electrical goods

(a) What uses the least energy?

(b) What uses about 25% of the energy?

(c) About how much of the energy is used in heating the house? Is it 20%, 40% or 60%?

3 Central heating can use gas, solid fuel (coke, for instance), oil or electricity.

Pick one of these.

Write a paragraph about your choice. You should mention both the good and bad things about it.

4 The bar chart shows the average amount of energy needed daily by boys and girls of different ages.

☐ boys
☐ girls

Daily amount of energy (kJ) — Age (years): 0–1 1–2 2–3 3–5 5–7 7–9 9–12 12–15 15–18

(a) How much energy does a 4-year-old boy need?

(b) How much energy does an 18-year-old girl need?

(c) Write a sentence about the pattern that the chart shows. Why do you think the pattern is like that?

5 Sheila's coalman said that small pieces of coal give out more heat than larger pieces. His competitor said that smokeless fuel is better than coal.

Sheila decided to find out which fuel was better. This is what she did.

She took two large pieces of coal and a piece of smokeless fuel. All three pieces were the same size. She broke one of the pieces of coal into small pieces. Then she burnt the large piece of coal, the broken piece of coal and the smokeless fuel under three pans of water. She made sure that each pan had the same amount of water.

Then she measured the temperature of the water in each pan after its fuel had burnt away. Here are the results.

	Start temp. (°C)	End temp. (°C)	Time to burn away (mins)
Small pieces of coal	20	56	8
One large piece of coal	20	48	13
One large piece of smokeless fuel	20	42	9

(a) Which fuel burned for the longest time?

(b) By how much did the temperature of the water rise for smokeless fuel?

(c) Write a sentence for Sheila saying what she found out.

Unit 8

6 Toy cars often have springs inside them that you can wind up with a key. As the spring unwinds, it makes the car move.

The spring is a store of energy. The more energy in the spring, the further the car goes.

Write a plan for an investigation to find out how the distance the toy car moves depends on the number of turns of the key.

7 Before steam engines, factories used energy from water to drive water wheels.

There were several types.

Undershot wheels

Undershot wheels

These were the earliest and most basic in design. The speed of the water is used to push the wheel. These wheels are not very efficient.

Breast-shot wheels

These were developed from the undershot wheels. They are more efficient because the water hits the wheel in the middle. This means that the weight of the water helps to move the wheel. But they were more expensive and complicated to make so they weren't used much.

Breast-shot wheels

water

Overshot wheels

These were very much more efficient designs. The water comes to the top of the wheel. It falls into the paddles, which are shaped like buckets. The weight of the water forces the wheel round. Then the buckets empty at the bottom.

Overshot wheels

(a) What are the main differences between the three sorts of wheel?

(b) The overshot wheel is the most efficient. What do you think that means?

(c) What makes the overshot wheel more efficient? Write a sentence in your own words.

Unit 8

8 Mrs Green was explaining to her children about atom bombs and nuclear power stations.

(a) How does energy come out of an atom bomb?

(b) How can cancer be caused thousands of miles away from the explosion?

(c) Radiation isn't always a bad thing. What does Mrs Green mention that is a good use of radiation?

A bomb is a bit like a nuclear power station, except that all the energy comes out in one big bang.

Some of the energy comes out of the bomb as heat, light and sound. Some comes out as a big shock wave – like a huge wind – that knocks things down.

Some of the energy comes out as radiation. Radiation is like invisible rays that can go right through you. They can damage your body cells so that you die of cancer a long time after. Hospitals can use these rays, called X-rays and gamma rays, but they aren't very strong. Hospitals use them to photograph bones or other parts of the body and to kill cancer cells that are already there.

When a bomb goes off, a lot of radioactive dust gets into the atmosphere. This is what happened when the nuclear power station at Chernobyl in Russia exploded. The dust eventually comes down in rain. It might come down many miles away. In a few weeks, the dust from Chernobyl reached as far as the Lake District in Britain.

This dust gives off radiation all the time. It can fall on the grass and be eaten by sheep and cows. And if we eat their meat or drink their milk, then it gets into our body. The radiation from the dust could cause cancer.

9 The information below is about one sort of Ford car. It comes with a choice of different features and with different engines. The table tells you about:

– whether the cars use petrol or diesel fuel
– the cars' top speed
– how quickly they can speed up (acceleration)
– how much fuel they use
– how much the cars weigh

Look carefully at the table. Your job is to advise different customers about buying a car to suit their needs. Often they aren't sure about whether to buy a diesel or a petrol car.

(a) Write a list of the good and bad things about petrol and diesel cars.

(b) A woman comes along wanting to buy a car to use as a taxi. What would you advise her to buy. Why?

Car type	Top speed (mph)	Acceleration 0–60 mph (secs)	How much fuel they use (miles per gallon) at 56 mph	Weight (kg)
Three-door				
1.3 Petrol			57.6	
1.6 Diesel	98	13.5	70.6	1275
	91	16.6		1350
Five-door				
1.3 Petrol			57.6	
1.6 Diesel	98	13.5	70.6	1300
	91	16.6		1375
Three-door estates				
1.3 Petrol			56.5	
1.6 Diesel	96	14.0	68.9	1350
	89	17.1		1425
Five-door estates				
1.3 Petrol			56.5	
1.6 Diesel	96	14.0	68.9	1350
	89	17.1		1425

Unit 8

10 Mr Aziz was getting some big fuel bills. And he was getting worried about them. He decided to find out where his house was losing most heat.

He put thermometers in four rooms in his house. Then he used the central heating to get all the rooms warm, and he shut the doors. He switched the heating off and measured the temperature in each of the rooms every hour for 8 hours.

His results are shown in the four graphs.

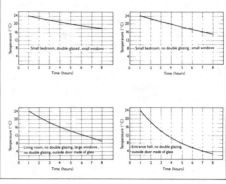

(a) The temperature in the entrance hall fell from 24°C to 3°C. This is a fall of 21°C.

Make a table like the one below to show the change in temperature for all of the rooms. It is started for you.

(b) Which room's temperature fell the least? Which room's temperature fell the most?

(c) Look at the information about each of the rooms. Why do you think the room temperatures changed like this?

(d) Write a sentence describing the pattern in the graph for the hall. Can you explain why the pattern is like that?

(e) What do you think the temperature outside was?

Room	Fall in temperature (°C)
Entrance hall	21

Unit 9 SENSES

1 Read this passage about lighting in rooms and then answer the questions.

There are two sorts of lights for use in houses and factories. The first uses filament lamps like the ones in most homes. The second type is strip lighting which is common in schools and offices.

The light from a strip lamp actually flashes on and off fifty times per second. This is so fast that you don't notice it. But if you are using a machine – a sewing machine or a lathe, for instance – the flashing can have odd effects.

As the light flashes, it can make a moving part – the needle in the sewing machine, for instance – look as if it is not moving. You get a similar effect when you see wagon wheels on television in a cowboy film. They can look as if they are not moving, or even going backwards.

Filament lamps don't do this. The law says that all machines in factories must have a filament lamp shining on the moving parts.

(a) What are the two types of lighting?

(b) How fast does a strip light flash on and off?

(c) What effect can this flashing seem to have?

(d) Why do you think the law says that all machines should have filament lamps? What might happen if they didn't?

2 Anna and her family were watching some slides from their holidays. After they had finished, she made shadows on the screen with cardboard shapes.

(a) She held the shape halfway between the projector and the screen. How big would the shadow be on the screen?

(b) What happens to the shadow as she moves the shape closer to the projector?

(c) Then she fastened the shape onto a piece of cotton. It twisted round slowly in the beam of the projector.

Describe what happens to the shadow as the shape turns one complete circle.

3 Here is some information about what you see if you look into different mirrors and lenses.

		What a distant object looks like	What a near object looks like
	Concave mirror	upside down and smaller	right way up and bigger
	Convex mirror	right way up and smaller	right way up and smaller
	Concave lens	right way up and smaller	right way up and smaller
	Convex lens	upside down and smaller	right way up and bigger

Use the information to answer the questions.

(a) What would a near object look like in a concave lens?

(b) What sort of mirror would you use to make an object look the right way up at any distance?

(c) Which type of mirror or lens would you choose for looking behind you when you are riding your bike? Explain why you chose that one.

Unit 9

4 Sally and Jim did an investigation to see whether they could taste things better if they could smell them as well.

Sally put a peg on Jim's nose and blindfolded him. Then she gave him a little bit of five different foods. He wrote down what he thought each of them was.

Then Sally did the same thing again, but without the peg. She gave the foods in a different order this time.

Here are their results.

Food	With peg	Without peg
A	✓	✓
B	✗	✓
C	✗	✓
D	✓	✓
E	✗	✗

✓ means that Jim recognised the food.
✗ means that he didn't or that he got it wrong.

(a) Why did Sally blindfold Jim?

(b) Why did she give the foods in a different order the second time?

(c) Use the results in the table to explain what Sally and Jim found out.

5 Modern rooms often have spotlighting from the ceiling on to different parts of the room. A simple spotlight is just an ordinary light bulb in a tube, like in the diagrams on the right.

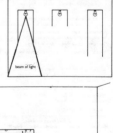

(a) Copy the diagrams. On each one draw in where the light will shine. The first one is done for you.

(b) Should the inside of the tube be shiny or black? Explain your answer.

(c) Suppose you want to put a spotlight on your ceiling to shine on a fish tank.

Copy the sketch of the room and draw in a tube spotlight with the bulb in the right position so that the beam just covers the fish tank.

beam of light

Unit 9

6 You are in charge of a TV quiz game. People in the audience keep on shouting the answers out, and your boss is getting cross because the contestants keep winning and the quiz is losing a lot of money.

You decide that you will have to make a soundproof booth for the contestants so that they won't be able to hear anything shouted from the audience.

Do a design for a box. Say what materials you would use for each bit of the box. Don't make it so that your contestant will suffocate as he or she answers the questions!

7 Some people say that sound carries for much greater distances over water than it does over land.

(a) Write a plan for an investigation to find whether this is true or not.

(b) Can you think of any reasons why it might be true!

8 Binoculars have numbers written on them to tell you something about them. For example, with 10×50. This means that they make things 10 times bigger. The second number, 50, tells you how big the lenses are, in millimetres. Binoculars with big lenses can collect more light and so the image is brighter.

50mm

Here is some information from a mail-order catalogue about different sorts of binoculars.

Type	Specification	Cost (£)	Features
A	10×50	30	10-year guarantee
B	12×50	33	10-year guarantee
C	16×50	35	10-year guarantee
D	8×30	20	10-year guarantee
E	8×30	43	Multicoated optics, lifetime guarantee
F	8×21	40	Rubber-protected for heavy use

(a) Which type will make things biggest?

(b) Which type would be worst for using in the early evening as the light fades?

(c) Look at the column in the table that tells you how much the binoculars cost. Why do the different binoculars cost different amounts?

9 Adam and his friends had invented a secret code. They used it to send messages to each other at dinner times.

His friends were called: James, Chi, Simon, Ahmed, Brian, Fatima, Penelope, Wendy, Maria.

The code for 'James' was ⊻ ◇ ⌒⌒ ℰ ⟨

Who is ⟨ ⊕ ⌒⌒ ▽ ⎰ !

10 If a ray of light goes from water into air, it changes direction as it leaves the water. The diagram shows this.

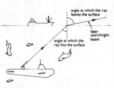

angle at which the ray leaves the surface

angle at which the ray hits the surface

laser searchlight beam

The table shows what happens at different angles.

Angle ray hits surface (°)	Angle ray leaves surface (°)
10	13
20	25
30	39
40	53
50	73

(a) At what angle does a ray leave the surface if it hits it at 20°?

(b) A ray leaves the surface at 53°. At what angle did it hit the surface?

(c) Draw a line graph for the data. Use the graph to work out what angle a ray must hit the surface if it leaves the surface at 35°.

Unit 10 SUBSTANCES

1 The pie chart shows the main uses of sulphuric acid.

fertilisers (30%)   other uses (30%)

cleaning (2%)
plastics (5%)
fibres (8%)
paints (11%)

detergent (14%)

Use the information from the pie chart to complete the table below. Put the uses in order with the biggest use first. The table has been started for you.

Use	Percentage
Other uses	30

2 Here is some information from a gardening book about different sorts of soils.

Soil type	Appearance	Physical qualities	Chemical qualities
Clay soil	Soil lies under water in wet weather. Sedges, rushes, buttercup, alder, willow in evidence.	Very slow to drain. Sticky, greasy if wet or hard and lumpy when dry.	Rich in plant food. Frequently neutral.
Heavy loam	Between clay and medium loam		
Medium loam	Strong-growing roses, shrubs and grasses.	Drains moderately quickly. Easy to dig over.	Usually well supplied with plant food.
Light loam	Intermediate between medium and sandy soil		
Sandy soil	Light coloured soil. Gorse, broom and Scots pine. Heather in acid sands.	Quick draining. Easily worked in most conditions. Gritty to the touch.	Low level in nutrients. Often very acid. Needs fertiliser.
Chalk or limestone soil	White or whitish subsoil. Dogwood, viburnum and clematis grow well.	Chalk is pasty when moist. Limestone is gritty to the touch.	Low in organic matter. Alkaline.
Peaty soil	Dark, fibrous soil. Alder and willow trees often present.	Spongy and fibrous.	Low in phosphates. Often acid.
Stony soil	Often light-coloured. Many stones on surface. Sparse vegetation. Mountain ash present.	Shallow soils with lots of rocks and stones.	Low nutrient content. Needs lots of fertiliser.

(a) Which soil is often very acid?

(b) Which soil is very slow to drain?

(c) Which soil will roses grow well in!

(d) What is a chalk soil like? What plants will grow well in it?

3 Here are the pH values of some everyday things.

Substance	pH
Lemon juice	2
Coffee	5
Strong household cleaner	12
Lemonade	4
Blood	7
Toothpaste	10
Water	7
Stomach medicine	11
Vinegar	3

(a) What has a pH value of 7?

(b) What is the pH of stomach medicine?

(c) Make a list of all the acids, with the strongest at the top.

(d) Make a list of all the alkalis, with the strongest at the top.

Unit 10

Countries that cause the pollution

Countries that suffer from acid rain

Hungary   Italy   Yugoslavia   Bulgaria   USSR   Sweden   Norway

4 The first bar chart shows the major polluters of the atmosphere. These are the countries which produce a lot of sulphur dioxide, which makes acid rain.

The second chart shows the countries which receive the most acid rain. These are the most polluted.

(a) Which country is the most polluted!

(b) Which country is the worst polluter?

(c) The map of Europe shows the same countries as the table. Where are the countries that are the most polluted? Where are the countries that cause most pollution?

Write a sentence about why this might happen.

USSR

Hungary
Italy
Yugoslavia
Bulgaria

5 Sarah and Iain were doing an investigation to find out what sort of paint was best for stopping rusting. They were given strips of steel, brushes and paint.

What should they do? Write a list of instructions to help them.

6 Jim and Brenda were doing an investigation to find out which was the best type of stomach medicine for neutralising acid.

They counted the number of drops of each medicine needed to neutralise the same amount of acid. They repeated their experiment four times.

Here are their results.

Medicine	Number of drops needed			
	First try	Second try	Third try	Fourth try
A Seltzo	4	4	5	4
B Fizzo	8	9	8	7
C Settlo	6	7	8	7
D Bubblo	11	12	13	11

(a) On average, how many drops of Settlo were needed to neutralise the acid?

(b) Which medicine neutralised the acid most quickly? Say why you think that.

7 Read the passage and then answer the questions.

Lead pollution

Lead is a poison which can build up in our bodies over many years. It seems to be stored there, rather than pass through like most other things. So we have to be very careful about lead pollution.

Pollution can be caused by the lead that is added to petrol for cars. When the petrol is burned, the lead comes out in the exhaust gases. Some people are worried about living close to motorways where there are a lot of petrol fumes.

Some petrol stations are starting to sell lead-free petrol, but not all car engines will work properly with it. All new cars can use lead-free petrol.

Another source of lead is lead pipes. Many years ago lead pipes were used to carry drinking water. Nowadays copper or plastic are used instead. Water that passes through lead pipes can pick up tiny particles of lead which we all drink.

Many scientists think that lead can cause brain damage, particularly in babies and young children.

(a) What are the two sources of lead pollution!

(b) What are the dangers of lead pollution?

(c) How does the lead in petrol get into people's bodies?

(d) What has been done to reduce lead pollution?

Unit 10

8 The descriptions below are about these metals – copper, brass, steel, iron and aluminium. Your job is to decide which description fits which metal. Write down which is which.

Metal A	Metal B	Metal C	Metal D	Metal E
rusts easily, is easily broken (brittle), is magnetic, is grey and the colour doesn't change much after heating.	rusts easily, comes in different forms which can be bendy or hard, is magnetic, is grey and the colour doesn't change much after heating.	is hard, is yellowy-gold and the colour doesn't change much after heating.	is very bendy, is orangey-gold and goes green or black when the metal is heated.	is hard when it is in a block, is not as heavy (dense) as the other metals, is silvery and the colour doesn't change when the metal is heated.

9 Look back at the descriptions of the metals A, B, C, D and E in the last question. Which metal would you use for each of these jobs? Explain why.

(a) To make a fancy ornament. Explain your choice.

(b) To make the handlebars of a lightweight racing bike. Explain your choice.

(c) To make a spring clip for a pen. Explain your choice.

10 The tables show some information about different metals. Look at them carefully as you answer the questions.

Table 1 Production of metals each year

Metal	Symbol	How much is produced each year (thousands of tonnes)
Aluminium	Al	12700
Chromium	Cr	6000
Copper	Cu	8000
Gold	Au	1
Iron	Fe	400000
Lead	Pb	3000
Silver	Ag	10
Tin	Sn	200
Zinc	Zn	6000

Table 2 Prices and amount of metals in the Earth

Metal	Price per tonne (1985)	How much there is in the Earth (%)
Aluminium	£750	8.1
Chromium	£3000	0.01
Copper	£1000	0.0055
Gold	£8.6 million	0.0000004
Iron	£130	5
Lead	£290	0.0013
Silver	£150000	0.000007
Tin	£9100	0.0002
Zinc	£500	0.007

How long the materials in the ground will last for

gold	26 years
zinc	27 years
copper	42 years
chromium	110 years
iron	195 years
aluminium	257 years

(a) Which table or chart tells you about how long the different metals will last?

(b) Which table or chart tells you about how much of each metal can be found in the Earth!

(c) Which metal is produced in the largest amount?

(d) Look at the information for gold. Write down all you can about this metal from the tables and chart. Write a sentence saying why you think gold is so expensive.

Unit 11 FORCES

1 Tom and Louise made a toy parachute from paper. Then they tried cotton, plastic and silk. For each one they timed how long the parachute took to fall. Here are their results:

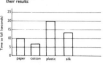

(a) How long did the paper parachute take to fall?
(b) How long did the silk parachute take to fall?
(c) Make a table to show this information. Put the parachutes in order, with the **slowest** first.
(d) What things could you do to make any of the parachutes fall faster? . . . or slower? Make a list for each.

2

Many people like eating nuts. Anne wanted to know what force was needed to crack different sorts of nuts. So she made some measurements with a force meter attached to the family's nutcrackers. Here are her results.

Type of nut	Force in newtons
Walnut	20
Brazil nut	25
Hazelnut	25
Almond	50

(a) Draw a bar chart to show these results.
(b) What do you think the force needed to crack an almond would be using these nutcrackers instead?

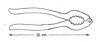

3 The sketch graphs below are about the stretching of a weak spring, a stronger spring and a strong rubber band.

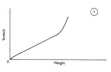

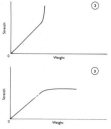

The three sentences below describe how each of the springs stretches. Your job is to match the paragraph to the sketch graph.

A The weak spring
When weights are put on to this spring, it stretches equally for each weight. It stretches quite a lot until it stops stretching evenly. Then it stretches even more.

B The strong spring
When weights are put on this spring, it stretches a lot less than the weak spring. When it stops stretching evenly, it stretches more than before, but not as much as the weak one.

C The strong rubber band
When weights are added to the rubber band, it stretches equally for each weight. After several weights it hardly stretches at all.

Unit 11

4 This table gives information about the fastest cars in the world.

Type of car	Name of car	Miles per hour (mph)	Metres per second (m/s)
Rocket-engined	Blue Flame	622	278
Jet-engined	Thrust 2	633	283
Wheel-driven (piston engine)	Goldenrod	419	187
Wheel-driven (turbine engine)	Bluebird	429	192
Rocket-engined (unofficial)	Budweiser rocket	740	331

(a) How fast did Thrust 2 go, in miles per hour?
(b) Which cars had rocket engines?
(c) Make another table showing the name of the car and its speed in metres per second. Put them in order, with the fastest at the top.

5 The graph shows the overall stopping distance for a car travelling at different speeds.

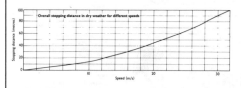

(a) What is the overall stopping distance when the car's speed is 20 metres per second?
(b) Your mother is driving along the road, when a dog runs out. The dog is 80 metres away. What is the fastest she could be driving if she can just stop in time?
(c) Write a sentence describing the pattern that the graph shows.
(d) What do you think the overall stopping distance would be for a speed of 40 metres per second?

6 Julie and Robert had five conkers of different sizes. They decided to do an investigation to see whether big ones were stronger than small ones. This is what they did.

They hung a brick on a piece of cotton 10cm from the bench.

They put the first conker on the bench underneath the brick and cut the cotton. They looked at the conker to see if it was OK. If it was, they put the brick 20cm from the bench and tried again.

They wrote down the height of the brick which eventually smashed the conker.

Then they did it all again with each of the conkers. Here are their results.

Conker size	10mm	15mm	25mm	28mm	40mm
Height to smash conker	40cm	50cm	70cm	60cm	90cm

(a) Draw a diagram or sketch to show what they did in their investigation.
(b) Write a sentence explaining what their results show.
(c) One of their measurements looks a bit odd. Which one is it?
(d) Can you think of any ways of making this investigation more accurate?

Unit 11

7

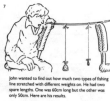

John wanted to find out how much two types of fishing line stretched with different weights on. He had two spare lengths. One was 60cm long but the other was only 50cm. Here are his results.

Load (g)	Length of line 1 (cm)	Length of line 2 (cm)
0	50	60
100	55	64
200	60	68
300	65	72
400	70	76
500	75	80

(a) What is the length of line 1 with 400g on it?
(b) How much longer is line 2 with 500g on it than it was with no weight at all?
(c) Which fishing line was most stretchy? Explain how you worked out your answer.

8 Car tyres are designed to have as much friction as possible on the road (whether it is wet or dry). Some tyre manufacturers claim that their tyres are 'better in wet weather'. Others say their tyres are 'better in any conditions'.

Suppose you work for the Automobile Association and that you have been asked to test the tyres.

Write a plan to send to your boss saying how you plan to test the tyres.

9 The table shows the average speed of the fastest men, women and horses when they run different distances.

Distance (m)	Speed (m/s)		
	Man	Woman	Horse
100	10.10	9.26	
200	10.15	9.21	
400	9.11	8.33	19.34
800	7.87	7.08	18.12
1500	7.11	6.47	17.52
3000	6.64	5.92	16.50
5000	6.41	5.56	15.33

(a) What is the fastest that any person has run?
(b) About how much faster can a horse run compared to a man over 400 metres?
(c) Look at the column for women's speeds. What pattern can you see? Describe the pattern and say why you think it is like that.

10 The diagram shows the gears on a racing bike.

The table shows the number of teeth on each of the cog's wheels.

Cog wheel	Number of teeth
Chain wheel	50
First gear	25
Second gear	20
Third gear	16
Fourth gear	13
Fifth gear	10

(a) When the bike is in first gear, the chain is on the chain wheel and the first gear cog.
How many times will the back wheel turn for each turn of the pedals?
(b) What difference will changing from first to second gear make? Explain why it makes this difference.
(c) How much faster could you go in fifth gear than in first if you turned the pedal at the same rate?

BASIC SKILLS (practical)

In this test you will have to do a number of simple experiments. You will have a few minutes for each question – the number of the question is the same as the number on the card by the experiment. When the teacher tells you to move on, go on to the next question. So if you start on question 3, then, when you are told to move, go to question 4. And so on.

Name_____ Form/class_____

1 Choose one of these force meters and use it to find the force needed to separate the halves of the magnetic door catch.
Instrument chosen ____
Force ____

2 Choose one of these thermometers and use it to measure the temperature of the room.
Thermometer chosen ____
Temperature ____

3 Choose one of the instruments and use it to weigh the plastic bag and its contents.
Instrument chosen ____
Weight ____

4 Choose one of the meters and use it to find the voltage of the batteries in front of you.
Meter chosen ____
Voltage ____

5 Choose one of these instruments and use it to measure the width of the door into the laboratory.
Instrument chosen ____
Width ____

6 Choose one of these instruments and use it to measure the width of the pencil.
Instrument chosen ____
Width ____

7 Choose one of these instruments and use it to measure how much water the yoghurt pot holds when it is full to the top.
Instrument chosen ____
How much water ____

8 Choose one of these instruments and use it to measure how much water the bucket holds.
Instrument chosen ____
How much water ____

9 Choose one of these instruments and use it to measure how long it takes for the toy car to run down the ramp.
Instrument chosen ____
Time ____

10 Choose one of these indicators and use it to measure the pH of the vinegar in the beaker.
Indicator chosen ____
pH ____

BASIC SKILLS (written)

1 Gordon and Julie were doing an experiment to find out which washing-up liquid lasted longest. They had three types of liquid:

Fiery Liquid
Moonlight
Longlife

They put 5cm³ of each type of liquid in 1000cm³ of hot water (at 60°C) in a bucket.

Then they put drops of hot fat into the buckets and stirred. They stopped putting fat in when all the suds went.

They found that Fiery Liquid needed 58 drops, Moonlight needed 70 drops but Longlife only needed 20 drops.

(a) Make a table to show these results.

(b) Copy and complete the bar chart which has been started for you.

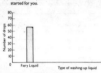

(c) Which do you think was the best liquid?

2 Emma and Winston were doing an experiment to find out whether tomatoes grew better in Bio, Growo or Nitro compost. They put the same number of plants in each of the composts and weighed the tomatoes that ripened.

Here are their results:

Type of compost	Weight of tomatoes (kg)
Bio	42
Growo	34
Nitro	47

Draw a graph or bar chart to show these results. You can choose between a bar chart and a line graph. You decide which is best.

Make your graph or bar chart suitable to put in an advert for the best compost. Make up a good slogan to go on your advert.

3 Abner and Bruce decided to find out how much their fishing line stretched when different weights were put on it. They hung various weights on a piece of the line. Each time they measured how much the line stretched.

Here are their results:

Weight added (g)	Stretch of line (cm)
500	13
1000	26
1500	35
2000	42
2500	46.5

Draw a graph to show these results. You can choose between a bar chart and a line graph. You decide which is best.

67

COMMUNICATING AND INTERPRETING

1 The drawings below show somebody doing an investigation into how a model bridge sags with different loads.

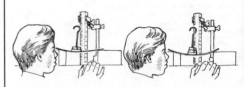

Your job in this question is to write a report about it. You should write the report so that someone who hadn't done the investigation would know exactly what had been done.

2 This piece of writing is about the Top Forge at Wortley in the West Riding of Yorkshire. Iron has been made there for a long time. The forge is now an industrial museum.

The molten metal is tapped from the furnace into rectangular moulds in a bed of sand. This metal is called cast iron or pig iron.

Cast iron is not very useful. It is very brittle and if you try to hammer it into shape it breaks. The only way to make it into a different shape is to melt it again and pour it into a mould.

Up to 4% of the cast iron can be carbon and it is this that makes the metal brittle. Cast iron can be made into wrought iron by removing the carbon which was absorbed into the metal in the furnace. Wrought iron is much easier to shape.

To make wrought iron, the cast iron is heated very strongly so that it melts and the carbon is burned off. But there is a problem. Cast iron melts at 1200°C while wrought iron does not melt until 1500°C.

So, as the carbon burns off, the iron will tend to solidify. So the furnace has to be very hot indeed. They made the furnace hotter by having a bellows to make a draught and a very tall chimney.

Now answer these questions.

(a) When the furnace was tapped, where did the molten metal go?

(b) What sort of iron comes out of the furnace at first?

(c) What temperature does cast iron melt at?

(d) Wrought iron has less carbon in it than cast iron. How did they get rid of the carbon?

(e) How did they make the furnace burn hotter?

(f) Why was it important that the furnace was hotter? Try to explain this carefully in your own words.

68

Communicating and interpreting

3 Sarah and Tony were talking about their little brother's party the following weekend. They knew they were going to be in a rush making the jelly.

Jelly comes in large pieces which have to be dissolved in water.

So they decided to do a test beforehand to see which was the fastest way of dissolving the jelly.

They made tables of their results.

Time without stirring		
	Time (mins) to dissolve in:	
	cold water	hot water
Small pieces of jelly	10	5
Large pieces of jelly	24	12

Time when stirred		
	Time (mins) to dissolve in:	
	cold water	hot water
Small pieces of jelly	8	4
Large pieces of jelly	19	10

(a) How long did it take small pieces of jelly to dissolve in cold water when the water was stirred?

(b) How long did it take large pieces of jelly to dissolve in hot water without stirring?

(c) Is it better to use hot water or cold? Explain your answer.

(d) What makes most difference, stirring or using hot water? Explain how you decided.

(e) When you are making jelly for the party, what will you do to dissolve the pieces of jelly as quickly as possible?

69

Communicating and interpreting

4 When people play squash they have to warm the ball up by hitting it hard for a while. When it is warm it bounces more.

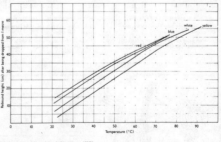

Some balls bounce more than others. The colour of the spot on the ball tells us how much the ball will bounce.

The graph below show some information about how the different squash balls bounce at different temperatures.

(a) How high did the red spot ball bounce at 40°C?

(b) Which ball bounces most?

(c) How much more does the red spot ball bounce than the white spot at 60°C?

(d) What bounce height do you think the yellow spot ball would have at 0°C?

(e) Write a sentence describing the pattern in the graphs.

70

OBSERVING

In this test you will have to do a number of simple experiments. You will have a few minutes for each question – the number of the question is the same as the number on the card by the experiment. When the teacher tells you to move on, go to the next question. So if you start on

question 3, then, when you are told to move, go to question 4. And so on.

Write your answers on the answer sheet – not on here. Don't forget to put your name on it.

1 Squeeze as much water out of the sponge as you can.

   (a) Put the sponge into the water. Describe how it floats.

   (b) Now hold the sponge under the water and squeeze it. Describe what happens.

   (c) Let the sponge go. Describe how it floats now.

   (d) Write a paragraph explaining why the sponge behaves like that.

2 In front of you are samples of different yarns. The manufacturer's label will tell you something about what they are made of.

   Take one of the small pieces of each of the yarns. Hold it in a pair of tongs and burn it. BE CAREFUL.

   (a) Write down what you notice for each of the yarns.

   (b) Can you see any pattern in the way they burn? Write a paragraph describing the pattern.

3 In front of you are samples of various materials.

   Material A is corrugated cardboard
   Material B is ordinary cardboard
   Material C is plywood
   Material D is ordinary wood

   Bend them in different directions.

   Corrugated cardboard is used in making cardboard boxes. Plywood is used in furniture and building.

   (a) Write a paragraph about corrugated cardboard saying why it is made the way it is. Say how this makes it better for making boxes.

   (b) Now hold the sponge under the water and squeeze it. Describe what happens.

4 Write a paragraph for a school science book describing this animal. Make sure you include the important scientific things.

5 In front of you are three different sorts of light bulb.

   (a) Pick one of them and describe the important things about it.

   (b) Write down as many things as you can that are similar about the three bulbs.

6 These teeth are from different animals. For each one write a paragraph describing the important scientific things about it.

7 The insulating materials in front of you can be used to stop heat escaping.

   Look at them carefully.

   (a) Which one do you think will be the best at keeping heat in?

     Why have you chosen that one?

   (b) Which one do you think will be worst?

     Why have you chosen that one?

71

Observing

8 Some mirrors have been set up for you. Do not move them.

   Look at yourself in the single mirror. Then look at yourself in the two mirrors.

   Do you look the same each time?

   (a) Write down any differences you notice.

   (b) Can you explain the differences?

9 You have been given some dilute acid, some dilute alkali and some water. Don't forget your goggles.

   (a) Put a few drops of acid onto one of the marble chips. Describe what happens.

   (b) Now put a few drops of water on to another marble chip.

     Describe what happens.

   (c) Now put a few drops of alkali on to another marble chip.

     Describe what happens.

   (d) Write a sentence saying why you think these things happened.

10 In front of you are a number of objects that are used at home or in the garden.

   Pick two of them and write a paragraph about each of them, describing how they work. Make sure you mention the important scientific ideas in your answer.

72

PLANNING INVESTIGATIONS

1 You can buy different brands of fertilisers to feed pot plants for the house.

   But which one is best?

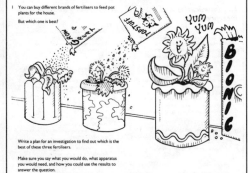

Write a plan for an investigation to find out which is the best of these three fertilisers.

Make sure you say what you would do, what apparatus you would need, and how you could use the results to answer the question.

2 If you open the wrong door of an aeroplane by mistake and fall out, then you hope your parachute works OK.

That will depend on whether the canopy – the material of the parachute – is the right size. If it is too small you would fall too quickly. If it is too large then it might get tangled up and not open at all.

Write a plan for an investigation to find out how the speed at which you fall depends on the area of the parachute.

Make sure you say what you would do, what apparatus you would need, and how you could use the results to answer the question.

73

Planning investigations

3 Some places have very acid soils. Many plants won't grow in these soils, so people put lime on the ground to neutralise the acid. Suppose you moved to a new house with a garden that was very acid.

COUGH COUGH   AAARGH

Write a plan for an investigation to find out how much lime you would need to add to a garden to neutralise the soil.

Make sure you say what you would do, what apparatus you would need, and how you could use the results to answer the question.

4 Simon says that his washing will dry more quickly if it is a warm day. Rachel says that it is more important that there is a wind.

Write a plan for an investigation to find out whether the strength of the wind, or how hot a day it is, is more important in drying clothes.

Make sure you say what you would do, what apparatus you would need, and how you could use the results to answer the question.

74

INVESTIGATING AND MAKING

Kitchen towels

Most people use paper kitchen rolls to mop up spills and clean things in their kitchens. Think about the sorts of things that you would want to do with a piece of one of these rolls.

Your job is to find out which of these kitchen towels is best. You must decide what you mean by 'best'.

You can use any of the apparatus that you have been given. You may not need to use it all. Choose the apparatus to suit your investigation.

Toy car

In front of you is a toy car. Wind it up – but not too tightly – and let it go.

Your job is to find out how the distance the toy car travels depends on the number of turns of the key.

You can use any of the apparatus that you have been given. You may not need to use it all. Choose the apparatus to suit your investigation.

Make a clear record of your results as you go along.

When you have finished, write a brief account of your investigation. Make sure you say what you have found out.

Make a clear record of your results as you go along.

When you have finished, write a brief account of your investigation. Make sure you say what you have found out.

© Coles, Gott, Thornley/Collins Educational 1989   *Active Science Copymasters 2*   75

Investigating and making

Soggy lawns

When it rains my lawn gets so wet that the water lies on top of the grass like a pond, yet when I look at other lawns the water seems to drain straight through them – they always look good!

The local park keeper told me the reason is that the soil under my lawn must have a lot of clay in it. Clay doesn't allow water to drain away quickly. He said that the rate at which water drains through a soil depends on the composition of the soil. A sandy soil drains very quickly but a clay soil does not.

Your job is to find out how the rate at which water drains away through a mixture of sand and soil depends on the amount of sand in the mixture.

You can use any of the apparatus that you have been given. You may not need to use it all. Choose the apparatus to suit your investigation.

Make a clear record of your results as you go along.

When you have finished, write a brief account of your investigation.

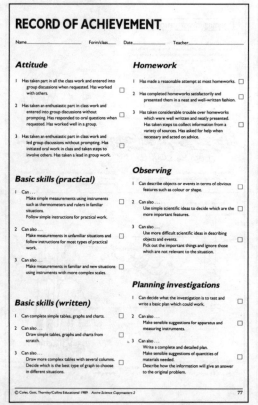

76   © Coles, Gott, Thornley/Collins Educational 1989   *Active Science Copymasters 2*

RECORD OF ACHIEVEMENT

Name_____ Form/class_____ Date_____ Teacher_____

Attitude

1 Has taken part in all the class work and entered into group discussions when requested. Has worked with others. ☐

2 Has taken an enthusiastic part in class work and entered into group discussions without prompting. Has responded to oral questions when requested. Has worked well in a group. ☐

3 Has taken an enthusiastic part in class work and led group discussions without prompting. Has initiated oral work in class and taken steps to involve others. Has taken a lead in group work. ☐

Basic skills (practical)

1 Can...
Make simple measurements using instruments such as thermometers and rulers in familiar situations. Follow simple instructions for practical work. ☐

2 Can also...
Make measurements in unfamiliar situations and follow instructions for most types of practical work. ☐

3 Can also...
Make measurements in familiar and new situations using instruments with more complex scales. ☐

Basic skills (written)

1 Can complete simple tables, graphs and charts. ☐

2 Can also...
Draw simple tables, graphs and charts from scratch. ☐

3 Can also...
Draw more complex tables with several columns. Decide which is the best type of graph to choose in different situations. ☐

Homework

1 Has made a reasonable attempt at most homeworks. ☐

2 Has completed homeworks satisfactorily and presented them in a neat and well-written fashion. ☐

3 Has taken considerable trouble over homeworks which were well written and neatly presented. Has taken steps to collect information from a variety of sources. Has asked for help when necessary and acted on advice. ☐

Observing

1 Can describe objects or events in terms of obvious features such as colour or shape. ☐

2 Can also...
Use simple scientific ideas to decide which are the more important features. ☐

3 Can also...
Use more difficult scientific ideas in describing objects and events. Pick out the important things and ignore those which are not relevant to the situation. ☐

Planning investigations

1 Can decide what the investigation is to test and write a basic plan which could work. ☐

2 Can also...
Make sensible suggestions for apparatus and measuring instruments. ☐

3 Can also...
Write a complete and detailed plan. Make sensible suggestions of quantities of materials needed. Describe how the information will give an answer to the original problem. ☐

© Coles, Gott, Thornley/Collins Educational 1989   *Active Science Copymasters 2*   77

Record of achievement

Communicating and interpreting

1 Can...
Read data from simple tables, graphs and charts. Describe patterns in straightforward data. Write a basic description of an experiment. Pick out relevant pieces of information from written materials. ☐

2 Can also...
Read data from more complex tables, graphs and charts. Write a complete description of an experiment. Pick out the most relevant pieces of information from written materials and assemble the information to answer more general questions. ☐

3 Can also...
Describe and interpret patterns in such data. Write a coherent and complete description of an experiment. Use library and other reference material. ☐

Investigating and making

1 Can...
Decide what a simple investigation is testing and carry out some measurements. Construct objects or apparatus that would work in principle. ☐

2 Can also...
Decide what more complex investigations are testing. Use apparatus to make suitable measurements. Construct objects or apparatus that work satisfactory. ☐

3 Can also...
Make sensible choices about quantities of materials. Make accurate measurements. Judge how many measurements are necessary to give reliable answers. Construct objects or apparatus that work well and incorporate ideas developed during the course. Criticise and refine the solution. ☐

Pupil's comment:

Teacher's comment:

Parent's comment:

78   © Coles, Gott, Thornley/Collins Educational 1989   *Active Science Copymasters 2*